BREAKING
RANKS

BREAKING RANKS

THE SHAPING OF CIVIL-MILITARY RELATIONS IN IRELAND

MICHAEL MARTIN

First published 2016

The History Press Ireland
50 City Quay
Dublin 2
Ireland
www.thehistorypress.ie

British Library Cataloguing in Publication Data.
A catalogue record for this book is available from the British Library.

ISBN 978 1 84588 515 1

Typesetting and origination by The History Press
Printed and bound by CPI Group (UK) Ltd, Croydon, CR0 4YY

Contents

Acknowledgements

There are hundreds of individuals past and present who dedicated themselves to the pursuit of better conditions in the Irish Defence Forces and played a crucial role establishing the basic democratic right of association. They are far too numerous to mention individually but groupings must be acknowledged in any written work about this subject. They include members of the National Army Spouses Association who first highlighted the many problems being experienced by soldiers in the late 1980s and were first to call for the establishment of a representative body. Soldiers of the Eastern Command who prompted others from the Western, Curragh, Southern Command and Naval Service and Air Corps, to consider the setting up of a representative body. Soldiers, sailors and Air Corps individuals who worked at local level throughout the country to organise committees, events and information at local level. The chaplaincy of the time who forthrightly outlined the extreme difficulties and poor morale being experienced by personnel. The individual serving officers who quietly supported the rights of their subordinates. The politicians who listened and raised questions in parliament about the unfolding crisis. Irish journalists who gave voice to concerns that many had never heard from the formerly secretive world of military service. The civil servants of the Department of Defence, who (once the decision had been made to provide representation) dealt in a most equitable and professional manner with the new and somewhat inexperienced representatives. And finally the fraternal associations of prison officers, An Garda Síochána, the European Organisation of Military Associations (EUROMIL) and the Irish trade union movement who all advised and encouraged the inexperienced military personnel who sought a legal means by which they could address their basic issues of pay and conditions.

Despite the lack of attention paid in the Irish context to the significance of the emergence of representative associations in the armed forces, in the research for this book I have been very fortunate to have had the kind co-operation and assistance of the Secretary General of the Department of Defence, Mr Michael Howard, in accessing Department of Defence files not yet in the public domain. These files are unique in the sense that they came to be produced at a time when the Irish Government were demanding explanatory perspectives from the military authorities with regard to their attitude and beliefs in the whole exercise of command and discipline, and the fundamental nature of the relationships between the military and the State. Equally, the assistance of the former Chief of Staff, Lt Gen. Dermot Earley, in gaining the co-operation of all units of the PDF paved the way for widespread co-operation from personnel of the Defence Forces. Unfortunately, in the period between the time he provided me with such assistance and commentary and the time of writing, he passed away. Former and current serving members of the army, navy and Air Corps were most helpful as were Permanent Defence Force Other Ranks representative Association (PDFORRA) national executive, their headquarters staff and secretariat. The presidents of EUROMIL and PDFORRA together with their general secretaries were most helpful. I am sincerely grateful to them all.

All those not directly involved in the events but supporting their spouses and loved ones through extraordinarily difficult challenges where legal proceedings and the threat of expulsion from their careers weighed heavily, among them my wife Geraldine. Thanks is due to all of them in helping to shape modern Irish military and social history.

Michael Martin
Cork, Ireland 2016

Introduction

The subject of this book concerns itself with the origin of PDFORRA (Permanent Defence Force Other Ranks Representative Association). Much is drawn from my PhD thesis entitled 'Breaking ranks, the emergence of representative associations in the Irish armed forces' and from my own considerable involvement in the events described. The influences that led to the enactment of legislation providing for statutory representative associations had many strands. These included a public campaign by army wives, a deliberate pursuit of the right of association by serving members of the Permanent Defence Force (PDF) and my own constitutional challenge against the State in the High Court. Military historians for centuries have exercised themselves on the weapons, campaigns and structural features of armies in a multiplicity of countries and conflicts. Few have managed to portray soldiers as a group in any capacity beyond their military persona. Bartlett and Jeffrey's (eds) very readable *A Military History of Ireland* sets out to address areas other than the above, but its contributors soon descend into types of warfare and strategy.[1] It seems the reality is that many modern-day soldiers are the only ones who see their soldiering as just one, albeit important, part of their daily lives. In a small country like Ireland where the vast majority of service personnel live off-base, their integration into mainstream society is probably more pronounced than elsewhere. Perhaps this is why comparisons with other members of civilian society became inevitable.

Since 1988 the Permanent Defence Force (PDF) in Ireland, comprising of the Army, Naval Service and Air Corps, has undergone significant cultural, regulatory and institutional change. These developments have impacted almost every level of the force and have wrought important change in two areas in particular: internal and departmental human-resource management. In addition and in a much wider sense, the framework, operation, and context of civil–military relations in Ireland has been transformed. Internally, the relationship between the officer corps and the enlisted ranks has changed significantly. New structures have redefined their respective roles in specified areas towards each other. These same structures have also altered the context and operation of the relationship between the civilian Department of Defence and the officer corps. In a very new departure there is also now a formal method of communication between the enlisted ranks and the Department of Defence. In the intervening period since the passing of the Defence Amendment Act of 1990, the political and structural profiles of the Irish armed forces have changed, and, with them, the political and structural contexts of civil–military relations in Ireland.

The activities and aims that precipitated the creation of representative associations for military personnel in Ireland were at one time thought to threaten the exercise of command and discipline in the force. These same activities and aims were most certainly in contravention of government policy. The level of control by a civilian government over its armed forces is a crucial matter and the balance of power between the two must always be weighted heavily in favour of the elected administration. This being the case, it is essential to have an understanding of the events in Ireland and the motivation for them. Matters that would prompt those in authority to believe there was a threat to the security of the State need to be understood. Equally, if fears proved unfounded regarding State security and army discipline, there is a benefit to be gained from the study of the particular circumstances in Ireland. Such a study may well help in the consideration of whether or not to provide similar structures to other forces in other countries.

To many soldiers, sailors and airmen who would have enlisted as members of the Irish Defence Forces or accepted a commission up to the late 1980s, the absence of representative associations or unions was accepted as a fact of life, a condition of service. Sgt Michael Gould (retired) maintained that during his entire military service of forty-two years in the Irish Army there was never a need for such bodies because, 'the forces always looked after their own very well'. He believed that membership of any type of a representative body would indicate ingratitude and disloyalty to the service.[2] In 1990 the Chief of Staff wrote that membership of any organisation (other than one approved by the military leadership and the State) would be 'unnecessary and divisive'.[3] One serving naval non-commissioned officer (NCO) remembers all personnel being assembled in the ratings dining room on board the Irish Naval ship *LÉ Deirdre*. It was a formal gathering that they were ordered to attend. The assembled ranks were then 'addressed' by the coxswain (who was officially the senior rating on the ship), who told them that the seeking the right of association, or membership of any organisation seeking it, would be 'tantamount to mutiny'.[4] The context of such a remark from a superior in the navy is important to outline. In any armed force the charge of mutiny is extremely serious. In Ireland if violence is associated with mutiny it becomes an offence for which conviction once carried the death penalty.[5] If this was the official attitude towards military representative bodies, it is understandable that any personnel at the time who felt the need for representative bodies in the forces would have been reluctant to express their view, particularly in the company of a superior officer. One Irish Navy senior figure at the time, Commander McNamara (retired) was commanding officer of the naval depot at Haulbowline Naval Base in County Cork, Ireland. He was fundamentally opposed to the introduction of representative bodies. 'I would have seen them impacting very negatively on the Defence Forces and still do.'[6] Yet despite these deeply held official views, there were others who evidently believed otherwise and who thought it sufficiently worthwhile to endanger their careers in the Defence Forces to try to establish representative bodies that could speak freely and represent the interests of those with whom they served. By 2007, after seventeen years of representation, the incumbent Chief of Staff, when asked about the impact of representative bodies on the Irish Army as a whole, emphasised the 'great contribution' made to all aspects of the armed forces by the Permanent Defence Force Other Ranks Representative Association (PDFORRA) and the Representative Association for Commissioned Officers (RACO).[7] These are the very same organisations that his predecessors thought would undermine the whole structure of command and discipline and represent a possible threat to the Irish State itself.

The question arises as to how this sea change in hierarchal attitudes occurred. What measures were adopted, if any, to allay the fears of those who believed that the right of association leading to the 'organising' of military lower ranks was a danger to State security or to the integrity and command structure of the Defence Forces? How was the government of the day, which was advised by the military hierarchy in these matters, persuaded to ignore that advice? After all, the General Staff of the forces were supposed to be the professionals in this area. Somehow, in Ireland, the difficulties that these scenarios would present to the delicate civil–military relations were overcome, but how? Does the Irish experience open up a new dimension to the conduct of civil–military relations worldwide?

Unlike the American, British or French armed forces, Irish military personnel of the Army, Naval Service and Air Corps now have a structure through which they can negotiate at all levels of the Defence Forces and, where applicable, with relevant Irish Government departments on matters of pay, allowances and certain conditions of service. For the first time, enlisted personnel are now part of the machinery that would not be envisaged in the usual concept of the operation of civil–military relations, particularly those espoused by Professor Huntington in his seminal work *The Soldier and the State*.[8] These structures provide the right whereby representatives of serving military personnel can speak freely to the press and media about certain matters in the Defence Forces. This constitutes another departure from Huntington's idea whereby only an officer corps is competent to advise the government in a 'professional' capacity.[9]

Until 1990, Ireland was similar to the above-mentioned nations in that its enlisted personnel had no input into the decision-making process that governed expenditure and policy on pay, allowances and normal human-resource considerations. A government-appointed independent commission established by the Irish Government in 1989 was chaired by Senior Counsel Lawyer Dermot Gleeson SC. It was tasked to look at the pay and conditions in Ireland's Defence Forces and offered the first-ever opportunity for enlisted personnel to express their opinions to any institution or body outside of the Defence Forces on matters that would have an impact on themselves.[10] Today the two statutory bodies, PDFORRA and RACO, that were set up under national legislation, provide for a system of consultation and negotiation on a wide range of matters. Negotiations take place with elected representatives in an industrial relations–type environment that was not ethically or legally possible before the passing of the Defence Amendment Act of 1990. The mechanisms by which this can now be done required significant cultural and regulatory change. This change did not occur from within. While most senior army officers in Ireland fully understood the

frustration felt by their subordinates in matters of poor pay and conditions, they nevertheless strenuously opposed any developments that
might have led to what they perceived as 'unionisation' of the armed
forces. Accordingly advised, the government not only opposed the
idea but actively prohibited the forming of any representative groups
in the Defence Forces. The eventual change in attitude of the government was brought about by a sustained public campaign carried out
initially by the spouses of soldiers and eventually by serving members
of the PDF. It involved and incorporated the use of the media, political
lobbying and, eventually, a High Court action. However, during these
events the government and the army, despite conceding that something
had to be done to alleviate what was then being called the 'army crisis',
still opposed the formation of an independent representative association.
What eventually changed their minds?

Many areas and disciplines were encompassed by these events.
They included the problems that prevailed in the Defence Forces in
the late 1980s, the responses of the serving men and women to what
they saw as low pay and poor treatment, the crucial role played by
the National Army Spouses Association (NASA) and the position and
activities of officers of the PDF (some of whom were in command
of dissatisfied subordinates) in their approach to representation. Also
the attitudes and activities of the various politicians who contributed
to the debate about professional representation and the right of association for soldiers. The influences of European political and military
perspectives, and in particular those of the European Organisation of
Military Associations (EUROMIL), were crucial. The law as it stood
in Ireland at that time and the interpretation of the Constitution
were also very important. All of these influences were set against a
background of genuine concerns of the General Staff of the Irish
armed forces, particularly with regard to their fears on the ramifica-
tions for managerial adaptation to any new structures. The subsequent
actions and reactions of the above stakeholders contributed to shaping
Ireland's response to the demand for representation in the armed
forces. The officer corps, some of whom were sympathetic and helpful
to the enlisted personnel, had problems of their own. Their right to
associate was affirmed in the wake of the initiatives that led to the
passing of the Defence Amendment Act 1990.

It is my intention that this book should help analyse the initiatives
surrounding the developments that led to the formation of representative

associations in Ireland. I hope to consider to what extent a type of
military 'intervention' took place and to shed light on the emergence
of the notion of the 'right of association' among Irish Defence Force
personnel and their families, and on the campaign that helped bring it
about. The following chapters will examine the ethical opposition of
the army and consider the public response to the arguments made by
those involved. Media reports and Irish parliamentary debates track the
lead-up to significant alteration of official attitudes towards the question
of the right to representation in the workplace and of fundamental
freedom of speech for a particular group of Irish citizens.

Was what happened in Ireland in the late 1980s a political radicalisa-
tion of an enforced apolitical section of the community or was it the
acquisition from a reluctant government of a fundamental human right?

This book will provide new knowledge in the study of civil–military
relations regarding how the State and the army in Ireland interacted
with each other during this period. It will do so in the context of
previous events such as the so-called 'mutinies' in the Curragh in 1914
and in the new State in 1924. It will seek to pinpoint the real issues that
led to the reversal of thinking in the sensitive area of State security and
policy. Thanks to unprecedented access to secret files of the Department
of Defence, it will provide an insight into the fundamental arguments
made by either side in their pursuit of, and opposition to, representative
associations in the army. Finally, it will contribute to our knowledge of
civil–military relations by highlighting and adding a new dimension to
it for scholarly consideration and, perhaps, for its application in other
countries in this field of study. According to Huntington:

> Military security policy deals with external threats to the State. Internal
> security policy deals with the threat of subversion – the effort to
> weaken or destroy the State by forces operating within its institutional
> and territorial confines. Situational security policy is concerned
> with the threat of erosion resulting from long term changes in social,
> economic, demographic and political conditions tending to reduce the
> relative power of the State.[11]

He goes on further to suggest that there are 'operating' and 'institutional' levels in the implementation of policy. While the operating
policy deals with the requisite resources to meet the contingency
threat, institutional policy is the manner in which operational policy is

formulated and executed. It is here that civil–military relations constitute the principal institutional component of security policy.[12]

In Ireland in the late 1980s issues emerged that gave rise to institutional consideration and responses in at least two of Huntington's designated areas of security policy, namely, the internal security policy, and the situational security policy. This book provides an opportunity to examine the motivations, considerations and catalysts for the process in the Irish context, in order to gain a new understanding of elements of civil–military relations as yet unexplored. It is all the more important, for the broader subject, that much of the evidence will be from internal sources, given the almost secretive nature of the day-to-day running of a military organisation such as Ireland's professional volunteer army. In addition to the internal traditions, codes and regulations of an operational armed force, there is a cultural reluctance and in most cases a regulatory prohibition on members of the armed forces to engage with the outside world in any public fashion. Traditionally there is even less opportunity for members of the armed forces to challenge and seek change to existing frameworks from within.

Everywhere, including in Ireland, the operation of any military unit is dependent on the exercise of command and control. The military environment is one where a strict hierarchal system of discipline is deemed to be of central importance to the successful operation of any military force. In this regard, Finer maintained:

Centralisation of command, the hierarchal arrangement of authority and the rule of obedience, are all necessary to make the army respond as a unit to the word of command …[13]

Orders are expected to be carried out immediately and without question. Welch and Smith acknowledge that soldiers are trained to: 'Follow commands quickly, efficiently and without questions'.[14]

Almost universally, there is a military cultural assumption that a superior officer, by virtue of his rank and training, will always be making the right decision in issuing an order. Even if that may not be the case, there is a regulatory requirement that his or her subordinate will carry out the order anyway. The underlying principle of 'do it now, and if there is a question raise it later' was well portrayed in nineteenth-century French military regulations, where the right to protest was permitted, but only 'after the order had been carried out'.[15] In an examination of the loyalty and obedience of the German officer corps, Demeter observes:

In any army there must be obedience; but in Germany every officer – senior officers included – had been taught for half a century (partly under pressure of the First World War) that obedience must be placed far away and above all other military virtues and treated as an absolute value, as a sacred taboo.[16]

Military training instils the need for immediacy of response to orders, an absolute requirement, which can often mean the difference between life and death. Institutionally and culturally, subordinates comply with the orders and requests of their superiors. There is no situation where a difference of opinion or a fundamental disagreement on how something should be done arises. In Ireland as in most countries, it is an offence against military law not to comply with all lawful orders. Paragraph 131 of Ireland's Defence Act 1954 is very specific:

Every person subject to military law who disobeys a lawful command of a superior officer is guilty of an offence against military law and shall, on conviction by court-martial, be liable to suffer penal servitude or any less punishment awardable by a court-martial.[17]

In addition to the strict code of discipline that prevails in military organisations, there is a highly defined demarcation of tasks. These can often be more dependent on rank than on expertise. Decisions of major managerial impact, together with those of seemingly minor import, are usually required to have the approval if not the actual authorisation of a superior. Although there are numerous strata of ranks in different armed forces, there is a universal constant, that is, the division of the officer corps and enlisted personnel who are made up of the privates and the non-commissioned personnel like corporals, sergeants and so on. All middle and senior management is entrusted to officers. Enlisted personnel are basically the workforce of the organisation. In the Irish forces as elsewhere, this rigidity of structural relationships is backed up by the physical reminder of the subordinate/superior hierarchy in the form of rank markings and uniform. It is ever present in military life. Rank differences are visible even in everyday working dress. Separate dining, recreation and living quarters are assigned to the three strata of private, NCO and commissioned officer ranks. However, the most distinctive differences really occur in the division of labour that rank imposes. Virtually nobody from among the enlisted ranks is ever tasked

with any duties that would involve making representations on behalf of
the military force or interacting with external agencies.

In the past, all proposals to the Irish Government regarding military
logistical and budgetary requirements were traditionally compiled by
senior officers of Defence Force Headquarters (DFHQ). All military
personnel assigned as aide-de-camp to the President and the Taoiseach
(prime minister) were and are commissioned officers. All captains of
State ships, pilots of State aircraft, and representatives at the United
Nations (UN) are drawn from the officer corps. In such a system there
was little requirement or desire for the upper ranks of the commissioned officer body to consult with the lower enlisted ranks on any
of these matters. It was not surprising that claims for pay for enlisted
personnel were traditionally processed by senior officers. There would
have been a number of justifications for this. Senior officers would have
had the resources, through various sections of DFHQ, such as planning
and research (P&R), where they could formulate claims. In these
military sections they could research past claims by both military and
civil bodies. They could gather information from public-service pay
trends, conduct research, and engage with employer organisations on
remuneration and allowances. However extraordinary it seems, it was
rarely the case that they would consult with enlisted personnel about
pay claims. From the senior-officer management perspective, pay for
the ordinary enlisted personnel was just one of many budgets they had
to seek from government. The same senior officers were often also
responsible for procurement, seeking resources other than pay from
government, and so would have been in a position to assign priority to
various segments of the defence budget from which all funding comes.
There would have been a traditional view that officers, having higher
educational entry requirements, would have a better understanding of
what needed to be done. In any event, it was the officers who always
made the case for increases in pay and allowance for all ranks.

In the late 1980s in Ireland, the whole question of poor pay and
conditions in the army ended up as a subject of national debate. Perhaps,
had enlisted personnel been better informed about the process whereby
claims for improved rates were being made on their behalf, and had they
been included in the process itself, the quest for the right of association
may not have arisen among them. The military hierarchy at the time
were making constant strenuous efforts to have pay and allowances
increased. Former Chief of Staff, Lt General Gerry McMahon, recalled

his own efforts to improve conditions in the Curragh command involving his making a decision to bring in and to consult NCOs about the amalgamation of colleges. General McMahon was the exception rather than the rule when it came to engaging with his senior NCOs in anything that resembled 'negotiations'; however, he conceded, 'it was a different army then'.[18] Whatever local commanding officers could do about local conditions, the fact remained that at that time senior military personnel formulated the claims in respect of pay. McMahon recalls:

> In the area of pay and allowances military management was tasked with that. The 1980s were truly appalling as regards the economy. The Defence Forces were stretched with the border.[19] The government were unable to support and pay an army that they were totally dependent on. They ignored them, the government, the Department of Finance, and their agents the Department of Defence ignored them. I remember being on the periphery of a conversation when the then Chief of Staff Lt. General Tadgh O'Neill expressed extreme frustration at the situation with the fact that nobody would listen to him anymore. I think the time for something like representation had come. But there were a lot of fears about it at the time.[20]

When the notion of a representative body to make claims for pay first began to emerge among enlisted personnel, there was little enthusiasm for it among military management. Commissioned officers who would have been aware of the process of making pay claims to the Department of Defence did not see the forming of representative associations as the answer to tackling the pursuit of better pay. 'Despite the extent of dissatisfaction with pay, allowances and others matters, the officer body never saw representative associations as being a part of the solution.'[21]

It is noteworthy that during the period leading up to the reported 'army crisis', continuous efforts were being made by the military hierarchy to seek better pay and allowances. Their efforts were not successful. Nevertheless, despite any ongoing disappointment in this or any other field, the nature of military thinking is to keep going, regardless of conditions, and to carry out the task in order to always complete the mission. From the time of the earliest fighting forces, this tradition has served armies well in the context of military conflict, in many instances being a matter of life and death and of survival itself. Arising from this need, one of the most important if not central ethos of the military is the 'can do' approach. What this means is that whatever the difficulties, the inconvenience, the challenges or perceived obstruction in the way of a task or the fulfilment of an order, it is imperative that orders are followed and that every attempt is made to fulfil the instruction as issued. In any army, complaints that might impede the fulfilment of a task or mission are neither entertained nor permitted. In recruit training there are a number of examples of how this culture is inculcated in newly enlisted personnel. One is taught to respond to any request or order from a superior by shouting, as loudly as possible, 'Yes sir'. During marching drill and exercises in 'square bashing' it is forbidden to use one's initiative to avoid obstruction and instead it is imperative to continue obeying the last order until a new one is issued. Petty Officer Jim Halligan, who served in the Irish Navy in the 1970s and 1980s and undertook his basic training in Cork Harbour, Ireland, on Spike Island and in Haulbowline, recalls:

> When we were doing our square bashing training, the Petty Officer in charge of us marched us around the drill square and then down along the depot lines where he gave the order for us to wheel left. This routing had us marching down an inclined slipway towards the sea. When the lads in the front stopped inches before entering the water, the instructor balled them out.[22]

Responding and acting on orders without question or hesitation regardless of how bizarre they may seem is an integral part of military training. It is also part of the process of removing individuality and the capacity for an individual (as a military person) to make certain assumptions or take certain actions based on their own view or experience. On enlistment in most armed forces, personnel are assigned a number that stays with them for their entire service. Every item of uniform, kit and clothing is marked by the recruit with the number and, when responding to questions about who a person might be, personnel are trained to give number, rank and name, in that order. The uniform itself prohibits the possibility of any individualism in terms of dress, as do the hair-length regulations, the dormitory-style accommodation and the prohibition of any movement or travel away from base without a pass granting permission. Enlisted personnel are required to do what they are told, not what they think they should do. Finer outlines the importance of the principle of military obedience thus:

This obligation to unquestioning and prompt obedience is enhanced by the depersonalisation of the soldier. The army is too big a machine to reek of individuals, and the soldier becomes a number. Extraneous considerations are thereby thrust aside, and obedience to superiors recognised by their rank and insignia becomes the dominant or sole criterion of action.[23]

These practices and this tradition are thought to be absolutely essential to any military force from recruit- or cadet-training stage up to and including situations when a unit will be expected to complete its mission, either in a hostile area of conflict or in a passive administrative situation in peacetime. Welch and Smith describe these organisational characteristics as 'military cohesion':

> In addition, a host of long standing army practices stress the totality of the institution and diminish the uniqueness of the individual. Consider the basic training given to a raw recruit in the American army. He is stripped of his civilian clothing, his hair, even his first name (Joe Jones becomes Private Jones); incorporated into a large, impersonal organisation; severed for several weeks from friends and family. The uniform, salute, PX [Discounted shopping outlets for military personnel] and clubs provide new forms of identification and stratification. Cohesion must be maintained in the stress of battle, hence the emphasis on solidarity found within the armed forces.[24]

Regarding these peculiarities of military life or any other matter in the Irish armed forces, the airing of any criticisms by serving personnel to outside parties was not tolerated. Communicating with any section of the media on any matters relating to the forces was strictly forbidden by military regulation paragraph 27 of A7, which is promulgated under the Defence Act 1954:

PART VII. – COMMUNICATION OF MILITARY
INFORMATION AND PERSONAL PUBLICITY.

Interviews, etc. - prohibition of:

27.   The granting of interviews or the divulging of information by any officer or man of the PDF to members of the public on matters pertaining to the service or to the conduct thereof is forbidden. Save

in the circumstances mentioned in paragraphs 30 and 31 no officer or man will authorise or purport to authorise the publication of any matter concerning the service or having relation to public business or questions of politics. Comment, if any, in publications, lectures, broadcasts or talks, touching on questions of a political nature – whether national or international – shall avoid strictly any reference which might be construed as being of a controversial nature.[25]

If personnel felt the desire to complain, there was an internal 'redress of wrongs' system provided under the same section of the DFRs, A7. This system set out a mechanism whereby soldiers who either had a complaint or felt that they had been wronged by a superior were entitled to bring the matter to a higher authority. This redress system required that a complaint be made at the lowest level and to the nearest superior. It would be considered first by an immediate superior and then sent to the next level for consideration, then to the next, and in theory the complaint could go right up as far as the Minister for Defence. Despite this provision, there was a perception among Irish military personnel that this self-regulated internal enquiry system was flawed and unjust towards the complainant. If a private had a complaint against his treatment by his or her superior officer, such as company commander, the first stage in administrative bureaucracy saw colleagues supposedly investigating colleagues. Richard Condron, a former company sergeant and vice president of PDFORRA, gave an insight into how this system was perceived in the army:

Other than pay we always had grievances. Mostly, they were about courses and promotion. We always had grievance procedure but it didn't work. The famous redress of wrongs never worked, the people that were involved in it were the same people that were hearing the case. It was an absolute joke. What happened with the likes of courses and promotion was that you would end up with someone who was dedicated, who was qualified, and who would probably be the senior person, now not being promoted for some obscure reason probably because some commanding officer did not like him or maybe didn't like the look of him. That person then became frustrated with the system.[26]

When an opportunity was afforded to military personnel to make a case to the Commission on Remuneration and Conditions of Service in the Defence Forces (later known as the Gleeson Commission), the team tasked with contributing submissions on behalf of NCOs did not spare any sensitivities. Part of their submission regarding the redress of wrongs system stated:

> The procedure is now held to be a meaningless ritual with little or no hope of actual redress in the end. There is also the perception that if a person applies for redress he may become the subject of 'special treatment' or some form of victimisation. The procedure has now lost all credibility and is now more or less ignored by most NCOs. This has led to a good deal of pent up frustration on the part of personnel with grievances of one sort or another and a more effective system of redress urgently needs to be put in place.[27]

The team went on to propose a whole new system of redress involving members of the judiciary, the labour court and even members of parliament. The officers' team recommended the establishment of a military ombudsman operating from outside the PDF with certain investigative powers and the capacity to make recommendations to the minister. The Gleeson Commission, in response, acknowledged the shortcomings of the system, recommending an examination of the procedures with a view to introducing new ones and suggested consideration be given to the establishment of a grievance board made up of a serving officer, an official of the Department of Defence and a member of the (as yet to be established) representative associations. Later, in 2004, legislation provided for the introduction of a military ombudsman following years of lobbying and negotiations by the PDFOR R A, who first raised the issue of the need for one as early as 1992. This sense among military personnel that their world was enclosed and complaints about it could not be articulated outside of the strict bounds of military regulation adds to the peculiarity of life in the profession. Furthermore, it increases the isolation and 'apartness' noted by Huntington and Janowitz as being one of the ingredients that need to be taken into consideration when assessing the state of civil–military relations in any particular situation.

From the inception of the legislation in Ireland's defence acts, orders from a superior officer were absolute. Any deviation from them resulted in a subordinate being guilty of a serious offence.[28] In a cultural environment such as that of the late 1980s, many would have believed it inconceivable to permit a situation whereby any of the activities of the

military body as a whole would ever be subject to a process of negotiation. Negotiations in an industrial-relations model would represent
the 'management' and the 'workers'. Such a means of engagement was
incomprehensible in the armed forces. The evolution of the trade-union
movement in Ireland and elsewhere sought to put management/owners
and their 'subordinate' workforce on equitable if not equal levels for
the purpose of negotiations. The process of respective consultation and
negotiation assumes at some level the right of the worker to disagree or
object to management initiatives or instructions. This concept, however,
would be alien to the structured command and control system that
was and is relied upon in countless armies around the world. Unlike
a civilian factory that may grind to a halt as a result of an industrial
dispute with little but financial consequences, it can be argued that any
impediment to the work of the armed forces could lead to loss of life or
even the undermining of the security of the State.

   Given the gravity of such scenarios and the subsequent establishment of statutory representative associations that now engage in
negotiations, a number of questions emerge. How did the army in
Ireland find itself in a situation where many of its decisions would
eventually become subject to the need for agreement or consultation? What changes took place in the defence policy and how did
they impact on civil–military relations? Were developments in Ireland
at the time indicative of an erosion of civil–military relations? To
what extent, if any, did the military intervene in politics? Does the
political intervention of enlisted personnel represent a greater or lesser
threat to civil–military relations? Does the evolution of representative associations lessen the susceptibility of military intervention? Has
intervention occurred in Ireland before? In the face of the emerging
reality that such a particular scenario was about to evolve, how did the
traditional military hierarchy respond to the request for the 'right of
association'? Did European resolutions and organisations help Irish
soldiers formulate a perspective on these matters? Did Irish soldiers in
turn influence European personnel in the pursuit of their aims? In the
military culture of the 1980s, how did the General Staff of the army
and the government perceive the effect of serving personnel and their
families publicly criticising conditions of service? The specific and
trenchant opposition that was cited by the army and the government
will be outlined later; so what triggered a change of heart?

1

Peculiarities of Military Life and Military Intervention

There are many ways in which to consider how Ireland's armed forces managed to acquire the right of association. This could be construed as a political study examining the ways and means by which politicians were persuaded or influenced to make changes and pave the way for new legislation. It could be looked at in the context of women's studies, whereby a group of like-minded women with a common purpose set in motion a series of events that led to the empowerment of a group of men. One could decide to approach the subject from a management or business point of view in which a particular workforce overcame the entrenched opposition of their leaders to acquire concessions that had been forcibly refused. It could even be considered from a human-rights point of view where one section of society had held itself as being denied a basic human right and worked within democratic and legal parameters to win that right. However, the discipline of civil–military relations is probably the best context from which to examine the emergence of representative bodies in the Irish armed forces in the late 1980s. This field of study has a broad corpus of work that deals primarily with the special relationship between a military force and the State in which it serves. Where this relationship is healthy, a military force serves the State through its government without question. Where this relationship breaks down, consequences can follow that, depending on cultural or geographical tradition, can range from minor fracture to full military overthrow. That special relationship became strained in Ireland during this period. The grievances of soldiers regarding their pay and conditions became the catalysts for their seeking the right of association, a right that neither government nor the military leadership were prepared to consider. As mentioned earlier, it could be argued that an examination or an analysis of these events should be grounded in the discipline of industrial relations or radical politics. Studies that concentrate a little outside of mainstream labour activities such as Devine, Lane and Puirséil (eds), *Essays in Irish Labour History* (Dublin, 2008), would be enhanced by the inclusion of how representation came about in the Irish armed forces. The continuing research of Forster, Edmunds and Cottey (eds), outlined in their series of studies such as *Soldiers and Societies in Post-Communist Europe* (Hampshire, 2003), could benefit from an examination of the events outlined in this book, events that occurred in Ireland during the very period in which they ground their analysis. It is conceivable that a new chapter could be added to the next edition of Coakley and Gallagher's (eds) *Politics in the Republic of Ireland* (Oxon, 2005), regarding how the Irish Government now interact with the military. However, while it is certainly true that there is an interesting study to be gleaned from these disciplinary perspectives, the primary impact of the events regarding the relationship between the military body and the government is more firmly positioned in civil–military relations. It is at this interface that new knowledge emerges regarding the hierarchal relationship between the military body and the government in Ireland. It is from this perspective that the extent of military intervention can be gauged. It is during the events that occurred between 1998 and 1992 that the deeply held attitudes to command and discipline in the Irish Army were not only forced to the surface, but became an issue of challenge between the army and the State it served.

Up to now, countries from the United States to Africa and from Asia to South America have been examined,[1] and although much has been written on the early relationships of army and State-makers in Ireland, there is still very little that has dealt with either enlisted personnel or representative associations. Throughout writings and theoretical proposals to date, a common assumption would appear to be that this civil–military relationship is gauged on the interaction between the officer corps and the government on one hand, and the officer corps and their ideal of 'the State' on the other. Much of the work examines the propensity of the military to 'intervene', a term that covers everything from political lobbying by the military of incumbent governments in relation to procurement, budgets and pay, to mutinies and the full final military coup d'état. In his examination of post-colonial African civil–military relations, Welch contends that there are three types of army 'involvement' in the politics of the State:

> the 'non-involvement', where there is a total absence of meddling in politics; the mutinous activity arising, in the main, over pay and conditions which he says is the first step in the involvement of the military in political life and, finally, the full political involvement embodied in the seizure of control.[2]

In *The Soldier and the State*, Huntington suggests that the more professional the officer corps, the less likely the possibility of intervention.[3] He dismisses enlisted personnel completely from any consideration in the context of civil–military relations on the basis that they are not professionals. Very little of the literature gives any consideration at all to a role for lower ranks. Finer's work *Man on Horseback* suggests that any political interaction with the government constitutes 'intervention' and asks how soldiers are 'politicised'.[4] Many consider officer training, officer-corps corporate identity and their bureaucratic functions as being crucial in the consideration of the level or complexity of civil–military relations in a particular country.[5] In Ireland the events that led to the emergence of the representative associations could easily be categorised as falling within a definition of 'intervention' in the context of civil–military relations. What is new to debate is an examination of the Irish context, and in particular the consideration of the fact that enlisted personnel played a central role in shaping a substantial alteration in the actual civil–military relations of the State.

The internal written requests of soldiers to establish a representative body, the political and social activities of the spouses group NASA, the political criticism of government by the opposition parties and the media, European parliamentary resolutions, European military representative associations and the propensity for a lengthy constitutional court case all seem to have culminated in the passing of the Defence Amendment Act 1990 in Ireland, which de facto sets out legislative parameters that define the basis on which elements of the military will 'relate', or engage with the government, in certain prescribed areas. These events at the very least constitute a shift in civil–military relations in Ireland and a new formal division of relations between

purely military matters and social/military matters. Before examining
the events that played out in the political arena that considered
the situation as it prevailed in the Defence Forces at the time, it is
important to outline the particular hierarchal environment in which a
soldier operates.

Taking into account the common perspective that the military are
unique in their responsibility to the State, in what Huntington calls
their capacity for the 'dispensation of violence', the fact that no threat
of violence was a part of the events in Ireland is worthy of consideration in the broader study of civil–military relations elsewhere. It will
be useful to highlight the attitudes of the Irish officer corps at the time,
which will give an insight into their particular perception of loyalty to
the State versus loyalty to the government, an area that appears to be
of great interest to the various contributors to the discipline of civil–
military relations. In Ireland, an examination of the sequence of events,
the relevant activities of the participants and the comparative issues in
the context of civil–military relations will best help contextualise and
define what happened, and what it means. Apart from issues of pay
and allowances, which are common to all workers, the consideration
of life under military law is a crucial element to the understanding of
what happened in Ireland.

PECULIARITIES OF MILITARY LIFE

Prior to the events of the 1980s in Ireland that this book will explore,
the day-to-day running of the armed forces was encapsulated in the
system of the military 'chain of command'. This system, which traditionally positioned members of the Irish forces outside of the sphere
of industrial relations as practised in the workplace of the civilian
population, relied on a hierarchal authoritarian system of discipline
supported by military law, Defence Force Regulations (DFRs) and a
tradition of obedience. Personnel, for reasons of discipline and State
security, could never be afforded the right to strike or withdraw labour.
Both ethically and culturally, members were deemed to be 'in the
service' of the State. As in most countries, the armed forces are seen as
the last line of defence in the event of either internal or external threat
to the people, institutions or jurisdictional integrity of the State.

MILITARY INTERVENTION

At the time of writing in 2016, the events that changed the context and operation of civil–military relations in Ireland are quite recent and may in time attract much more attention. In the broad corpus of work examining civil–military relations, there has been little scholarly attention paid to the Irish context. Much has been written on events that have helped shape Ireland's social and military history, such as the War of Independence and the Civil War, but they have not been contextualised with regard to the wider study of the subject. Professor Huntington does not examine the Irish context in his work, although it has to be noted that, at the time of his writing, the Irish Army structure differed little from other structures such as the British and the American. He did not consider any possible role or impact of enlisted personnel in influencing civil–military relations in the Irish or any other army, nor did he, or anyone else, look at representative associations. This is not because they did not exist then. The Dutch armed forces sought to form representative associations as early as 1896. At the time of Finer's research in civil–military relations in 1962, the German and Danish forces were forming or had already formed representative bodies for their serving personnel. He defines democratic and legal means of military intervention; he does not deal in any way with military representative associations. Broadly speaking, very little attention has been paid to the role of enlisted personnel and their effect, if any, on the relationship between the military and the organs of State and even less so on the role, if any, of representative associations. Although military intervention is widely considered in the context of the use of arms, there is a dearth of material regarding 'democratic intervention' by members of armed forces and even less material regarding intervention by enlisted personnel. Military 'intervention' in Ireland is probably seen in the collective memory as the use of the army to maintain essential services such as dustbin collection or public transportation during the withdrawal of labour by civilian unions.

Finer does grade different levels of military intervention and includes among them a level where the *influence* of the military authorities is exercised in a legitimate way with the level above being where *pressure* is applied.[6] Although these grades could be applied to the Irish situation, his only reference to Ireland is in relation to the Curragh mutiny and the constitutionality or otherwise of British Army actions that occurred before the foundation of the Irish State.

It is clear that in the emergence of representative bodies for the armed forces in Ireland, an informal code of honour among enlisted personnel exists. That perspective places the integrity of the State at the highest level. Nevertheless, little has been written about the concept articulated in Ireland by Irish soldiers (influenced by EUROMIL) of the citizen in uniform, and of the notion given expression in the European parliamentary resolutions that in peacetime a soldier should be afforded the same democratic rights as all other citizens.

Since few have considered the Irish context of civil-military relations, it is not surprising that an examination of what happened in Ireland has not yet found its way into the broader studies. This book presents the opportunity to acquire a new perspective on Ireland's civil–military relations and hopefully further afield. If, through its pages, we acquire an understanding of the background, motivation and methodology of Irish military personnel in the pursuit of the right of association, we will understand better how and why these relations in Ireland were affected. This will lend knowledge to the field that may assist us in a greater understanding of civil–military relations elsewhere. Culturally, governments may embrace them or dismiss them; academically, scholars may ignore them as a legitimate part of the study of civil–military relations, but either way representative associations and the pursuit of the right to form them has been a missing link in the study of civil–military relations so far. Despite an Irish military thesis regarding the establishment of the associations, and the readiness or lack of same by the military authorities there, and another thesis that deals with the operation of representative bodies at barrack level, there is little else. Commandant Michael Gannon examined the advent of representative associations in Ireland. However, his focus was primarily on the events themselves and his conclusions were about apportioning blame to government and, to a lesser extent, to the military authorities on the emergence of the associations, which he appeared to view as an undesirable development. This interesting study was about the internal responses of the army and their preparedness, and as might be expected for a military thesis, the perspective is grounded in command and control.[7]

Oliver O'Connor, a former member of PDFORRA, explored the actual operation of the associations' committees at barrack level. This study encompasses the years after the body was set up and sheds no light on the broader impact of the emergence of the associations on the field of civil–military relations.[8] Apart from these studies, an examination of some of the leading works that follow reveals a complete absence of consideration of the Irish context or of the role and position of representative bodies as a whole in the conduct of civil–military relations.

The Gleeson Commission report outlines the findings and recommendations of Ireland's first-ever independent commission, set up in 1989 to address what was being described in the Irish Parliament and the newspapers as the 'army crisis'.[9] It was chaired by Senior Counsel Mr Dermot Gleeson and had the following terms of reference, 'To carry out a major review of the remuneration and conditions of service in the Defence Forces having regard to their separate and distinct role and organisation and to make recommendations.' The commission report presents its findings as a result of twelve months of deliberation, during which 215 written submissions were considered, eighteen oral hearings were conducted, thirty military installations and posts around Ireland were visited, 3,000 Defence Force personnel were met and the commission itself went to consult with the Irish members serving in the United Nations Interim Force South Lebanon (UNIFIL). Although a detailed submission was made by the NCOs Team to the commission seeking the right to establish an association to be known as the Permanent Defence Forces Other Ranks Representative Association (PDFORRA), the report only refers once to representative bodies quoting impending legislation as a reason not to respond to or comment on the request. Apart from the findings of the report, what is significant in the context of civil–military relations is that this was the first time members of the armed forces had an opportunity to express their views to an incumbent government without having to go strictly through the usual 'chain of command'. However, the report itself does not address the issue of representative bodies and their possible alteration of the civil–military relations of Ireland. In addition to the many individual and organisational submissions made to the commission, the one compiled internally by the Defence Forces represents the most comprehensive of all.[10] It records the wish lists of the officers, non-commissioned and privates in relation to pay, allowances and conditions of service. Only fifty copies were made. It is interesting to note that, through the process of setting up rank-orientated teams making submissions to the commission, a temporary framework was established which provided an opportunity for the military to interact with the government for a specific purpose and a specific timeframe in a specific way.

In *The Soldier and the State*, Huntington proposes a theoretical framework from which to study the relationship between civil authority and the military.[11] His has become a leading reference text in the field. He examines in detail the role of the military in society and how it interacts with its various levels but, in particular, with government. He contends that the relationship between the two is unique given the skill set of the military, their possession of arms and the capacity of an army to interfere with or overthrow their political masters. Having established the necessity of a State to raise an army for internal and external defence, the point is made that there is therefore a dependency on an entity that of itself can also be the greatest threat to the very State that raises it. Given the capacity, through possession of arms, of an army to turn on a government, Huntington explores the propensity of intervention by members of the armed forces and concludes that the higher the level of military professionalism, the lower the risk of intervention. He expounds the skills of the military officer and the officer corps, concluding they are a profession on par with the civilian medical and legal professions. He dismisses the enlisted ranks as not having any impact or role in civil–military relations. His theoretical framework is set in an American setting but he did not consider the Irish context.

Writing much later, Finer seeks to provide an informed insight into the general structure of command in an army and sets out the strengths, weakness and desirability or otherwise of peripheral or full involvement of the military in politics. In his *Man on Horseback* he provides examples of the organisational cohesion and efficiency of a military body, but he argues that an army is incapable of running even the most primitive of societies.[12] Finer disagrees with one of the central contentions of Professor Huntington that the increasing professionalism of an army is a factor in diminishing the likelihood of military intervention in political affairs. Finer does not examine the attitudes of the military in Ireland despite the fact that they now have formal interaction with politics through the representative bodies and that, in his own 'table of intervention', the Irish armed forces were at least at the first level. A study of the Irish situation could lend some clarity on his musings about the fine line between 'influence' and 'blackmail'.[13]

There have been some examinations of post-communist European civil–military relations – particularly in the light of the 'democratisation' of former Soviet bloc countries. Edmunds, Cottey and Forster assess the transition of civil–military relations from the communist era to the post-communist era at a distance of fifteen years.[14] Although their book examines military–societal relations, it does not include consideration of the existence of representative associations and what role they may have played in that process. In another work on a similar theme, *Soldiers and Societies*, they looked closely at the relationship between the military and the society it serves.[15] This book examined the role of armies in a number of central and eastern European States in the wake of the fall of the eastern bloc. The events considered are set in the late 1980s and early 1990s. The book does not refer to the role, however small, played by western European military representative associations in the 'democratisation' process of the military personnel of former communist regimes. Nor does it consider the role played by Ireland's representative association PDFORRA in the process.

In his book *Democracy and Military Force,* Philip Everts considers the growth in the influence of democratic societies' input in the decisions made regarding entering conflict.[16] The book explores the changing level of acceptability of war with regard both to the motivation for it and the perceived casualty levels that may result from it. It combines and updates a number of previous papers by the author and considers the issues raised with regard to the western societal responses to military intervention in Kosovo and Iraq. The author does not consider the views held by European and Irish representative associations that a soldier in peacetime is a citizen in uniform and has a stake in decisions made by society about war and armed conflict. An understanding of the representative bodies that this book will explore could contribute richly to the issues raised in his book. The methodology of those seeking to establish an input into how decisions that affect them as soldiers are made could be considered to be intervention.

Welch and Smith examine the propensity of military organisations to intervene in politics. In *Military Role and Rule* they draw on five examples of varying degrees, from military influence in day to-day-government decision-making, up to a full coup d'état.[17] The countries examined are Peru, Nigeria, France, Thailand and Egypt. In attempting to identify any particular pattern or factors that contribute to the likelihood of intervention, they consider matters such as political awareness of the officer class and the social class or strata they are recruited from, the use of the military for civilian operations, military organisational cohesion and the perceived effect of government policy on both the economic welfare of the State and its attitude to the military. A recurring theme is the question of military loyalty and the difference between whether the officer body feels subservient to the government or to the State and its people. They conclude that while there is great variation in the instances and circumstances of military influence and intervention, 'throughout most of the world the military appears to be in politics to stay.' The authors do not consider the Irish context, and despite the proximity of the activities of representative bodies (in some European countries at the time of writing) to the body politic, they do not consider them either.

In an American context, Waterhouse and Wizard related their personal experiences in their efforts to assist GIs to 'organise'.[18] In their account, *Turning the Guns Around*, they indicate that the organisational aims of this group were more to do with being allowed protest against the war and the practice of compulsory drafting than with the right to organise themselves. When taken as a comparison to what happened in Ireland, this highlights the much narrower aims of Irish soldiers to have only the right of association and explicity to renounce their right to comment on operational matters and policy. It illustrates the response of the military in the US to the notion of soldiers 'organising' for whatever reason, and the threat that was felt by those in authority.

Despite parallels of that fear among the military personnel in Ireland, it was their spouses that initially confronted the government in the seeking of better conditions for their husbands in the army. They argued at the time that their spouses' poor conditions were reflected in the quality of their own lives. An American study regarding military spouses and the challenges surrounding their employment and education was undertaken in 2004 under the auspices of the US National Defence Research Institute, and its results were prepared for the office of the secretary of defence.[19] The study took place against a background of the US administration being mindful of the impact of domestic contentment on the retention of serving military personnel. The work examines which factors of military life inhibit or restrict the capacity of the spouse to seek or acquire education or employ-ment. As part of the research, 1,100 subjects were interviewed from all levels of enlisted and commissioned ranks. The research confirms that although the occupational choices of military spouses are the same as those of civilians, the former are less likely to be employed than the latter, and when they are employed, they earn less than their counterparts for the same work. There are numerous recommendations regarding making life in the military more harmonious for families. The report does not consider an Irish context or the evolution of the National Army Spouses Association (NASA) in Ireland in 1988, which articulated a view that military personnel and their families were being treated differently from the rest of society.

In *The Political Influence of the Military*, Perlmutter and Bennet provide a variety of extracts from well-known and some lesser known scholars and authors on the subject of civil–military relations and, in particular, on the influence or otherwise that the three types of military soldier proposed by Perlmutter have on the political system.[20] This work does not consider the operation of representative bodies comprising exclusively of soldiers who can have a direct influence on the political system, albeit in a regulated fashion.

In other studies of this subject of intervention, Welch and others analyse factors that lead to military involvement in politics in Africa and the impact of military rule upon individual African States.[21] As part of the analysis, the primacy of the loyalty of the soldier to either government or State is raised. Three types of military involvement in politics are suggested: abstention from politics, mutinies aimed at forcing governments to improve pay or conditions and coups d'état considered to be full-scale military intervention. Comparisons might be drawn between the 'political' influences brought to bear by Irish soldiers on politicians in the Irish Parliament (Dáil Eireann) and those mentioned by Welch, but, at time of writing, the Irish situation had not yet evolved.

Throughout the period when soldiers were seeking the right of association in Ireland, the officer corps there were never publicly involved. In one sense they stood apart, seeing themselves as dependent on the goodwill the government had towards them in relation to improving pay and conditions. In a later chapter, the attitude of officers and their approach to the problems of the late 1980s will be explored, in particular their sense of a two-way code of honour between themselves and the government of the day.

Karl Demeter, drawing on extensive German national archive sources, presents conclusions having looked at the whole establishment and evolution of the German officer corps, their corporate identity, *esprit de corps* and code of honour.[22] He examines the role of obedience of the military to the State versus the government, and among other things he details the moral, legal and professional dilemma of officers having to pledge allegiance to leaders such as Hitler. Demeter confines himself to the Prussian and German officer codes, and Ireland, before or after independence, is not considered.

A study by Paul Smith of the relationship between the armed forces and the British government between 1856 and 1990 sheds no light on the arrangement that hitherto had existed in Ireland. His book *Government and the Armed Forces in Britain* traces and comments on the relationship between the government of Britain and its military chiefs.[23] In particular, it focuses on the process of procurement and defence-budget determination. The arrival of representative bodies and their competing for scarce resources from the national budget undoubtedly could impact on those relationships, but they are not considered in his work.

There has been a variety of studies and scholarly interest on the whole question of civil–military relations. The political, economic and security issues that have hitherto been considered by authors and researchers have not been able to take account of the impact or potential impact of representative associations because they have been generally unaware of them. Equally, studies that attempt to understand the complexity of loyalty and what prompts intervention have not had the added benefit of considering the new knowledge presented by the examination and analysis of the events in Ireland that brought about the emergence of representative associations in the armed forces there. Such a consideration may well provide a whole new factor that has to be considered by scholars when assessing the relationships that exist between military bodies and their civilian governments. It is useful then to re-examine two dimensions of Ireland's military history in the context of civil–military relations.

Professor Huntington in proposing a theoretical framework from which to study civil–military relations suggested that any system of such relations involve the 'complex equilibrium between the authority, influence and ideology of the military, on the one hand and the authority, influence and ideology of non-military groups on the other'. They are, he said, 'two elements that are interdependent on each other, and no one of these elements can change without producing further changes in the other.'[24] The two broad elements to which he refers are the military body itself and the civilian community from which it receives its direction. In a technical sense, any armed force cannot exist in isolation – they must have a community to serve. Even if this is not a single community, armies are headless alone, directionless unless a higher authority gives instruction and identifies objectives that utilise the unique skills that they possess in the application of violence.[25]

Finer suggests that armies are precluded 'save in exceptional circumstances, and for brief periods of time, from ruling without civilian collaboration and openly in their own name. Soldiers must either rule through civilian cabinets or pretend to be something other than they are.'[26]

Apart from armed criminal gangs who exist purely for financial gain, rebel bands, insurgent armies and revolutionary groups serve some higher purpose or aspiration always bigger than the sum of the individual. In such cases they may well be seeking to establish a nation or a community, but few armed groups exist purely for the perpetration of their existence. Given that most societies feel the need for an armed force to protect and defend their citizens and vital interests, a relationship based on service arises. That the nation's interests are being served is usually the justification for maintaining an army in the first place. However, given that an army is going to be the most lethal force of any particular society, nominally capable of destroying those whom it serves, the way it provides service, receives its instructions and relates to those it is obliged to obey is what constitutes the various elements of civil–military relations.

Identification of the ultimate authority for the armed forces to act becomes crucial. Do they serve the nation? If so, who or what is the embodiment of the nation? Democracy and other forms of governance usually identify a person or group who supposedly represents the wishes of the community. This representation, if the elective process is legitimate, serves to provide the necessary leadership for the armed forces and embody the imperative to send them to war. But there are other scenarios. There can also be constitutional, legal, royal, governmental arrangements or tradition. In the case of the US there is provision for congressional approval of the decision to go to war, yet according to Professor David Kennedy this has only been exercised in five out of 234 decisions over the last two centuries that sent US military personnel into armed conflict. All other occasions were by executive order.[27] If the legitimacy of the decision to go to war is in doubt, if the motivation of the figure or body who has made a determination of necessity is in question, then serious moral and social issues arise. The structures that govern who is responsible to who, with regard to the national interest being served, and the taking of decisions that impact upon it are crucial elements of civil–military relations. Is it the military themselves who decide when and where they are to act in the application of violence? Is it the entirety of government or a part of it which is responsible? Is there a point at which a military body acting in the belief that it will serve the public interest will challenge and/or threaten a sitting government or ruler? If not, what of the officers in the German Army who tried to assassinate Hitler?

Most societies abhor the very notion of military intervention, which by and large takes the form of armed soldiers using their weapons to either forcibly remove or change the decisions of a sitting government. Such action is clearly recognisable and easily defined. A military force refusing to carry out the order of the government could be categorised similarly. Such manipulations of the government by the military are based on the threatened use or actual use of arms. Though skilled and exclusively trained in the administration of military force, can armies exert political pressure without them? Or is it reasonable to assume that any intervention, whether using arms or not, carries an implied threat to do so? Finer classifies military intervention in politics as 'The armed forces constrained substitution of their own policies and/or their persons for those of the recognised civilian authorities.' He suggests that the factors that inhibit intervention include professionalism and *esprit de corps*, the principle of civil supremacy, and the possibility of self-destruction or eventual abolition when a civilian power structure is re-established. Of them all, he quotes civil supremacy as being the most effective means of inhibiting military intervention. In considering motives that dispose the military to intervene, Finer suggests the following:

> The 'manifest destiny of the soldier' in which it is claimed that the soldier enjoys a 'sacred trust', almost a divine duty to act in the public interest. The belief that they hold most precious the national interest of the nation in their actions and finally the motivation to act out of self interest, for improvements in their own careers or conditions.[28]

Huntington, however, wrote that the disposition to intervene was made greater or lesser by the actual professionalism of the army officers – the more professional in training and ethos, the less likely to intervene. However, both this argument and Finer's see soldiers somehow outside of the political process. Finer admits 'we know little or nothing about the mechanism by which rival political ideologies are transmitted into and throughout the armed forces. On the whole, the military are effectively prohibited from participating in civil political party parties; and it is not through such participation that political ideologies are usually transmitted to and through them'. He maintains that most countries strive to prevent military involvement in political parties, and advances some 'obvious' reasons as to why.[29] While it is true that many countries prohibit the active participation of soldiers in political parties in an attempt, one presumes, to give effect to civilian supremacy, the fact remains that soldiers have a vote and are able to exercise it in favour of one party or another, albeit in a secret ballot, which is also true of any other citizen. The issue then is not about the exercise of the franchise, which has long been established as a citizen right and in some cases such as in Australia as an obligation, but about the democratic activity that goes together with having the right to vote. The exercise of democracy, however, is not only about casting the vote. Citizens often wish to consult their politicians, to try to influence them in some way or another for community or personal entitlements. Politicians also want to garner support and will speak to all who have the capacity to install them in office, or remove them from it.

The thorny question that arises when considering political intervention is as to whether the military should be assumed to be a different entity at all. If all citizens are free to engage in political lobbying as is their right in a democracy, is there not a case to be made for soldiers? Professor Kennedy suggests that there was a time when the bearing of arms was considered an obligation which was conferred on those who were full and active citizens. There was a direct link between citizenship and the necessity of a community to defend itself.[30] This effectively meant a direct link between citizenship and service in the army. If a community or group legitimises itself with democratic principles in the election of its leaders and the conduct of its business, and it further asks of some of its citizens to undertake the commitment to lay down their lives in defence of those principles, can it be argued that there is an inconsistency at play? On one hand seeking the ultimate sacrifice for something that is deemed a fundamental human right and on the other denying that right to the very people who are willing to defend it? The argument about political-party membership causing division in the army could be equally applied to military personnel who support rival

football teams, or enjoy being members of different religious beliefs.
According to Professor Kennedy, the Weinberger doctrine sought
to extend part-time membership of the armed services to 'ordinary
citizens' in the hope that more thought would be given before commit-
ting the country to war.[31] Even though there can be a distinction made
between the traditional 'citizen' armies in countries such as Greece and
post-revolution France and the 'professional' armies of the UK, US
and Ireland today, are not all soldiers full citizens of the country under
which the army is raised? Given that to serve in the armed forces is
usually a prerequisite to be a citizen, are we to assume that the citizens in
the full-time forces are less deserving of consideration in the decision-
making process that leads to war? Are there degrees of citizenship? It
seems on the other hand that there are examples of soldiers interfering
with the political process in such a way as to hinder the work of government, and this is clearly undesirable.

In the events that led to the emergence of representative associations in Ireland, the idea of the democratic rights of soldiers was raised
on many occasions during the soldiers' campaign to acquire 'the right
of association'. The soldiers, at the time, perceived that the basis of this
right was grounded in the Irish Constitution, where all citizens are
conferred with the right to form associations for professional interests.
They clearly saw themselves as being entitled to rights that came with
actual citizenship.

2

The Origins of the Irish Armed Forces and the Evolution of Civil–Military Relations in Ireland, 1913–24

In identifying the origins of the Defence Forces of Ireland there are numerous starting points that can be taken depending on one's perspective. A question that emerges is at what point an army is 'the army of the State'. Is it correct to identify a pre-independence group as a State army, or an army in waiting? To what extent can a revolutionary army, an unrecognised government and their relationship with each other be considered? The current definable continuous Irish Permanent Defence Force (PDF) was set up by proclamation in 1924 as authorised by Section 22 of the Defence Forces (Temporary Provisions) Act 1923 [1] It was from this date that the current PDF became subject to government control. From 1923 the 'temporary' provisions were re-enacted by legislation each year until the Defence Act 1954 was passed, providing a more permanent nature to the legislation governing the forces. Prior to the passing of the original 1923 Act, the army can be said to have originated from elements of a revolutionary group that had participated in the armed struggle for Irish independence. Humphrey and Graves, in their work on military law in Ireland, set the point of origin at the foundation of the Irish Volunteers, established by Eoin MacNeill in November 1913.[2] In his history of the Irish Army, Duggan also sets this date but acknowledges the changes in emphasis, name and focus of the group with a split in September 1914 over the thorny issue of

fighting for the British Army in the First World War.[3] The formulation
of an oath of allegiance to the Irish Republic and the first Dáil Éireann
that was sought by the government on 20 August 1919 were seen by
some as facilitating the establishment of an official State army. When
the oath was tabled, it was pointed out that the present constitution of
the Volunteers 'prevented them from being subject to any other body
but their own executive'. It was proposed that at their next convention
they would be asked, as a standing army, to swear allegiance to the Dáil.
The Minister for Defence on the day said he regarded the Volunteers as
a standing army and that as such they should be subject to the government.[4] It could also be argued that it was not until 1921 that the army
was formally connected to the government when, in the second Dáil on
11 March 1921, at the height of the War of Independence, the government finally took responsibility for it and its actions. The President of
the Dáil, Eamon De Valera, said he felt that while in America and since
he came home, the Dáil was hardly acting fairly by the army in not
publicly taking full responsibility for all its acts. He suggested that formal
acceptance of a state of war being in existence would also position them
to seek 'belligerent rights' abroad.[5]

   Ireland had, up to this point, a long history of struggle that had mani-
fested itself in a variety of insurrections, attempted revolutions, uprisings
and paramilitary activity. Earlier in history, the assistance of other nations
was sought to encourage Britain to leave her earliest and probably most
troublesome colony. France and Spain in particular had been encouraged into the ongoing conflict of Anglo-Irish affairs. Being on the side
of the Irish and against the British coincided with their own strategic
interests. Neither was successful. Even the nominal villains of the First
World War, the Germans, were courted for a time leading up to the Easter
Rising in Dublin in 1916. The Easter Rising, as it became known, was
a military failure, but certain events during and after it contributed to it
being seen as a milestone in the lengthy history of Irish armed resistance.
It was perhaps at this point that a relationship between those bearing arms
for a nationalist ideal and the general populace began to grow into the
particular brand of civil–military relations that was to evolve in Ireland.
On Easter weekend of 1916, the proclamation of the establishment of a
republic was first read out by Padraig Pearse on the steps of the General
Post Office in O'Connell Street, Dublin, the epicentre of the insurrection. Although many Irish people seemed indifferent to the events that
weekend, and some Dubliners were more than annoyed at the disruption

the fighting caused, the subsequent rounding up of the insurgent leaders and the manner of their executions by Britain's imperial forces appeared to coalesce people's views towards the merits of independence and armed struggle. The shooting at dawn on 3 May 1916 of Pearse, McDonagh and Clarke followed the next day by the executions of Plunkett, Daly, O'Hanrahan and Pearse's brother Willie and by that of MacBride the following day shocked the Irish population. After a one-day cessation, Colbert, Kent, Mallin and Heuston were also shot. Finally, on 12 May, Seán MacDermott and James Connolly (in his wheelchair) were both executed at Kilmainham Jail, Dublin. Other death sentences followed but were commuted to imprisonment. Robert Kee suggests:

> In the Irish situation an extremely tense and sensitive emotional atmos-
> phere had been created by these measures ... even so it cannot be said
> that they need inevitably, in themselves, have led to the pronounced
> swing round of public opinion to the rebel's way of thinking which
> took place. They merely created a needlessly favourable climate for
> such a transformation.[6]

The hardening of opinion against British military treatment of those involved in the Easter Rising was seemingly balanced by an equitable softening of attitudes towards those who suffered execution, incarceration and internment. Augusteijn noted:

> The virulent British reaction to the failed rising of 1916 swayed the
> allegiance of many and, by identifying with popular issues such as the
> opposition to conscription, the republicans established themselves as
> the main representatives of nationalists in 1919.[7]

The armed struggle did continue despite the execution of the leaders of the Easter Rising, the imposition of martial law, and the arrest of over 3,400 people, 1,841 of whom were interned, and the ninety death sentences that were issued.[8]

In 1801 Great Britain had passed the Act of Union. This effectively abolished Ireland's parliament and subsumed it into the parliament at Westminster. Two years after the crushing of the 1916 Easter Rising and the execution of its leaders, the 1918 parliamentary elections for Westminster were held on 14 December. They resulted in a massive swing of support for the new Irish political party Sinn Féin (meaning 'ourselves alone') who had identified themselves closely with the events of 1916 and their aftermath. Of the 105 seats contested, six former members of the Irish Parliamentary Party candidates were returned and twenty-six unionists. In a huge upset for the traditional parties, Sinn Féin won an incredible seventy-three seats. Despite their success, they had adopted a strategy wherein their new members of parliament (MPs) would not take their parliamentary seats at Westminster. Instead, on 21 January 1919, twenty-eight of the available Sinn Féin elected representatives met and established the first Dáil Éireann (Parliament of Ireland) declaring themselves to be the government of Ireland. It was also on this date that the War of Independence began.[9] These new 'parliamentarians' were men who had advocated military struggle and were identified with those who claimed they bore arms in the national interest.

For those who had advocated the struggle itself it had not been a smooth transition from armed revolutionary group to subordinate disciplined national army. Prior to the establishment of the State, the armed elements that constituted a revolutionary army had taken their orders from, and pledged allegiance to, their own 'army council'. Many of the leaders of that council were also members of this first Dáil, which had been formed arising from the legitimate parliamentary election of 1918 albeit for a different parliament. In March 1921, the government of the first Dáil endorsed the armed struggle that had become known as the War of Independence.[10]

Two months later, as a result of the Government of Ireland Act being passed in December 1920, another set of elections were held for two new parliaments in Ireland, one for a new jurisdiction comprising six of the nine counties in the province of Ulster; the second for the remaining three counties in Ulster together with the twenty-three counties in Leinster, Connaught and Munster. Many of the same candidates who had made up the first Dáil were re-elected. The same approach was adopted as had taken place previously. The successful candidates established the second Dáil and ignored the institution for which the elections had been held. Throughout a heightened guerrilla war against the British military and administrative presence in Ireland, Michael Collins had been the Minister for Finance of the government and at the same time the director of intelligence who coordinated and directed the military strategy of the War of Independence.

When Britain finally agreed to talks, Collins was directed by the then government to participate in the group of plenipotentiaries that went to London to engage in a conference there on 11 October 1921. The resultant treaty signed by them was a source of sharp division among members of the republican government on their return. It fell short of the ideal of recognising the previously declared republic for all thirty-two counties and yet took cognisance of the parliament that had been already set up for Northern Ireland, enshrining partition. The divisive debates that took place were to be aired in Dáil Eireann and the country at large. That same division was also prevalent among the men of the armed force who had been engaged together in what they saw as the fight for Irish freedom in the War of Independence. Robert Kee suggested it was the 'army who had brought the situation in which there was to be a treaty debated at all'.[11] Nevertheless, it was hoped that with a full debate in the Dáil, all views could be expressed and a democratic vote could be taken to resolve the matter finally and either accept or reject what had been offered by Britain. The plenipotentiaries who signed the Treaty on behalf of the provisional government saw it as a stepping stone to acquire full freedom. Michael Collins stated:

> I am responsible for making the nation fully understand what it gains by accepting it, and what is involved in its rejection. So long as I have made that clear I am perfectly happy and satisfied. Now we must look facts in the face. For our continued national and spiritual existence two things are necessary – security and freedom. If the Treaty gives us these or helps us to get at these, then I maintain that it satisfies our national aspirations.[12]

The government debate split the Dáil almost down the middle with those politicians opposed to the Treaty losing the vote on 7 January 1922 by a small margin of fifty-seven votes to sixty-four. Immediately after the vote was taken, Eamon De Valera contextualised his perspective on the authority of the parliament. He relegated the parliamentary debate to being just a 'resolution' and suggested that there was already a 'republic' which somehow had more authority because it had been established by the 'Irish people':

> There is one thing I want to say – I want it to go to the country and to the world, and it is this: the Irish people established a Republic. This is simply approval of a certain resolution. The Republic can only be disestablished by the Irish people. Therefore, until such time as the Irish people in regular manner disestablish it, this Republic goes on.[13]

In this stated perspective it would seem that the government of the day in De Valera's view was secondary to a higher idealist entity. Perhaps at this point civil turmoil was inevitable. Led by Eamon De Valera, those who opposed the Treaty walked out of parliament and political debate degenerated into physical conflict. What had been a relatively united government with its own united, though somewhat independent, army during the struggle for independence was now a divided group of politicians followed by a divided group of armed personnel. This was a crucial point in the very birth of the new nation State and an immediate crisis in civil–military relations was about to emerge. Peter Young suggested that the foundation of the military organisation had been established before the War of Independence.[14] Prior to the parliamentary walkout, it could be argued that the civil–military relations were at their peak, with the body politic and the military establishment, such as it was, united in their aims if not in their strategy. Instead, a military body, although not a formal one, had many of its members rejecting the authority of the parliament and the democratic decision it had made, thus reflecting the wider social and political division among the population. Kee maintained that it was anti-Treaty sentiment inside the Irish Republican Army (IRA) and their allegiance to their own leaders, not De Valera, which brought about Civil War.[15]

It could be argued that this rejection and what followed was full military intervention. The ensuing Civil War consolidated the political division and the loyalty of the men of arms to the respective sides of the conflict. Those who did not accept the provisions of the Treaty fought against those who did. De Valera argued that the army were the army of the republic and that the disestablishment of the republic by the government could lead to civil war.[16]

The conflict and the targeted violence it generated was not confined to the fighters themselves: government ministers of the new 'Free State' became 'legitimate targets' in the conflict as did those who had left the government. During the Treaty debate itself, Cork deputies had been circulated with a notice that they would be shot if they voted in favour of it. When it was brought to the attention of Cathal Brugha, in the Dáil, on 16 December 1921, he refused to deal with rumours and asked for evidence.[17] Later when he received a copy of the actual document he read it to the House:

To all T.D.s (members of parliament) in the Cork No. 1 Area:

(1) On December 10th the Staff of the First Southern Division and
    all Brigade Commandants met and sent forward to G.H.Q. a
    unanimous demand for the rejection of the Treaty proposals.
(2) You are reminded it is your duty to support this demand.
(3) To act otherwise would be treason to the Republic to which we
    have all sworn allegiance.

Now I have given you my assurance that I am going to deal with the
persons responsible for sending out that.[18]

If the Irish armed forces of the fledgling republican government were
perceived to be the official army of the day, it may be construed that
the Civil War constituted the highest level of military intervention
by a large number of those forces as defined by Finer, Huntington
and others. Those soldiers who rejected the provisions of the Treaty
and fought against it were placing the pursuit of an ideal above civil
authority. It could also be argued that since the ideal of the revolutionary army had not been fully met, then the government that was
constituted before the realisation of the ideal was not a legitimate
government, and rejection of their resolutions was merely a continua-
tion of the original struggle and not intervention. Lawlor maintained
that De Valera was responsible for the prolonging of the conflict in
transforming what had previously been local allegiance of IRA units
into a broader part of an ideal of the republic.[19] That position would be
somewhat weakened by their earlier participation in the deliberations
of the government and their leaders' participation in the democratic
vote. Lynch wrote that the signing of the Treaty divided Sinn Féin
between 'separatists who wanted the reality of an independence that
would enable Ireland to look after its own affairs, and those who
wanted more, who opposed the Treaty for a principle – the republic'.[20]
   The details of the military engagements that constituted the
Civil War are not relevant to this book, however the perspectives of
those involved in it and their allegiance to a particular ideal or an actual
government are important to the understanding of early civil–military
relations in the new State. Although the anti-Treaty forces were
thought to have been finally overcome in April 1923, doubts remained
among cabinet ministers as to whether those who fought in the Free

State Army on the pro-Treaty side did so out of loyalty to the new State or to their former military commanders. It was imperative that in order for the new State's civil–military relations to be set on a solid footing, provision would have to be made to establish the supremacy of civilian rule and not have the country depending on the sometimes transient loyalty of those skilled in the use of arms. At this early point in the nation's new circumstances, it was very clear that the concept of loyalty to the State far outweighed loyalty to the government. This was an important period in the establishment of the Irish State; that point at which the revolutionary soldiers hitherto dedicated to the downfall of the previous British civil authority had to recalibrate their efforts to support rather than suppress the new object of civil authority.

The timing of actions by 'soldiers of the State' during a period when the very definition of statehood was in question may well absolve those who opposed the democratic resolution of the new parliament whose legitimacy was being questioned, when they took up arms against the civil authority. However, there were two other instances not far removed chronologically from those events which raise a more serious question about the nature of military intervention in Ireland. In one case prior to the foundation of the new Irish State, soldiers of a different army owing allegiance to a different government threatened to take action that would result in orders not being followed. There was no confusion in the British Army in Ireland in 1913 about the legitimacy of the civilian government in London. Although the threat of armed insurrection did not arise in that instance, nevertheless there were certain soldiers who questioned the legitimacy or morality of government intentions and took a position that could be construed as mutiny. Equally, very soon after the foundation of the State and the subsequent Civil War, Irish soldiers of the new legitimate army brought influence to bear on political decision-making by threatening intervention.

In attempting to contextualise the events in the Irish armed forces of the 1980s from a civil–military perspective, it will be useful to look briefly at these two other periods in Ireland in the early twentieth century when the relationship between the military body and their government were strained to the point that intervention was threatened and may have occurred albeit without the eventual use of arms. Unlike in 1922, in both cases the State had long since established its legitimacy to govern the armies they now directed. The so-called

'Mutiny at the Curragh' by British Army personnel in 1913 and the threat of mutiny by members of the Irish Army in 1924 provide interesting comparisons when considering later events. It might be useful to examine briefly the stated motivations and perspectives that surrounded these events.

THE CURRAGH MUTINY

A series of events that became known as the Curragh mutiny occurred in Ireland among British armed forces there in 1913 and 1914. It could be argued that the institutions of the State were unable to implement democratically made decisions as a result of resistance in the army to a particular government policy. It could also be argued that a number of officers made personal decisions to resign their commissions in the face of what they saw as impending immoral orders. It would appear that the officers' loyalty to their own command structure may have been superior to that of the civil authority. The incidents in question arose between December 1913 and the end of March 1914, when the British parliamentary democracy at Westminster had indicated their intention to implement Home Rule for Ireland, providing the country with its own parliament in Dublin.

Strong opposition among Protestant unionist citizens of Northern Ireland had been a continuing feature of the public debate on the issue. In February 1912, during a specially convened general assembly of the Irish Presbyterian Church, unanimous resolutions were passed at a series of eleven meetings in which the 'unalterable opposition' to Home Rule was recorded.[21] Edward Carson, a leading unionist from Dublin, organised a protest campaign across Northern Ireland that rejected any notion of Home Rule and went on to threaten that if such a law was to be passed, the new Dublin parliament would be ignored and Northern Ireland would set up its own parliament and State. Significantly, this was to include the raising of its own army. Many leading British and unionist politicians at the time pledged their intention to participate in this new Ulster government should it become necessary. Volunteers were sought from all over Ulster to come to the defence of the province and of their religion. Their leaders used existing laws to justify the gathering of large numbers of personnel who were about to be trained in arms and foot drill.

Colonel Wallace, one of the members of the provisional executive of the Ulster 'government', applied to the courts 'for lawful authority to hold meetings and drill men in the use of arms'.[22] The result was an army of volunteers openly drilling on the streets of Northern Ireland at first with mock rifles but later with the real thing. They rapidly became a formidable and well-disciplined army, complete with signallers, motorcyclists, service corps and intelligence officers.[23] Over 100,000 men marching in military formation were assembled for a march past their leaders at Easter 1912. With the situation deteriorating and the defiance and arming of the Ulster volunteers, it seemed serious resistance against the expected Home Rule legislation and the State itself was imminent. With the police force, the judiciary and the body politic in Northern Ireland (and a section of it in Great Britain) seemingly acting in concert with the volunteers, it appeared that it was going to be left to the British Army to uphold the implementation of the will of parliament and maintain law and order and the protection of property.

One key player in the midst of the politicians at Westminster was the director of military operations, Sir Henry Wilson. He was on record as being sympathetic to the Ulster volunteers. He supplied Carson and opposition leader Bonar Law with ongoing updates regarding the intentions of officers of the British Army stationed in the Curragh in Ireland to resign. He also provided much of the information that would fuel fierce political debate in the House of Commons and the House of Lords. Wilson is credited with suggesting to Carson and Law that they should argue that the volunteers would be willingly deployed to 'fight for England' in any upcoming European conflict.[24] The government and opposition parties continued into the spring of 1914 attempting to resolve their differences or at least reach some sort of a compromise that would avert an armed confrontation and civilian casualties. They were not successful – the rumours regarding a crisis in the British Army in the Curragh and the threat of defections and mutiny only exacerbated the difficulties in the talks. Increasingly worrying intelligence reports coming from Ulster suggested that advanced plans were afoot by the Volunteers to raid government military arsenals and installations and commandeer their arms and munitions for their own use. These developments coupled with the declared intention of Carson to resist with arms any implementation of Home Rule persuaded the government to move to protect

installations and mobilise the requisite British Army and Royal Navy
units to Ulster. In a newspaper report at the time, these actions were
considered to be a 'bullying' of the people of Ulster. *The Irish Times*
reported on a *Daily Mail* article in which news of threatened resignations by officers in the Curragh were made public:

> Officers in Ireland on being ordered north to Ulster are resigning.
> This catastrophe faced the government last night and threatens to bring
> to nought all their plans for bullying Ulster.[25]

While *The Irish Times* was broadly unionist, there was a very different
perspective to be read in the nationalist *Irish Independent*. The lead
article on 23 March 1914 stated:

> If it be true that any army officers have refused to accompany their
> troops to Ulster then we are face to face with a transaction that is
> discreditable to the army, menacing to the very existence of England
> and the Empire and awkward for the government.[26]

The strategic arrangements designed to prevent raids and lawlessness
in Ulster were organised by a committee of the cabinet that had been
set up in early March. They decided that mobilisation would begin so
that troops and ships would be on station by 20 March. Wilson leaked
the military arrangements to Carson who interpreted them as an act of
aggression against the province. All the necessary military arrangements
were completed by 19 March and British military forces stood by to
go into Ulster and restore Westminster's authority there. On 20 March,
when deployment should have commenced, the War Office in London
received a telegram from Ireland advising that all except two of the
officers in the 5th Lancers had resigned and there were fears that the
same was about to occur in the 16th Lancers and that the enlisted men
would refuse to mobilise. It also reported that fifty-seven officers of the
3rd Cavalry indicated their preference to accept dismissal if ordered to
Ulster.

It is important to note here that senior professional officers of the
British Army questioned the detail of a future action to be undertaken
in a deployment that was 'in aid to the civil power'. Furthermore, they
adjudged that the orders at some future point may lead to illegal or
immoral use of force. In the ensuing crisis, Brigadier General Gough,

who was the senior officer in Ireland responsible for the mobilisation to Ulster, was called to London and given written reassurances that officers would not be deployed to 'enforce' Home Rule on Ulster. At this point a civil authority, democratically elected, found itself subservient, in the implementation of its policy, to a force it should have commanded. Although Finer contends that Gough did not disobey the civil authority,[27] the placing of conditions on the circumstance in which one does obey amounts to the same thing. It would seem in this case that army senior personnel who had intervened in government, and effectively chosen to select which orders they would choose to obey, won the day.

There are a number of possible motives and a number of possible reasons for the officers' actions in this whole matter. Before exploring them it is evident that there was a very high level of interaction between soldiers and politicians. Aside from motivation or explanation, it seems clear that the democratic process of government was impeded. The decision, democratically taken, to extend Home Rule to Ireland was watered down not just by political objectors who had a right to protest, but also by the threat of inaction by the British Army units in the Curragh, so-called defenders of the State. As a result events in Ulster took a particular course. A legitimate plan of action by the sovereign British Government in response to a perceived threat, crafted, as such things are, in secrecy, was leaked by the military to those that represented the threat. The implementation of the government decision was further impeded by senior-ranking military personnel who bore responsibility not just for their own actions, but for their subordinates too. The biggest impact of the officers' action in the Curragh was to erode the civil authority's control over the army.

To what extent it damaged the army is unclear, although the apparent triumphant reception Gough got on returning with his written guarantee probably indicates that the internal morale of the force was strengthened rather than weakened by the affair. It is in the arena of civil–military relations where one must look to assess the extent of the damage. A parliament had to pander to the demands of a military civil servant because he was prepared, by whatever label one might attach to it, to withdraw service or labour from the State in an extraordinarily volatile situation. Why did the mutineers behave as they did? The question of pay did not arise. Neither was fear a factor as many of the soldiers involved had accumulated very real combat experience in various theatres of war around the Empire. It is difficult to claim that their refusal to deploy to Ulster was humanitarian because mobilisation against the civilian population in other parts of Ireland or industrial workers in Great Britain had not precipitated a similar response. The idea of imposing by force a political reality on a reluctant population was hardly a new departure for the British Army. Perhaps the officers in question had been taken in by the opposition's claims that an ill-intentioned government was prepared to orchestrate a bloody encounter in Ulster to pander to nationalist demands in return for parliamentary support. They may also have believed from the same source that the arming of the Volunteers there and the moves to create a counter-government in the event of Home Rule were the last patriotic stand of a group whose only crime was the desire to stay loyal to, and remain a part of, the British Empire. If they believed, as undoubtedly some of them did, that they were to be the instruments of nefarious bloodshed, perhaps their position is somewhat understandable, but there are other possibilities not raised by Ryan in his research. Were the officers of the opinion that the citizens in the rest of Ireland were somehow not of their kind and that the upstanding citizens of Ulster were just like them? Did they have a military cultural abhorrence of the Irish people but considered unionist causes to be just causes? Did this racial perspective indicate racism in the army? Whatever the motivations, the Curragh mutiny of 1914 taught the Westminster government that the British Army were not indefinitely resolute in their loyalty to the instruments of civil power and that in certain, albeit rare, circumstances they would usurp that authority by their actions on a political level and their inaction on a military one. The stand taken by the officers of the Curragh defied a democratically elected government, chosen by an electorate that would have included the soldiers themselves. This constitutes interference by military personnel in operational matters that should only be within the remit of a legitimate government. Although no government minister was threatened with violence, their capacity to act in a manner they thought appropriate was impeded by the threat of inaction of the military. Though the implications of this may seem minor, the fact remains that a paramilitary force, established in Northern Ireland to oppose the decisions of the State was supported by a legitimate army supposedly deployed there in the defence of the State and its decisions. These events come well within the parameter of military intervention explored by Huntington, Finer and others and raise questions about how such actions should be considered. It would appear that, in this particular case, the theory of increased professionalism among officers reducing the possibility of intervention did not apply. Perhaps another feature that needs to be inserted in the quest for answers about the disposition to intervene is the political perspective of the soldier and his social identity with the target population of government policy. It seems evident that there was a huge empathy within the ranks of British officers with the unionist population of Ulster. There was also a judgement made on the morality of imposing a particular political decision on a people with whom the military empathised. This is against the grain of most military training, and if it had been the case in other theatres of war in which Britain found itself, the Empire would have been a much smaller geographical entity than it grew to be.

The Curragh mutiny also raises questions about the strength of internal military loyalty. Does the regimental loyalty supersede loyalty to the government or to decisions it makes? Are there considerations of morality and legality in the minds of soldiers deployed on missions that bring them into contact with a civilian population? As pointed out by the lead *Irish Independent* article:

> We take it that the government decided to send troops to Ulster, as a precautionary measure, for the protection of life and property. They are entitled to the services of the military for that purpose and for the repression of any armed violence which may be attempted within the State.[28]

Clearly, for those who advocated the Home Rule Bill or feared the wrath of unionist armed opposition to it, the failure of the army to respond to threatened violence was a worry. Following their conceding, the government put a brave face on events and played down how close the British Forces in Ireland had come to full-blown refusal to obey orders and effect a mutiny. The actions of the senior military officer in the Curragh who threatened to resign if deployed to Ulster must also be noted. If a commanding officer announces his intention to proceed with a course of action that may be outside of the law or regulation, one must consider who may follow. The events in the Irish Army that led to the emergence of representative bodies at times raised these very questions.

IRELAND'S 1924 ARMY MUTINY

The issues that surrounded the so-called mutiny of 1924 contrast somewhat with the Curragh events of a decade earlier. In the case of the Curragh it was clearly a concerted effort by military personnel to influence legitimate decisions of the civil authority, and in the traditional sense can be defined as an incident of military intervention. The events of 1924 deserve a deeper analysis as they mark a very early opportunity to explore the relationship between the Irish military and the State. The definition of military intervention may not apply; however, political intervention into the military ethos may well have taken place. For the most part, the study of civil–military relations concerns itself with the relations between existing governments and their armies. That relationship is often determined by a combination of law, tradition and political history. In countries such as Great Britain, the United States, France, Germany and others, the relationship between government and military has been there for many years. Although trends and events such as war, internal upheaval, or even a change of government may alter the relationship, there still exists a tradition upon which the military and governments can engage with each other. Usually both groups claim a pedigree of entitlement to interact, one on the basis of the right to govern, the other on the premise of the tradition of service to the emergence and/or the survival of the 'State' itself.

In Ireland's case, the government of that State and the army it expected to serve it evolved at almost the same time and in some cases from one and the same group of men. In fact the army, although not a regular 'professional' one, was in place before the State. This was the army that fought for independence and the creation of a new country, independent of Great Britain. They fought against the institutions of the British State, which they deemed to be an oppressive, occupying regime. That so many of this group of armed personnel had by 1925 fully accepted a new civil authority so swiftly is of great import because in doing so they were often acting in such a way as to undermine their own interests.

Until the emergence of representative associations seven decades later, there were three distinct phases of the development of the relationship between the army in Ireland and its government. Firstly, the phase encompassing the War of Independence and the origin of the

Irish forces, in which those bearing arms acted in unity to rid the country of what they saw as the common enemy. Secondly, the phase of Civil War, in which the armed elements had split into two distinct groupings, both of which had opposing views on the extent to which their military objectives had been achieved. Both of these phases have been referred to in the previous chapter on the origin of the Irish Defence Forces. Finally and perhaps as a consequence of the so-called 1924 mutiny, the third phase led to the acceptance by the military that the ultimate authority was that of the civil government.

Prior to the establishment of the new State, although the army fought on behalf of the ideals of a proclaimed 'republic', the elected government who were established long after armed resistance had begun took no responsibilities for the actions of the armed force until four months before the cessation of hostilities in July 1921.[29] In a technical sense, then, during the War of Independence and before it, the army were fighting for themselves in the pursuit of an ideal. That the ideal was, to some, not realised later in the formulation of the Treaty goes to the heart of the issues that resulted in civil war and to the core of the peculiarity of Ireland's early civil–military relations. In their 'struggle for independence', groups of Irish men and women fought side by side as one to defeat a common enemy in the form of British military forces and government agencies. They sought to establish a legitimate government to rule a re-established idealistic nation-State. When that fighting brought their opponents, the British Government, to the negotiating table, it was at a time when neither party had completely defeated the other militarily. By its very nature, an 'agreed settlement' that was painstakingly difficult to arrive at was never going to contain everything for everybody. The Treaty proposal that emerged from the negotiations was brought back to Ireland by Michael Collins and placed before the Irish Parliament for acceptance or rejection. Although many were unhappy with the proposal, there was an option to reject it and many elected members of the government did so. The first fracture in civil–military relations emerged at that time before any 'tradition' of relationships had had a chance to take effect. In the wake of the Civil War that followed and the attempts to round up all armed elements that had opposed the 'Free State' forces of the new government, instances arose where there was uncertainty about on which side armed personnel had previously fought.

Some members of the fledgling civilian government, despite the fact that they had defeated their opponents, feared an internal insurrection from among the armed forces. The Ceann Comhairle (speaker of the House) stated there was a 'question of national security arising' in March 1924, and Deputy Baxter asked:

> The ordinary citizens are wondering where they stand to-day between the armed forces, and want to know … what the real position is. We also want to hear from the other side what the position is as regards these officers in the Army and ex-officers. What do they really want, or what is the cause of their dissatisfaction? What do they want to do, or what is it they want to do with the country?[30]

As will be seen later in the chapter, there certainly seems to have been also circumstances where politicians such as Deputy McGrath encouraged, or at least tolerated, insurrection for nothing more than political gain. Members of the army who sided with the anti-Treaty politicians and lent their military expertise to the opposing of the Treaty could be said at that point to have been engaged in 'military intervention'. And although it is not generally deemed as an attempted military coup, primarily because there were elected politicians who fully endorsed the military activities, it could be said to be an attempted coup nonetheless, given that these armed actions were undertaken in opposition to a democratic vote of the parliament to accept the Treaty.

Kissane, however, is satisfied that the conflict met all the criteria of a full civil war, including that which requires, 'a government fighting an organised opposition that seeks to replace it by armed victory'.[31] That these soldiers had used their arms and skills to oppose the new reality of government identifies them very clearly as personnel whose allegiances were not, at that point, to the democratically elected body. It would be argued that their loyalty was instead to a higher ideal, that of a thirty-two-county republic which they felt the Treaty would not provide. Thus they could argue that their military objectives in pursuit of the 'ideal' had not yet been attained, and from that point of view a military action must go on with continued loyalty to their military leaders. The Irish Government's acceptance of the Treaty thus became an impediment to their 'ideal' and as such another obstacle to be overcome by force of arms. In this context it could be argued that they were not guilty of any intervention but were merely continuing a military campaign for an objective not yet achieved, albeit against different enemies of or obstacles to that ideal. Many of them had never deemed themselves subservient to the State in the first place. Their former colleagues, and people with whom they had previously been comrades, were, on the other hand, now expected to give allegiance to the new government. This, however, was not straightforward either. Although they fought and many died in defending the decision of the majority to accept the Treaty, and were afforded legitimacy by the government itself, there had still been no formal pledge of allegiance, so it could be argued that until a republic had been achieved it would be premature to take the final step in swearing an oath of loyalty to the new Free State Government. This 'previous' pledge was certainly referred to later as a bargaining position for those who wanted to be considered more favourably in the demobilisation process.[32] Even after the army of the new government had suppressed the insurgents, some of the Free State fighters themselves did not pledge allegiance to the civilian government. This, it seems, was because they had previously done so to their military leaders during the time when they were a 'rebel' movement. These men had been sworn into the volunteer movement where membership required a particular oath of allegiance that included never laying down arms until an independent republic was achieved. No convention of the previously named Volunteers to alter this provision took place. It could therefore be considered a matter of contention that until such an amendment took place, allegiance could be said to be due only to military leaders pursuing the ideals of the proclamation. Cognisant of this, the Minister for Defence, Cathal Brugha, sought the introduction of a new pledge of allegiance to the government in an effort to strengthen civilian supremacy.[33]

At this point, it was in the interest of the government to formalise its army and the relationship between it and the process of democratic leadership. It was not to be easy. A revolutionary army fought a foreign occupation succeeding in bringing it to the negotiating table. They had not been subservient to any government during this time. Talks took place, a Treaty was proposed and, although there was sharp division, a democratic vote was taken by parliament resulting in an acceptance of the Treaty. Members of the same army who had fought to obtain independence saw the acceptance of the Treaty as a betrayal to what they had achieved in driving Britain out of most of the country. It was at this volatile period at the very birth of the new nation that future positive civil–military relations had to be established. Adding to the difficulty of the government in creating a peacetime structure for the armed forces was the need for demobilisation. During the preceding years of conflict, the War of Independence had seen thousands of men under arms, most of whom continued fighting on one side or another in the Civil War that followed. At the end of the Civil War, most of those who had fought on the anti-Treaty side had been disarmed and either imprisoned or dispersed. The armed forces of the new Free State were the victors, but with the War of Independence won and the Civil War over the new government had no need for such a large army. Cutbacks in numbers left many soldiers disaffected. Many lost their positions as the army transformed itself from a wartime unit to a peacetime institution. There was a feeling among many soldiers that they had fought and risked their lives both in the War of Independence and in defence of the new State in the Civil War. Now they were to be disbanded and, as some saw it, cast aside. Lee commented on the implications thus:'The most potentially dangerous threat to Cosgrave after the Civil War came not from Sinn Féin but from a Free State army swollen in size to 55,000 men and 3,300 officers by the end of hostilities.'[34]

Eventually this relationship between those who saw themselves as the ones who facilitated freedom and those who were trying to establish the supremacy of the civilian government came to a head in what has been described as the army mutiny of 1924. The events of that year and the army officer challenge to the government had their roots in the foundation of the State and the nature of the struggle that had precipitated independence. Thus the relationship between the men of arms and the politicians was central to the challenges that emerged. Irish civil–military relations had not had the benefit of tradition. The only formal military presence in Ireland for previous centuries had been the British armed forces. Their government and institutions had highly developed civil–military relations. Anybody that had taken up arms in Ireland to try to achieve independence had, of necessity, to belong to a revolutionary group that had only a violent relationship with the military presence of the British Government of the day and virtually none with any civilian leadership. Many Irish personnel had served in the British Forces for many years and understood the tradition of the military ethos, but there was no existing tradition of how the military might interact with a wholly different Irish State structure.

In a general sense, the normal convention is that a government raises an army from citizens. It demands loyalty from them. Senior departmental and military personnel are appointees and at all times subservient to government, usually through a Minister for Defence. In independent Ireland's embryonic period, the group that was to become the new State 'army' was in place before the government. This was part and parcel of the evolution of the State itself.

Under rule of Westminster, a British garrison army had been loyal to the London Government. As has been described earlier, in 1913 the impending introduction of Home Rule for Ireland had precipitated the formation of a very large Protestant volunteer army in Ulster. Set up to oppose plans to introduce Home Rule and forcibly resist any attempts to bring Ulster under any new Dublin Government jurisdiction, the group with its threat of violent resistance won sweeping political concessions and eventually their own parliament. South of the border and disappointed with the progress that parliamentary and peaceful endeavours had achieved, a southern volunteer force was assembled to protect and promote the interests of those who sought independence from Britain. The vigour and effectiveness of Ulster militancy inspired nationalists with a mixture of outrage, admiration and envy, culminating in imitation.[35] This was the volunteer force in the South that was to eventually become involved in the War of Independence and different elements of it in the Civil War that followed. Importantly, however, the Volunteers were assembled and operating before the elections of 1918. That year, in the elections that had taken place to elect MPs to Westminster, Sinn Féin won a landslide victory. They did not take their parliamentary seats in London but used the mandate they had to set up an alternative Irish Government, establishing the Dáil.

Co-operation between the Dáil and the volunteer force was immediately established and they merged with leading figures from one group, occupying leading offices of the other. Richard Mulcahy was at this time Assistant Minister for Defence while also being Chief of Staff.[36] At this point the government that had been formed and the men of arms who were to be engaged in the War of Independence all had the same aims. As the counter-government of the Dáil continued to meet, it remained unrecognised by Britain. Political attempts at establishing the new State were matched by military initiatives, and at this time the volunteer army, which had come to be referred to as the 'army of the State', conducted their operation independently of the government but kept them appraised at all times. The fact that both the Chief of Staff of the Volunteers, Richard Mulcahy, and the director of intelligence, Michael Collins, had cabinet responsibilities to ensure that the government was both informed and had some influence, at least theoretically, in the activities of the army. Mulcahy was also assistant Minister for Defence and Michael Collins was Minister for Finance. This procedure worked reasonably well; however, there were no formal civil–military relations, no institutions, and agreed relationships. Arrangements based on personality, familiarity and cohesion of purpose, sufficed until the government and the Volunteers both split over the Treaty. It transpired that being referred to as the army of the State was somewhat premature in light of the differing views on what constituted the legitimate 'State'.

The devastating effect of any civil war sees former comrades and family in conflict with each other. In Ireland men who had been fellow combatants now faced each other in a spiralling war of bitterness and division. Although the pro-Treaty side won a barely discernible victory, for the fledgling government these early years were full of uncertainty. There were many concerns among successive government ministers regarding the loyalty of those in the forces with access to weapons and trained personnel. Valiulis contended that:

> The aura of uncertainty disturbed the government. It was worried about the loyalty of the army it had authorised and on whom its very existence depended ... Had soldiers simply followed their local officers or the leading figures at general headquarters in choosing sides in the civil war, or did their decision to support the Free State reflect a commitment to democratic rule?[37]

These matters of relations came to a head in what Dr Maryann Valiulis called 'almost a rebellion'. Also known as the Irish Army mutiny of 1924, the series of incidents that occurred underlines the necessity of formal institutions and clear-cut relationships in the conduct of civil–military relations in an operative democracy. As the new government tried to recover from the ill effects of the Civil War, the thorny matter of downsizing the army emerged. An army council was set up to oversee this work. On 9 November 1923, nine army officers who were served with demobilisation papers refused to accept them. Their reasoning and defence was that they had undertaken a solemn oath not to lay down their arms until a republic had been achieved. This was a classic case of the army feeling that they owed an allegiance to a national ideal rather than any manifestation of it in the form of a democratically elected government. Had the officers in question been representative of the whole army corps, clearly there would have been questions about the extent of control of the Irish Government of the day. According to Welch and Smith:

> The establishment of effective political authority thus requires (1) the aggregation of consent, and (2) control over the means to organised coercion. If the armed forces thus exercise nearly total autonomy over their internal organisation and, in time of crisis, over the decision to support or not support the civil government, then civilian control clearly does not exist.[38]

3

Early Strained Relations

A civilian and unarmed government, in order to operate effectively, would always have to be secure in the knowledge that there would be no possibility of a military takeover or coup d'état, whether this was by way of an army acting alone or refusing to act. Such must have been the considerations of the Irish fledgling government of the day. This significant incident, particularly the notion of a body of officers remaining loyal to an aspiration that had been set aside by the government, challenged the whole idea of the supremacy of civilian control over the army and was a definite threat to the new State. In Huntington's theory it could have been passed off as a lack of professionalism, one of the major contributing factors he suggests as being the cause of military intervention.[1] But the situation was to get worse than a few officers refusing their orders. Members of the army who had been Old IRA, those who had fought in the War of Independence, began to meet and discuss the moves being made by government to demobilise the former soldiers who had been active then. They eventually formulated a letter and sent it to the President of the Dáil, requesting a meeting. These former officers stated that they had accepted the Treaty only as a stepping stone to the 'Republic' and quoted Michael Collins saying that he had sworn an oath of allegiance to the republic, 'Treaty or no Treaty'. In the ensuing meeting and conferences, the officers claimed that in the present army 40 per cent were Old IRA, 50 per cent were former British Army personnel and 10 per cent civilians, which they claimed would lead to a diminution of the ideals of a Republic. They threatened to intervene by 'taking steps' to 'secure the Republic'.[2] This kind of threat derives from among one of the motives, Finer suggests, that disposes the military towards intervention:

Sectional bodies all plead the national interest when making claims for their own benefit, but the military are especially well placed to do so.[3]

About sixty officers eventually refused to accept their demobilisation orders, but they were demobilised anyway and ordered out of barracks without any financial remuneration. Amid continuing complaints, the government established a committee to oversee the question of demobilisation and investigate claims of preferential treatment for British Army personnel. However, none of the sixty officers were reinstated. Reports were received that other Old IRA officers up and down the country were organising themselves. These activities culminated in an ultimatum being delivered to government on 6 March 1924. They reiterated that the Treaty had only been accepted by them as a stepping stone to a republic and that the government were now betraying that ideal. President Liam Cosgrave, to whom the letter had been addressed, read it into the Dáil records:

To President Liam Cosgrave.

Sir,—

On behalf of the I.R.A. Organisation we have been instructed to present the following Ultimatum to the Government of Saorstát Eireann.

Briefly, our position is this:—

The I.R.A. only accepted the Treaty as a means of achieving its objects, namely, to secure and maintain a Republican form of Government in this country.

After many months of discussion with your Government it is our considered opinion that your Government has not those objects in view, and that their policy is not reconcilable with the Irish people's acceptance of the Treaty.

Furthermore, our interpretation of the Treaty was that expressed by the late Commander-in-Chief, General Michael Collins, when he stated: "I have taken an oath of allegiance to the Irish Republic and that oath I will keep, Treaty or no Treaty." We claim Michael Collins as our leader, and again remind you that even after the Treaty was signed, that drastic action was taken against enemies of the unity and complete independence of our country. Both in oath and honour bound, it is our duty to continue his policy, and therefore present this ultimatum, to which we require a reply by 12 noon, 10th March, 1924.

We demand a conference with representatives of your Government to discuss our interpretation of the Treaty on the following conditions:–

(a) The removal of the Army Council.
(b) The immediate suspension of army demobilisation and re-organisation.

In the event of your Government rejecting these proposals we will take such action that will make clear to the Irish people that we are not renegades or traitors to the ideals that induced them to accept the Treaty.

Our organisation fully realises the seriousness of the action that we may be compelled to take, but we can no longer be party to the treachery that threatens to destroy the aspirations of the Nation.

LIAM TOBIN, Major-General, President of the Executive Council.
C.F. DALTON, Col., Secretary to Executive Council.[4]

It would be expected that any head of government would make a robust response to such a letter and President Cosgrave did. He said:

Having heard the text of the document Deputies will have no difficulty in agreeing that it constitutes a challenge which no Government could ignore without violating the trust conferred on it ... The attempt, such as it is, is not against a particular Government; it is a challenge to the democratic foundations of the State, to the very basis of Parliamentary representation and of responsible Government. As such, it is the concern of every Deputy, of every party and of every citizen.

In his statement it appeared that the government had moved swiftly to contain the situation and protect the integrity of the State. However, the Minister for Industry and Commerce, Mr McGrath, resigned in protest for actions taken against men who were responsible for the 'birth of the State and its life since'; in the Dáil he stated:

I am thoroughly satisfied in my own mind that I will convince you this is brought about by absolute muddling, mishandling and incompetency on the part of a Department of the State.[5]

It transpired that following the ultimatum, forty-nine officers resigned and a further fifty absconded, some taking arms and munitions with them. General Mulcahy, in addressing the Dáil, read out the letter of resignation that had been signed by the officers involved. Having indicated that the total number of officers involved was at the maximum ninety, he reassured the Dáil thus:

> So that from the point of view of national safety and security, the military position in the country is quite sound and the incidents that have taken place have been incidents of absconsion rather than of any definite attempt to take military action of any kind.[6]

Despite Mulcahy's optimistic interpretation, this series of events, occurring, as they did, after the legitimacy of the government had been established, represent a more concrete example of the type of military intervention which the study of civil–military relations analyses so often. This was a direct threat of action on the State by a minority group of serving officers. It marked a change in their allegiance with the government of the day, which they had supported not just in the War of Independence but also through the Civil War. Now this appeared to have been only on a transitional basis. The military personnel involved were setting aside their 'transitional allegiance' to the government that, in their minds, had some finite limit. Because their original and steadfast allegiance to the ideals of a republic had not been realised, they were now setting aside the transitional for the original. In effect they were categorising the supremacy of the ideal over that of the civil government. But were their motives so idealistic or were there other influences at work? General Mulcahy reported to the Dáil some interesting commentary that may indicate a more mundane motive for the activities of the mutineers, such as positions and pensions. By acting in such a fashion they chose the route of intervention. As the crisis unfolded, it became a matter of contentious debate in the Dáil. The following day matters had taken a very different turn: the President read another letter from the original signatories indicating that they accepted fully the authority of the State, in a seeming reversal of the letter dated six days earlier. It stated, among other things, that the authors recognised that the army must be subject to the 'absolute control of the civil authority'.[7]

The letter was signed 'Liam Tobin, Major General and C.F. Dalton Colonel'. There was a lot of confusion in the Dáil chamber. Only the previous day the President had talked about the threat that no government could ignore in referring to the ultimatum of 6 March. On the face of it, the officers had written again, this time pledging their allegiance to the democratic institutions of the State. Now it seemed that the second letter and the decision to set up a committee of enquiry was all that was needed to gloss over the threats that had been made to the security of the State. It certainly seemed at this point that the government had done an about-face and were conceding to the threats made in the original letter by not confronting the authors with the full rigours of military or civil discipline. The threat of violence in British and Irish military law is usually deemed sufficient to impose harsh penalties.

Tom Johnson spoke with great clarity about the import of events and their impact on civil–military relations. He also referred to Ireland's embryonic stage in the establishment of civil–military relations, stating:

> The army, I say, must not be judged as rigidly as, perhaps, an older army in an older State would need to be judged. But offences of this nature must not be condoned or overlooked … The Dáil has a right to know, and to insist upon knowing to-night, whether the Government is maintaining authority, or whether it has submitted to the ultimatum.[8]

Kevin O'Higgins also had a very clear view of what type of relationship the army should have with the institutions of the State:

> That fact has to be faced just as the other fact had to be faced, that the disciplined forces of the State must be the disciplined forces of the State, that the people who pay the piper must call the tune, that we turned on a section of our own countrymen and fought the conflict of the last two years for one issue, and one issue only, and that was the supremacy of the people – that the people in their collective wisdom or unwisdom in their collective judgement or lack of judgement must decide the future policy of the country.[9]

It seemed that the government had completely changed its approach overnight. That an enquiry should suffice to get to the bottom of what many called mutiny is at least suspicious. Acceptance of the second letter also indicated that the authors had not been arrested as had been intimated. There was, however, a different perspective – regarding the all-important *esprit de corps*, Major Cooper said:

> The spirit of an army is a very delicate and sensitive thing, and if people outside of the army are going to inquire into its organisation, into the whole manner in which it is carried on, you run a very grave risk of sapping the esprit de corps, the vague, intangible something, that makes a thing an army, and not an armed mob.[10]

This position, directly from the mouth of a military officer, could be interpreted as indicating a higher value being attributed to the *esprit de corps* than to the stability of the State. It is interesting to consider the status of the *esprit* at a time when officers were divided among themselves and in their loyalties. The signatories of both the ultimatum and the letter of partial retraction were intervening on the basis that the policy of the civilian government was inconsistent with what they believed was the in best interests of the nation and what they thought was their duty in continuing the policy of their former leader, Michael Collins. Huntington proposed very specific responsibilities for the 'military man', including representing the claims of military security in State machinery, professionally advising the State in military matters and executing the strategies of government.[11] It would seem that the actions of the officers in Ireland at that time in sending the ultimatum would fall well outside of what Huntington proposed were the desirable modes of practice for their profession and would constitute 'intervention'.

In discussing the various modes of intervention, Finer has categorised it into six levels, ranging from 'influence' to 'blackmail'. He further contended that discussing or attempting to persuade a government to a particular view was legitimate; however, 'threats of physical coercion or of disobedience are unconstitutional in any circumstances and that views accompanied by such threats are, clearly, blackmail.'[12] In view of Finer's definition, it would appear that in Ireland at that time the whole integrity of the State and its authority over the military was under threat. President Cosgrave described the ultimatum as, 'a challenge that no government could ignore' on 11 March, yet the next day, he was happy to report to the Dáil that everything was resolved and that the measures that were to be taken, including the commissioning of an enquiry, would suffice to address the problems at hand.[13] The brevity of his statement and the comments of Deputy McGrath, who had proffered his resignation the previous day, indicated that some sort of a compromise had been arrived at, or some sort of deal had been done. McGrath announced that he felt the President had 'met the situation' so he would not be making any further statements until the enquiry took place.[14] However, others, including Deputy Johnson, were dissatisfied with the events as they were unfolding. He referred to the announcement of a 'mutiny in the army' the previous Saturday, the response that had been given by the President and finally the meagre statement issued by him.[15]

These exchanges in the Dáil were indicative of members of a government wanting to elicit change in the army or perhaps not trusting those who were currently charged with responsibility for it. The previous army council, comprising of Minister for Defence and Commander in Chief Richard Mulcahy, Chief of Staff General Sean McMahon, Adjutant General Gearóid O'Sullivan and Quartermaster General Seán O'Muirthuille had listened to criticism by the cabinet regarding their lack of progress in rounding up republican activists and in the general running of the army. This criticism continued to such an extent as to drive the council members to present their resignations.[16] The complaints arose from numerous members of the cabinet who were impatient with the process of apprehending former Civil War opponents, some of whom were still engaged in insurgency around the country. While this may have been the reason proffered, it is difficult not to contemplate that disgruntled former IRA soldiers were placing political pressure on their politicians to intervene and have them spared in the mass demobilisations that, inevitably, had to take place.

The resignations were initially rejected; however, that was to change in light of the ultimatum and the proffered resignation of McGrath. It would appear at this point that political consideration rather than civil–military relations became the focal point of the events as they played out. Firstly, the ultimatum and the threat it contained did not come from the appointed official leadership of the army. They did not see a widespread mutiny in the making, so the question arises as to how much the claims of a 'crisis' were in fact scaremongering for political purposes. General Mulcahy, as Minister for Defence, assured the Dáil on a number of occasions that the revolt was not widespread and generally the situation around the country was secure. In contrast, politicians of the executive council were questioning the loyalty of their own army. Deputy

O'Higgins said there was a view forming that the army were no longer an instrument of the people's will.[17] These comments flew in the face of the initial government reaction to the mutineers. It was the mutineers who were not 'instruments of the people's will.' On the other hand, Mulcahy and others were discharging their duties in very difficult circumstances. Secondly, those who issued the threat almost certainly had the support of members of government. Although McGrath claimed to be resigning as a result of the mishandling of army administration and management, he announced it on the day of the reading of the ultimatum, and in any event his reason was found not to be valid by the enquiry that followed. Thirdly, the army officers who were in the invidious position of having to cull the numbers of their former comrades were being accused of favouring British soldiers when, in fact, this was found not to be the case. It seems there may have been political expediency at play in not wishing to confront the painful task of selection required for downsizing and demobilisation. Politicians at cabinet level would seem to have taken the side of the mutineers, and in doing so undermined the integrity of the rest of the army and of the State itself. There were arguments put forward by members of government to justify the requested resignations of men who had served the State with distinction. O'Higgins suggested that the men had fulfilled their function and it was now time for others to build on those contributions.[18]

In the midst of the debates around these issues, a routine military operation exacerbated the acrimony of the exchanges after a pub in Dublin was raided and a number of army personnel, who, unauthorised, had gathered there with arms, were arrested. The arresting officer's report stated that Deputy McGrath came to the pub in question and interfered in a way that was sympathetic to the armed group. He highlighted McGrath's attitude regarding the authority of the Defence Forces to act, when he claimed that the government had not authorised the raid. McGrath even insisted on buying the detained soldiers a drink.[19]

The cabinet called for the resignations of the army council after the arrests, and following this Mulcahy proffered his own resignation explaining that he could not 'stand over condoning mutiny to such an extent as to foster it and prejudice discipline in the army'. He quoted the provision of the Defence Act as being the basis on which the assembled soldiers had been acting illegally.[20] The Act to which Mulcahy refers is the Defence Force (Temporary Provisions) Act 1923. There were many provisions under that Act that placed the mutineers in breach of military law. Among them, paragraph 36 which dealt specifically with mutiny and laid down the possibility of the ultimate punishment, that of the sentence of death.

> Every person subject to military law who commits any of the following offences, that is to say:–
>
> (a) The offence of causing, conspiring to cause, attempting to cause, or joining in any mutiny or sedition in any of the Forces; or
> (b) Being present, the offence of not using his utmost endeavours to prevent any mutiny or sedition in any of the Forces; or
> (c) The offence of persuading, inducing or compelling or endeavouring to persuade, induce, or compel any person subject to military law to join in any mutiny or sedition in any of the Forces; or
> (d) Having come to the knowledge of, or having reasonable grounds to suspect any actual or intended mutiny or sedition in the Forces, the offence of failing to inform without delay, a superior officer of the same; or
> (e) The offence of seducing or endeavouring to seduce any person subject to military law from allegiance to the State,
>
> shall, on conviction by Court-Martial be liable to suffer death or such less punishment as is in this Act mentioned.[21]

As can be seen from this legislation, not only is it an offence to commit mutiny, but under paragraph (b) there is a direct obligation for somebody who is aware of such activity to prevent it. These provisions under what was then the law of the land underline a strong basis for the argument that Mulcahy was acting in compliance with the law. That his actions were not compliant with a policy procedure by the government designed to bring the mutineers round is arguable too. The dismissal of the General Staff in the immediate wake of the raid without any possibility of defending their actions is within the remit of the government, and was provided for under the Defence Act; however, while it may have been legal, it does give rise to a question of fairness. These men were legally endowed with the obligation of defending the State and maintaining discipline in the army. In doing so on this particular occasion they found themselves on the wrong side of supposed government policy. It would be difficult to accuse such men of plotting intervention. Those who threatened it, on the other hand, were protected by the political consideration of the government of the day. In this context, the fledgling State got off to a very bad start in the establishment of civil–military relations.

General Mulcahy then addressed the whole question of the real reasons, which he believed had led to the situation at that point. He believed that the so-called mutiny was not so much about the defence of ideals as the posturing for position in the new, slimmed-down force that had to be gleaned from the existing inflated force. He heavily criticised the way in which the whole episode was approached by the executive council and its impact on the force. He pointed out the unsuitability of the appointment of General O'Duffy to take charge at a time of possible armed crisis:

> The extraordinary position has been taken up of placing a man who was away from military work – who had not been in touch with the work of the army, or the development of the army for many months past.[22]

When the committee of enquiry finally reported to the Dáil, Deputy Mulcahy made a scathing attack on the conduct of it and felt vindicated in his criticism of the executive council. The whole basis of the resignation of Deputy McGrath, which had escalated the perception of a pending crisis, had been based on his charge of the muddling and mismanagement of the army. Mulcahy pointed out that the committee had found 'no evidence to justify a charge of muddling, mismanagement or incompetence on the part of the late Chief-of-Staff in carrying out his duties.'[23]

The so-called mutiny of 1924 was probably not a mutiny at all or at least not a full-blown military one. It bespoke of political intervention in military affairs rather than vice versa. While it is certainly true that a number of disgruntled members of the Old IRA sent a threatening letter to the government and that a number of officers absconded or stole arms, the vast majority of middle-ranking officers, NCOs and privates did not participate. Kissane's contention that socio-economic considerations might have more to do with the longevity of civil conflict than higher principles can probably be applied when contemplating the motivation of those involved in the mutiny.[24] Had the episode ended some other way, the conflict or a part of it may well have resumed. It would appear, however, that the intention of the mutineers was not so much to 'take over' the country as it was to threaten violence to get their own way. What is manifest in this case of 'mutiny' is the compliance or even participation of a faction of government in the manipulation of public fears about instability.

The army leadership of the day appeared balanced enough in their approach to demobilisation. The figures given in the Dáil do not support the claims by the Old IRA that total favouritism was being afforded to former British Army service men. In the case of their approaches to the downscaling of the army, the subsequent commission of enquiry could find no evidence of favouritism. Likewise, the charge put forward by Deputy McGrath of muddling and mismanagement in the administration and running of the army was reported as being unfounded. If this was the case it would seem that elected members of parliament manipulated the integrity of the army officers who had tried to undertake the difficult task of demobilisation as fairly as possible. Equally, the primary excuse that was proffered in the call for the resignation of Mulcahy was hardly sustainable. He is purported to have undermined the authority of a superior, the recently appointed General Eoin O'Duffy, by not informing him of the raid that took place on the premises of Devlin's in Parnell Street, and to have compromised the policy of government in doing so. However, military regulations and tradition would prohibit the gathering of any armed members in circumstances outside of normal duties. The authority to intervene in such circumstance does not ordinarily require a reference to a higher rank, and in fact it is usually the duty of any NCO or officer to intervene in any such circumstance.[25]

One could expect that the apprehension of a group of armed men meeting in secrecy – men who had threatened violence to the State – would have been lauded as a heroic act. On the contrary, a politician saw fit to arrive on the scene and buy a drink for those who had been caught, and to later seek the resignation for those responsible for the capture of men who were prepared to use arms against the organs of the State. The fact that the enquiry subsequently confirmed that the Old IRA had, at no time, any intention of recognising the authority of the State, and that those who had quoted Michael Collins had also been fermenting dissent even prior to his death, is indicative of the validity of Mulcahy's policy in launching the raid. It would appear that in Ireland, at that time, the civil–military relationship between those charged to run the army and those in power was not what it should have been. However, more blame can be attached to the government side than the military. Kissane alludes to the possibility of government not always being in concert with the wishes of the wider population. He distinguishes between civil society and the government of the day and highlights many instances where organisations, movements and groups of interested citizens disagreed with, and tried to dissuade both sides from engaging in violence against each other in the conduct of the Civil War. In defining what constitutes civil society, he excludes not only the anti-Treaty forces but also the State forces, on the basis that they too were part of the conflict that civil society did not want.[26]

The Old IRA members in the army were part of a group that, despite their positions, did not recognise the supremacy of the civil authority of the State and were not prepared to respect its democratic right to govern. At their Army Council Convention in March 1922, they had resolved that the IRA should remain 'the Army of the Irish Republic' without regard for the authority of the provisional government, the Dáil, or Mulcahy's headquarters staff.[27] Their political influence among members of the cabinet was to muddy the civil–military relations at a time when the utmost of clarity was needed. A request for Mulcahy's resignation may have been justified on the basis that he had joined a secret organisation such as the Irish Republican Brotherhood (IRB), but this organisation was not the one that had threatened the State. In fact, its founders had claimed they were reconstituted to prevent irregulars and members of the Old IRA from undermining the army from within. The fact that the Old IRA managed to do so is more a reflection on the politicians of the day than it is on Mulcahy and his comrades.

That the government should have taken any action other than to arrest the mutineers has probably a lot to do with the volatile period that marked the early years of parliamentary democracy in Free State Ireland. Nevertheless, in the context of civil–military relations, it was an episode that weighed the desired relationship in favour of a rogue element of the military. It was fortunate for the establishment and growth of those relations in Ireland that this should be short lived. It was not for another sixty-five years that the notion of something approaching a widespread mutiny was even contemplated. The emergence later of an organised body within the Defence Forces, bringing pressure to bear on the government, albeit political pressure, rather than the threat of arms, was to raise once again questions regarding the relationship between the civil authority and that of the forces. And while during this period there was never a threat of armed insurrection, it could be argued that a political insurrection took place. The similarities between what happened in the late 1980s and in the early 1920s lies in military personnel influencing a government in both cases against the better judgement of the Chief of Staff. To what extent this is detrimental to civil–military relations is a moot point, but one thing that it does prove, however, is that civil-authority supremacy has been the profile in Ireland since the 1920s even if that supremacy was abused or misguided on occasion. Huntington, writing long after the events in Ireland, recognised the conflict between military obedience and political wisdom but argued the supremacy of the political system in all cases:

> The criteria of military efficiency are limited, concrete and relatively objective; the criteria for political wisdom are indefinite, ambiguous and highly subjective. Policy is an art, military science is a profession. No commonly accepted political values exist by which the military officer can prove to reasonable men that his political judgement is preferable to that of the Statesman. The superior political wisdom of the Statesman must be accepted as a fact. If the Statesman decides upon war which the soldier knows can only lead to national catastrophe, then the soldier must fall to and make the best of a bad situation.[28]

Valiulis looks on the impact of the political manoeuvring that went on during the crisis as positive, a demonstration of the changes that had taken place within the army.[29] However, these positive changes wherein the military were conscious of civil supremacy were already well under way before it, and the threat of instability and a return to violence that year came not from the established senior generals of the army but from a disgruntled Old IRA vying for better positions in the aftermath of demobilisation. Different forms of this dissidence would evolve in later years, and even in the present day there are remnants of an organisation that do not recognise the supremacy of the State. They are no longer in the army of today. They never held any sway in Mulcahy's vision of the army either. Whether or not the intervention by political figures in the Irish Army crisis of 1924 prevented national disaster will probably never be known. To what extent the threats of the Old IRA would have been implemented is equally unclear. That they were assuaged by the political wisdom of the day may or may not have averted another civil conflict. One way or another, the incidents clearly outline an

established civil supremacy that sustained itself even at the expense of
decent men. The professional attitude that has marked the civil–military
relations between the Irish armed forces and their government since
then survived despite the sacking of Mulcahy, not because of it.

In the intervening period between the 1920s and 1980s, the
Defence Forces underwent significant change. The demobilisation
of the Civil War period reduced strength in terms of manpower, but
new services and units were established in accordance with perceived
needs and the emerging complexity of the PDF grew in parallel with
that of the nation. The 'command' system of the early 1920s that had
been established by Mulcahy divided the operational areas into eight
zones: the East (HQ Dublin), the West (HQ Athlone), the Southwest
(HQ Limerick), the Northern (HQ Stranorlar), the Cork (HQ Cork),
the Kerry (HQ Tralee) and the Waterford (HQ Kilkenny) areas.
The number of commands was later halved to four, comprising of the
Eastern, Western, Southern and Curragh commands. Formations such
as the Air Corps and the Naval Service would come later. Further
demobilisation took place into the late 1920s.[30]

The raising of a volunteer force in the late 1930s facilitated an
expanded body of men under arms for the period of the Second
World War when the Irish Government were adamant that they would
maintain their neutrality. Reductions in numbers had to take place again
in the post-war period. The establishment of the United Nations (UN)
soon after it resulted later in a basis for some new roles for the Irish
Army. Despite the new roles, the PDF seemed lacking in up-to-date
means and equipment. Col Walsh in his thesis remarked that:

> Irish governments have failed to address the Defence needs of the State.
> During the 1920s the pattern established was to be repeated by succes-
> sive governments, the armed forces were placed in a disadvantaged
> position relative to the manner in which the armed forces were treated.
> In the Congo there was obsolete dress, equipment and failure to exert a
> proper command and control system.[31]

Pay and allowances may always have been an issue. Duggan notes a
Department of Finance Order from 1924 that lays down that the army
was not professional enough to merit full pay and suggests 'It is arguable
whether it ever subsequently changed its mind'.[32] The late 1960s were
marked by increasing civil strife in Northern Ireland, which over time

drew the Irish armed forces into duties that provided aid to the civil power along dangerous borders. By the 1970s, Irish Army personnel were being formally posted along the border with Northern Ireland as the administrations in both jurisdictions were grappling with deteriorating internal security. In addition to the expansion and contraction of the physical size of the Irish armed forces and their changing role since their foundation, there had been no satisfactory standard set in the determination of military pay and allowances between the 1920s and the 1980s. In 1924 wage rates were fixed by a pay commission. Although there had been an expectation of parity with the Gardaí, this was not to materialise. The military authorities would contend that many proposals were made over the years to the Department of Defence to improve matters, to no avail. In 1969 a working group was set up by the Minister for Finance, and after a protracted period of over three years they recommended an improvement in pay. National wage agreements in the 1970s heralded a linkage of some grades to the civil service, but by the 1980s dissatisfaction with pay in the army continued. [33]

In the Gleeson Commission report, no fewer than twenty-seven instances are listed during these decades where some element of army pay was reviewed, reported on or implemented.[34] In the context of civil–military relations, serving members of the military had developed a very loyal if somewhat frustrating relationship with their civilian masters.

4

Civil–Military Relations after 1924 and Dissatisfaction in the 1980s

In the stable democracy that is Ireland today, fears of the propensity for a civil-war conflict or a mutiny may seem remote, yet in the period between 1924 and the present there have been many instances elsewhere around the world where military personnel intervened in, influenced or even dramatically usurped elected governments. The close mixture of military power and political authority sharing the same chamber and an equality of influence is seen as clearly undesirable. Writing in 1974, Welch and Smith observe that:

> Nearly half of the member States of the United Nations are ruled by outright military regimes, in which officers fill senior political positions; or by military-civilian coalitions, in which officers exercise paramount influence behind a façade of civilian control.[1]

While any government may concern itself with civilian disaffection and protesting, having an army hierarchy or part of it openly dissatisfied and critical of the government is an entirely different matter. In his compelling *Political Order in Changing Societies*, while comparing the threat posed by protesting citizens to that caused by protesting soldiers Huntington contends that: 'The military can be cohesive, bureaucratised, and disciplined. Colonels can run governments; students and monks cannot.'[2]

Finer believes that armies are incapable of running anything other than a very simplistic society. Among other reasons quoted regarding their competence in administration, he highlights lack of moral mandate as being the principal restriction on which armies may fail. If they are in a position as a result of the threat of violence, it will not be too long before they are usurped themselves: 'Rule by force alone, or the threat of such force, is inadequate; in addition, government must possess authority. It must be widely recognised not only as the government, but as the lawful, the rightful government.'[3]

In Ireland, the soldiers who had fought in the War of Independence certainly wanted a government to be established in order for the population to be able to rule themselves. While some of them went into politics, it had not been with the intention to 'take over' the country at the end the War of Independence. As was already shown, the early leaders of the military, such as Mulcahy and his General Staff, deferred to the greater authority of a civilian government. This was evidenced by their willingness to resign at its request even when the stated reasons were hard to justify and were not subsequently proven. Nevertheless, other elements of the army who were members of the Old IRA maintained divided loyalties. In an effort to formalise the subservient/superior relationship between soldier and State, and as a result of the 'army crisis', an amendment to Ireland's Defence Act copper-fastened an important element in the context of civil–military relations in law. Enacted on 1 August 1924, the Defence Forces (Temporary Provisions) Act, 1923 (Continuance and Amendment) Act, 1924 contained a provision that updated oaths for those joining the forces. This provision was intended to prohibit any recurrence of divided loyalties and 'secret society oaths' to another cause above that of the State. The chain of command in Ireland since 1924 is clear-cut and unambiguous. The President, acting with the approval of the government, is the supreme commander of the Defence Forces. The powers are set out in Article 13 of Ireland's written Constitution and command itself is exercised through the government by way of the Minister for Defence under the Defence Act, 1954.[4]

As the army in Ireland evolved there were increasing administrative consequences in the way in which the superior/subordinate relation-ship was maintained. Today the Department of Defence, for which the minister is responsible, is unique among other government depart-ments in Ireland in that it has two distinct sections to it, the civilian section and the military section. Both sides have responsibility to the Minister for Defence. The military Chief of Staff has direct access to him or her as does the Secretary General on the civilian side. Until

recently, the civilian departmental side administered the entirety of
the department and controlled its budget. That has changed following
a number of reviews that placed more budgetary responsibility
on military commanders, but up until the 1990s it was the civilian
section of the department that was responsible for implementation of
government legislation, ministerial instruction, statutory regulations
and government pay-and-expenditure policies. All matters relating
to government budgetary policy, including what was to be allocated
to the military section, came through and from the civilian section.
This included pay, allowances, capital expenditure and day-to-day
budgetary subheads that dictated how much could be spent in a
particular area. As a result, all capital expenditure requests emanating
from the military section, even the most minor of purchases, had to be
eventually approved or processed by the civilian side. One administrative result of this is well demonstrated in the commentary of a former
naval officer. Petty Officer Jim Halligan served in the army with the
Corps of Engineers for three years before transferring to the navy.
Being a technician he was frequently exposed to delays and frustration caused by difficulties in acquiring stores or spare parts that were
needed to complete his work: 'Somewhere along the administrative
purchasing line there could be an eighteen year old civil servant with
little life experience and no military inkling who would be endowed
with the capacity to delay, question or even seek justification for the
purchase.'[5]

While such arrangements were probably manifestations of the
supremacy of the civilian authority, they often led to the military
section becoming dissatisfied and frustrated with what they saw as
a burdensome system which was being administered by a civilian
section that had little understanding of the needs of a military force
in a general sense, and of the specific needs of individual members of
such a force. Gleeson observed:

> The centralised bureaucracy and the slow processing of decisions through
> extended chains of command create a sense of powerlessness and disillu-
> sion among military personnel, resulting in lower morale and widespread
> feeling of frustration.[6]

In some respects, the present structure of the Irish Army hierarchy
reflects the earlier concerns that prevailed at the time of the 'army

mutiny' of 1924. All of the leadership of the military are subservient and reporting to the civilian Minister for Defence. The supreme command of the Defence Forces is vested in the President of Ireland; however, the actual command is exercised through the government by the Minister for Defence. All of these are civilian. The Minister is advised by a Defence Council comprising of Minister of State for the Department of Defence, its Secretary General, the Defence Force Chief of Staff, Deputy Chief of Staff (operations), and Deputy Chief of Staff (support). Although the military General Staff officers may report directly to the minister, it is the civilian Secretary General who is the principal officer of the entire Department of Defence. In Ireland the military Chief of Staff does not himself exercise command over any troops. Command of the soldiers throughout the country is exercised through four brigadiers, each of whom is on an equal rank to his colleagues, the inference being that no one officer could mobilise the entire forces of the State. In addition, the three members of the General Staff – the quartermaster general, the adjutant general and the Chief of Staff – have independent access to the Minister for Defence. In the years following the foundation of the State, these arrangements were to consolidate the subordinate relationship of the army to the government. They became the enduring ethos that permeated the modern Defence Forces. To this day the army has no authority to deploy any armed force of its own volition. Operational armed soldiers engaged in any security operations in Ireland are deployed only when requested by the civilian police force, An Garda Síochána. Although the broader intention of the structures and reporting arrangements in the Irish armed forces had its origin in the well-intentioned imposition of civil authority, their strict boundaries and observation often led to strained relations between the constituent parts of the Department of Defence. In addition, the role of the army and the type of mission assigned also impacted on the relations between the army itself and the government or the soldier and the government.

SIGNIFICANCE AND ROLE OF CIVIL-MILITARY RELATIONS

The legislation governing the respective roles of the elements of the Department of Defence outlined in the preceding paragraphs provides a framework for the intended boundaries and practice of civil–military

relations in Ireland. For the most part it establishes the supremacy of
civil authority and removes the presence of the military from political
activity. However, the statutory provisions are not the only influence.
Relationships are also influenced by role and perspective. For much
of the period between the 1920s and the 1980s, the stated mission for
the Irish Defence Forces had been to, 'defend the State against external
aggression'. The current mission amends the phrase 'external aggression' to 'armed aggression'. While the distinction of dropping the word
external may seem small, much has been written about the importance
of the mission for an armed force, with particular regard to its relationship with the civil authority. According to Finer:

> The army is a purposeful instrument. It is not a crescive institution
> like a church; it comes into being by fiat. It is rationally conceived to
> fulfil certain objectives. One may be to assist the civil power, but the
> principal object is to fight and win wars. The highly peculiar features of
> its organisation flow from this central purpose, not from the secondary
> one, and in it find their supreme justification.[7]

In considering the impact of 'internal' missions on the propensity for
military forces to become involved in politics, Smith and Welch proposed:

> State involvement of the armed forces in internal pacification – in short
> duties usually assigned to the police – inherently and inevitably
> brings the military into political disputes. Accordingly they suggested,
> 'the likelihood of military intervention rises should the armed forces
> become involved in primarily domestic police type or counterinsur-
> gency activities.[8]

In light of these observations it is interesting to consider the emergence,
in 1988, of the political campaign by spouses of soldiers and later the
soldiers themselves in Ireland, at a time when troops were deployed in
aid to the civil power that was operating on the border with Northern
Ireland. The question remains whether these duties and the soldiers'
exposure to internal, police-type duties resulted in an increase in
their 'political' activity and posturing. If Smith and Welch's proposal
were to be accepted, Irish troops being deployed along the border
in aid to the civil power contributed in the politicising of the troops.
Certainly soldiers had already begun to consider the remuneration

they were receiving in a different light. If a soldier's function, as has been suggested by Huntington, Janowitz, Finer and others, is combat, then while engaged in it soldiers only have their own compatriots with whom they can compare. If on the other hand they are utilised as a kind of gendarme force or a militia, it is perhaps inevitable that they will draw comparisons with their civilian counterparts. Does this then lead to the soldier considering him or herself something other than a unit of combat? Does the public perception of the soldier up to now disregard the social dimension of his or her life? And, if they are not off fighting wars, where do they fit into the normal non-military routine of the civilian community in which they live?

For many personnel in the Irish Defence Forces, they were only really soldiering on overseas missions such as UNIFIL in South Lebanon. Most soldiers who have served overseas enjoyed the experience; the proof of this is in the fact that in the Irish Defence Forces, until very recently, all deployments of personnel to UN missions were voluntary. While this has now changed, it was the case for most of the duration of the mission in Lebanon which went on from 1978 in one form or another to the present day. In the marital profile of Irish soldiers of the late 1980s outlined by Secretary General Michael Howard, many soldiers while deployed in Ireland would have been returning home from duty on a daily or weekly basis. There would have been the requisite daily or weekly transition from soldier to father/husband or wife/mother and the necessity for the military men and women to adjust, and at least while at home, begin to consider themselves in the context of their family role as opposed to the classic image the public would have of the toughened military personage. Studies undertaken on the impact of this on/off role and the difficulties that it precipitates in family life have been undertaken both in the Irish Army in respect of overseas missions, and in the navy in respect of the absence from home while ships are deployed.[9] In some cases the time spent throughout the year on three- and four-week sea patrols around the Irish coastline far exceed the total number of days a soldier may spend away from home in any given year while deployed on a UN overseas mission. While these observations reveal that there are consequences for the family in this on/off adjustment, little consideration has been given to the fact that most personnel of the armed force in Ireland live among the local civilian population. This differs to living in the larger isolated self-contained bases that would be a feature of the armies of the US, Great Britain and elsewhere. In countries such as the US and UK, recruitment is conducted on a national level with personnel being deployed to any number of distant locations from their home. Another important distinguishing factor of military life in considering civil–military relations is the physical isolation of the troops from the wider community. In Ireland, the practice of large-scale barracks being built in remote locations, isolated from the community, never really arose. The historical positioning of barracks around Ireland was mostly the result of Britain's military needs through the years. These varied from coastal defence from archrivals France and Spain, to the consideration of a good geographical spread that would enable speedy response to the threat of internal attack by those who saw military resistance as the best way of achieving Irish independence. As a result, the barracks system was spread geographically all over Ireland. Apart from the Naval Service and Air Corps, most recruitment was traditionally conducted at a local level where new recruits were drawn from the local community. One of the effects of this system was that the soldier lived out of barracks and maintained ties with family, friends, local organisations and clubs. In 1989, the Gleeson Commission found that, out of 13,233 soldiers, only a small number lived in barracks:

> A survey conducted at the request of the commission indicated that a total of 1,608 army personnel were classified as 'living in' on the 30 November 1989, while only 1,424 actually slept in barracks on that night.[10]

This represented only 11 per cent of the total Defence Forces and in the intervening period this figure has probably reduced even further. Thus the question arises: in the absence of larger isolated military communities and considering the propensity on the part of Irish military personnel to 'live out' of barracks, are Irish soldiers in fact more exposed to or involved in political activity?

Membership of any political party is prohibited to personnel of the Defence Forces by the Defence Act, 1954. This states: 'A member of the Permanent Defence Force shall not join, or be a member of, or subscribe to, any political organisation or society or any secret society whatsoever.'[11]

The reality is that most soldiers in Ireland who live in traditional civilian communities would be well aware of who their local politicians are, and may even be active for certain political parties, if not actually members of those parties. During the spring and autumn of 1989, when soldiers had taken matters into their own hands in the pursuit of the idea of a representative body for serving personnel, active members of the fledgling Permanent Defence Force Other Ranks Representative Association (PDFORRA) made daily visits to Dáil Eireann. There, they engaged with sitting politicians and lobbied for the necessary changes in legislation, while at the same time informing them first-hand of the deteriorating conditions that prevailed in the Defence Forces at the time. In this instance, there were serving soldiers not quietly influencing politicians in the background but physically visiting elected representatives in the parliament of a democracy and making their case. This very direct influence certainly made the political debate in the Dáil chamber far more interesting and better informed that it had been before. Richie Condron was a company sergeant in the Eastern Command involved in the initial stages of the establishment of PDFORRA and served at all levels of the organisation, from barracks to national executive. He became the vice president of the association and probably had more contact with the politicians of the day than did any other activist. He was passionate about the political system and how it might be best utilised to improve matters in the army. He remembers visiting the public chamber of the Dáil while he was still a company sergeant in the Irish Army, in the late 1980s, and listening to a lengthy parliamentary debate about the wisdom of using loose-leafed tea or tea bags, and which would be best for the army to purchase. 'I couldn't believe that so much importance was being afforded to such a trivial issue, when there were huge very real problems with pay and conditions'.[12]

While many issues contributed to great dissatisfaction being expressed by soldiers in their local communities to their local politicians during 1988 and 1989, they rarely seemed to have complained about conditions while on overseas service, when these would have been sometimes worse than anything at home. Most soldiers spoke in glowing terms about service overseas, in which they clearly perceived themselves in a different role. It is also noteworthy that when on overseas missions, the subordinate/superior relationship between the military and the occasional visiting civilian members of the Department of Defence was very much reversed. In the field, the supremacy of the military function and role of the soldier was very much the dominant force. The role and mission of the army in Ireland, consisting mainly of aid to the civil power and overseas peacekeeping missions, are significant in determining how the individual soldier perceives his or her role in the local community, and their relationship with it. They are also factors in influencing perspectives among others, including civilian personnel of the Department of the Defence, about the value or status of members of the armed forces. Military personnel would have had a very different view.

PERSPECTIVES ON STATUS AND ROLE OF THE MILITARY

Military personnel in Ireland perceived themselves as unique in their service to the country, prepared to lay down their lives if necessary in its defence. They believed that for this unswerving loyalty, the State should 'look after' them, and that they were special. The military felt they should not have to argue about getting decent pay and condi-tions because of the very special place they occupied in society and their role in the protection of its interests. Loyalty to the State was a given in the officer corps. In 2008, Brian O'Keefe, general secretary of the Representative Association for Commissioned Officers (RACO), was already a colonel who had come through the Irish Army cadet-training scheme. Having served at all the officer-rank levels from second lieutenant to colonel, he was an officer proud of his rank and status and protective of his subordinates. His perspective on the rela-tionship between the military and the State was clear: 'Officers were of the view that we owed absolute loyalty to the government.'[13]

This is an important perspective from a career officer, particularly when you consider it comes from a person trained in the application of violence. The uniqueness of the military and its role in society has been acknowledged throughout the study of civil–military relations. Welch and Smith maintain that the responsibilities of the armed forces are unique in the burden of protecting the State which is their only patron.[14] Janowitz suggests that their uniqueness derives from the requirement that members are specialists in making use of violence and mass destruction.[15] Desch contends that the military are undemocratic because of their hierarchical organisation and their near monopoly on coercive power in a State, which, he says, if not under firm civilian control, can represent a serious threat to democracy.[16]

Consistent in these perspectives is the belief that the military and their role are unique in society, but that they can pose a threat to the very body they serve. In Ireland in the late 1980s the well-established tradition among military personnel was that the use of such violence was only at the request of, and in the interests of, the State. Given the deadly skills that are inherent in military expertise, it is all the more important that personnel perceive themselves as being especially loyal to the State. This loyalty manifests itself in numerous ways. Military personnel in Ireland appear to accept their responsibilities to the furthest extreme, willing to give their own lives for the greater good of the society in which they live. Even in peacetime, long hours, absences from home and the rotations to and from foreign missions all require a special dedication from soldiers in their service to the country. In considering the dual nature of the Department of Defence as earlier outlined, it is not surprising, perhaps, that the civilian employees did not share the perspectives of 'uniqueness' held by the military personnel. Civilian departmental staff did not see their own role as unique; they saw their function as being similar to that of any other department operating within the same government policy and budgetary constraints as everybody else. It was a job for them. Nine to five Monday to Friday, holidays off and all the benefits that go with steady employment. While many were as dedicated to their job as anybody else, they did not have the requirement of 'living' on the job, of ever having to lay down their lives for it.

These different perspectives of the military and the civilian elements in the Department of Defence were to have an important impact on the respective responses of both sides to problems that arose in what was termed a 'crisis' in the Irish Army in 1988 and 1989. Both parties had very different views of the situation with regard to pay, allowances and conditions of service in the armed forces. Both on occasion blamed each other for some of the problems that were highlighted across the front pages of the national media at that time. Reports of very bad pay, poor opportunities for promotion and unfair treatment were soon to be the topic of national newspapers, radio chat shows and prime-time national television. *The Irish Times* articles in 1988 reflected the mood:

> Inevitably, what has come to be seen within the Defence Forces as a consistent policy of official neglect, is beginning to take its toll on morale. Last year 35 army officers voluntarily resigned, the highest number of voluntary retirements since 1960 and it's not just the lack of clear Defence policy that is causing this haemorrhage. Many army officers are finding that they are poorly paid in comparison to civilian colleagues, while there is also a lack of career structure for many younger officers.[17]

In recent months the National Army Spouses Association (NASA) has
enjoyed great success in highlighting what they believe are appalling
levels in pay in the army and a general crisis in morale, which has been
sapped by the virtual embargo on promotion and recruitment.[18]

Although there was a certain amount of sympathy among the civilian
section of the Department of Defence for the poor pay and conditions
being described as prevalent in the army, it would be argued that they had
little real understanding of the source of the soldiers' complaints. In the
departmental side, the issues of pay and allowances were perceived as parts
of a very broad public-service-sector pay policy. Individual members of
the Department of Defence had no role in determining pay. It was the
Department of Finance, acting on behalf of government, that usually
set the rates and ceilings. Michael Howard was the Department of
Defence press officer in 1989. He was a witness to, and actively involved
in, the events and strategies that precipitated the introduction of representative bodies. He was fully informed of the claims military personnel
were making about their pay and conditions, while at the same time
cognisant of the government's need for pay restraint. Eventually rising to
the highest position of Secretary General of the Department of Defence,
he recalled that a very stringent budget had been introduced in 1987 and
that there was little room for manoeuvre in relation to pay. It was felt at
the Department of Defence, at that time, that military personnel had a
poor understanding of the constraints of public-pay policy, and that the
increasing age and marital profile of soldiers influenced dissatisfaction
rather than the actual level of pay itself. 'Although the military perspective
on their uniqueness in their service to the State has merit, for the purpose
of pursuing better pay, a case was often made seeking comparable rates of
pay with other uniformed services such as on the occasion of submissions
to the Gleeson Commission.'[19]

The problem was that the practice and traditional manner of according
them payment was not recognised as being in need of any unique arrangements for remuneration. Gleeson remarked:

The commission could understand why military personnel would make
comparisons with other uniformed services which they would have
come into contact with in the course of their work. However, having
considered all the claims, the commission concluded that military
duties were clearly in a distinctive category and that it would not be

appropriate to fix military pay on the basis of a direct comparison with the pay of the Gardaí, prison officers and fire fighters. The commission decided that the fairest way to deal with military pay would be to compare the rates of pay in the Defence Forces with the pay of a wide range of jobs with roughly similar levels of responsibilities in a variety of employments in the public and the private sectors.[20]

This seems somewhat contradictory. If they were not comparable with the other uniformed services of the State, and in a 'distinctive category', why bother comparing them to others at all? Gleeson appeared to advocate that soldiers could expect no additional consideration over any other workers regarding their wages. These perspectives were also prevalent in the section of the Department of Defence that dealt with pay. The army was no different to any other public sector in terms of administration and being subject to government policy. Although Gleeson did acknowledge the uniqueness later in the same chapter of his report, he did so to justify recommended increases in allowances but not pay:

> In addition to comparison with other employments other factors were also taken into account. In particular the distinctive features of employment in the Defence Forces are reflected in the recommended revised rates of military service allowance, which compensates Defence Forces personnel for the special conditions associated with military life.[21]

In the context of having a uniform mechanism for the payment of all public servants, the Military Service Allowance (MSA) was some official recognition of the uniqueness of military life. But it had been a very small allowance and was not reckonable for pension purposes. The Gleeson Commission addressed both of these issues in the final report and made recommendations for a formative increase in the allowance and a new status which made it reckonable for pension. The recognition of the uniqueness of the military mission only extended to a recommendation to increase a military-service allowance and underlined the different perspectives of the value of the military to the State. It came about long after matters had taken a new turn and after the relationships between the military hierarchy and the State had come under considerable strain. These relationships, established under pressure at the time of the foundation of the State, were being tested in the respective responses of the two parts of the department in the unfolding crisis.

ORGANISATIONAL RELATIONSHIPS IN THE 1980s

Many civilian observers and commentators in Ireland in the late 1980s had little understanding of the makeup of the Defence Forces. In listening to the daily complaints about pay and conditions, the civilian population began to identify and sympathise with the members of the Irish armed forces. It transpired that the issues that came to the fore at the time were not only about pay. Internal relationships in the forces were being criticised too. Some of the events that led to the establishment of representative bodies, where it seemed members of the army were being critical of the civilian department and the government, may have brought some of the former doubts about loyalty and allegiance into sharp focus once more. The entire department struggled with the problems that arose from the campaign that sought better conditions for soldiers. There were problems for the government in the Dáil – it seemed that, in late 1988 and the first quarter of 1989, the Minister for Defence was being challenged and criticised by members of a very vocal opposition on a daily basis. The civilian departmental side, responsible for the compilation of answers to parliamentary questions, constantly had to prepare and brief a sometimes bedraggled minister, under pressure from the media and others. The Department of Defence press officer had to contend with new stories, emerging unexpectedly, of depravation in the army. From mid-1988 military commanders were having their barracks gates picketed by women with their children, seeking better conditions for their husbands. Soldiers had to be deployed on missions that took them from their homes and for which the commander had no means of recompensing them. The Chief of Staff himself appealed to the department to have something done about pay. All were concerned with the suggestions of low morale, and all felt the need to defend their particular record in the abundance of criticism being aired by all sections of the media in what became known for a second time as 'the army crisis'. Although there are distinct operational, cultural and physical differences in the respective missions and roles of the three sections of the PDF, control and supervision of the armed forces is quite centralised. In all cases, senior management of the various military units is provided by commissioned officers who for the most part have been trained in cadet school where they learn the craft of military management, motivation and leadership. The junior managerial functions are undertaken by non-commissioned officers (NCOs) from among enlisted personnel who enter the military as recruits. The *esprit de corps* and the morale of the troops are extremely important elements of any military institution. The officer corps, who manage all armies, make constant reference to that spirit that binds them. They are the military professionals. Their craft is military leadership, logistics, resources and strategy. They are expected to be leaders and in the conduct of any military operation, this is their most valuable skill. In all branches of the forces, officers will often require additional specialist skills. At the base of the three-part hierarchy beneath the officer and NCO body is the largest group comprising of the privates. These far outnumber the other two and in the past were thought to be the essence of an army's strength. It was the privates who were most needed to fight wars. It was the privates who needed to be motivated and it was the privates who, by and large, gave effect to whatever weaponry and arms an army possessed for utilisation in pursuit of its military aims. They were also the 'manual labour' detachment of an army. The middle group of the military force is the NCO body. They are supervising managers, with all the skills honed as privates added to by further training, education and most importantly experience. They are the constant feature of the lower army-management structure. Their time in a particular posting or position is usually far longer than that of either privates or officers.

In many countries there is a practice of utilising the skills and experience of selected NCOs by training them to become 'commissioned' officers. These are generally referred to as 'commissioning from the ranks' schemes (CFRs). The French Army at one time had almost half of their officer body coming from the ranks.[22] Although such a scheme does exist, there are relatively few officers in Ireland commissioned from among the enlisted ranks. Professor Huntington suggests the transition from one to the other is problematic as one has a vocation while the other has a profession. He claimed in 1964 that 'enlisted personnel have neither the intellectual skills nor the professional responsibility of the officer.'[23] Huntington's generalisations regarding the intellectual skills of enlisted personnel may well have been valid in the US in 1964, but certainly such conclusions would not be sustainable in Ireland twenty-five years later. It is not unusual today to find many instances in which the enlisted personnel are better educated and have greater intellectual skills than their military 'superiors' in the commissioned ranks. Nevertheless, there is reluctance in the Irish Defence Forces to promote their enlisted personnel into the commissioned ranks. Despite the existence of the Irish CFR scheme, the frequency and application process make it little more than a token gesture to the principle. In the twenty-five years between 1962 and 1987 there were only six courses under this scheme with an average of twenty-five NCOs on each.[24] That represents about five enlisted personnel per year in a force of over 12,000. In the British Army, while 80 per cent of commissioned officers are cadet-trained, the remaining 20 per cent come through various other schemes including officer-training courses for serving soldiers.[25] This was one of the issues raised by enlisted personnel themselves in their submission to the Gleeson Commission when it was felt that not enough of them were given the opportunity to go on training courses that would lead to a commissioned-officer rank.[26] Contrary to the impression that Professor Huntington might have expected, Gleeson, in responding to their proposal, found something altogether different:

> During the course of its investigations, the commission formed the impression that considerable scope exists for greater involvement of NCOs in the management of the Defence Forces. A number of senior NCOs in particular, appear to have extremely good middle management qualities which are not fully utilised merely because they are not officers.[27]

In a footnote to the above, Gleeson records the fact that between 1962 and 1989 only 140 NCOs were commissioned from the ranks. Despite the recommendation by Gleeson in the final report of the commission that a review should take place, little has changed.[28] In the subsequent scheme that was introduced, the actual criteria for eligibility was narrowed rather than widened by reducing the age eligibility and specifying the number of years served, so the number of opportunities that personnel had to apply for officer training actually narrowed.

Perhaps Huntington's conclusions still carry some sway among the military hierarchy in Ireland. It may also be that the perspective in the armed forces in Ireland comes from the early British military model where the officer class came from the aristocracy and maintained a cultural separation from the enlisted ranks by institutionalising their social differences in the day-to-day operation of the army as an entity. While the aristocratic system was not present in Ireland in the late 1980s, the tradition that had prevailed was that, once a candidate successfully completed cadet school to become an officer, the seniority and career progress were generally assured, regardless of ability or suitability. Janowitz maintained that because of the simplicity of the skill structure and static nature of the military organisation, military authority was derived, among other things, from social position. He contends that where authority was ascribed, rather than earned, promotion came on the basis of age and not ability.[29] Although commissioned officers, NCOs and privates operationally work and live in very close proximity to each other, there are many imposed divisions that separate them, from pay, conditions of service, allowances, career expectations and pensions down to where they eat, sleep, live and socialise. It is a highly hierarchal institution. Janowitz remarks: 'Since by definition the military establishment is a comprehensive and all-embracing hierarchy, the career soldier is assumed to be an ideal example of the professional operating under bureaucratic authority.'[30]

This system facilitates a managerial/worker or superior/subordinate type of management that defines the organisational relationship which is further solidified by the wearing of a uniform. Such uniforms, in all cases, externally portray the actual rank of the individual. Thus, as in most armed forces of the world, any subordinate coming into contact with any superior will be immediately and explicitly aware of their superior/subordinate relationship and vice versa. This causes the smoothing of the imposition of authority. It helps speed the response and context of military orders and instructions. Finer comments:

> Further to this each echelon in the hierarchy is immediately and objectively identifiable by rank and distinctive insignia. Authority is de-personalised it is owed to the rank not the man ... The importance of subordination and superordination is further enhanced by social practices prescribing a social distance between the superior and the inferior ranks.[31]

The heavy importance that the Irish armed forces attached to rank, insignia and uniform were to fully emerge in the period leading up to the establishment of representative associations. In 1990 and 1991, during the negotiations that preceded the setting up of the representative bodies (which will be examined later), the military authorities were to contend that the wearing of uniforms and the display of rank were 'inextricably' linked to the exercise of command and discipline.

The issue almost derailed the talks that were set up to compile new regulations for consultation mechanisms for elected representatives at all levels of the army chain of command. These talks, commencing in July 1990, were made up of the elected representatives of PDFORRA on one side, and, on the other, by officials from the Department of Defence and senior officers of the army hierarchy. The matter of contention was that PDFORRA wanted elected representatives, in future consultation with army management, to be in civilian attire. They argued that if meaningful 'negotiation' was to take place then all people at the table were to be deemed, for the purpose of the talks, to be 'equal'. Both sides were there in legitimate roles, either conferred on them by lawful orders as in the case of the military, or by elected mandate under statutory legislation in the case of the elected representatives of the associations. Nevertheless, the army side felt that the 'shedding' of the uniform for such talks in barracks or elsewhere in the army system would be totally unacceptable. The issue rumbled on for eleven months of discussion but was finally concluded when both sides seemed to concede on the issue. The resultant arrangements were set out in the Defence Force Regulation (DFR) S6. The details of the arguments made will be outlined in a later chapter.

While the lesser ranked person are in all cases subordinate to their superior, and are compelled to carry out all orders or instruction received from them, the relationship is not just one way. The commissioned officer body have an ethical, regulatory and definitive 'duty of care' to their subordinates. They are responsible for every aspect of their subordinates' lives in the service, from providing them with clothing, accommodation and food, to granting them permission to get time off, apply for promotion and even get married. This duty of care is taken very seriously by most military commanders. In an earlier part of his military service, Col Brian O'Keefe recalled the long days spent on military exercises at the end of which all troops were cold, exhausted and hungry in the Dublin Mountains: 'Your first priority as a commander was to ensure the troops were fed and quartered; this was even before you had anything to eat yourself, famished though you may have been.'[32]

In Ireland as in many other countries the relationship was paternalistic. There were continuing instances whereby military commanders used their all-encompassing authority to assist their charges in times of difficulty. Conscious that they had no control over pay rates, they did utilise their ability to provide time off to soldiers who were suffering family bereavements, domestic difficulties or even health problems. Commanders were also aware that there were personnel under their charge who were having difficulty in trying to make ends meet. A number of privates in the army were eligible for a supplementary social-welfare allowance as a result of the low level of their pay. To compensate, commanders often deployed such people on duties that attracted a subsistence allowance. Lt Colonel Adrian Ryan had wide experience as a company commander. He had witnessed, first-hand, soldiers taking on additional civilian part-time jobs to try and supplement the pay they received in the army in order to survive. 'You turned a blind eye to them having second jobs in civvy street (*sic*), which strictly speaking was in breach of regulations.'[33]

The Defence Act, 1954 distinguishes only two groups among the members of the Permanent Defence Force (PDF); these are officer ranks and 'other' ranks. The cultural differences between these groups and their relationships with each other not surprisingly resulted in different approaches to the whole idea of representation and associations in the forces. Many of the officers serving in 1988 saw the calls for a representative body as the manifestation of their failure to provide good pay and better conditions for their soldiers. They sympathised with them and often articulated their frustration in being unable to assist in these crucial areas. Low pay and insufficient remuneration were areas that officers felt were outside their control, and although the military authorities submitted proposals to the Department of Defence for improvements, they could only do so in the context of the constant struggle for more resources to run the PDF and ensure it fulfilled its mission. Much of the blame for perceived penny-pinching was laid at the door of the civilian section of the Department of Defence, and, in this regard, officers, NCOs and privates were often united in the negative perception they held regarding the department's approach to pay and allowances. 'We are all in the same boat' was a phrase often used by superiors to their subordinates in any discussions that arose about pay. But as has already been pointed out, while everybody may well have been in the same boat with regard to their dissatisfaction with pay, there were different degrees of privilege in that boat. For many enlisted personnel there were far more problems in the service than just the levels of pay. Promotion through the ranks, career development, selection for overseas service, standards of food and accommodation in barracks, accreditation of training received, and subsistence eligibility were all matters that attracted criticism among enlisted personnel. The difference between these issues and that of basic pay was that the commissioned officers, in their managerial role, did have control and were directly responsible for the procedures, delays and defects in many of the areas where problems arose. There was a service-wide criticism among enlisted personnel that when officers retired from service or were deployed out of their units, a replacement was in place immediately. Applications for promotion by those eligible in the officer ranks, and the interview process that preceded promotion, were all carried out and in place prior to the vacancy arising, so that when an officer did retire, the vacant position was filled immediately. With such a promotion there was a domino effect down the line that occurred literally on the day of departure. In the case of enlisted personnel, vacancies for promotion were only generally acted upon after the NCO had retired. The potential promotion created often remained unfilled for months or even years. It was in these areas, where the officer body did have control over the timing of interview boards, that criticism of the higher ranks in management arose among enlisted personnel. In their submission to the Gleeson Commission, the NCOs team highlighted a 21 per cent discrepancy between the permitted full strength of units and the actual numbers. They also criticised an overuse of personnel put into 'acting' ranks where they had all the responsibilities but not the actual promotion.[34]

Internal relationships between military commanders and their subordinates were therefore complex. While they shared their military uniqueness and both perceived the Department of Defence, in areas such as pay, to be the 'common enemy', there was also the internal dissatisfaction with the way in which non-pay issues were managed by officers in a position where they had absolute control of outcomes that impacted on the service of the enlisted personnel. Thus in the very public campaign that was about to unfold, organisational relationships between enlisted personnel and officers, between the Department of Defence and the army, between military body and the government were to come to the fore in a way that had not been experienced in Ireland before. This exposure of the nuances of Irish civil–military relations was precipitated by the conditions that led to the call for improvements in the army and the establishment of representative associations in the Irish armed forces.

SOURCES OF DISSATISFACTION
WITH PAY AND CONDITIONS

Despite the complexity of internal military relations and the broader civil–military relations, soldiers involved in the day-to-day operations of the army were confronted with what they saw as deteriorating conditions of service and pay, which none of the structures were able to address. From the late 1960s, the continuing civil strife and paramilitary violence in Northern Ireland resulted in increasing numbers of Irish soldiers being posted along the border between Northern Ireland and the Republic. They were there by request of the Irish Civilian Police Force, An Garda Síochána. The practice of army support for policing operations in Ireland arises as a result of the main police force being unarmed. If at any time the Gardaí require armed assistance, there is a mechanism in which they can request what is termed in the army 'aid to the civil power' or ATCP. Much of the Irish Army's activities by the 1980s were associated with ATCP operations in support of what was, essentially, police work. Cash being transported to and from banks had come under attack from different armed paramilitary groups. The Gardaí sought the aid of the army in the protection of the vehicles being used, and the 'cash escort' military duty came into being. There were similar duties that emerged in the movement of legitimate explosives around the country for the purposes of mining. Finer expressed reservations about armies being used in this way for 'domestic' duties, and not for the role for which they were trained. He further maintained that the strain which such duties put on the loyalty of the armed forces is often too great and impels them to disobey or even to act against their government, giving the Curragh mutiny as an example.[35]

There is a certain irony in the fact that the British Army, as a result of developments in Northern Ireland, was accused of being mutinous and that Irish soldiers as a result of their work in the same area seventy years later would be labelled, by some, similarly. Finer's comments suggest the use of a standing army against mere 'nationals', the implication being unarmed civilians or citizens. In fact, as has already been pointed out, the British Army of the day were supposed to be there to protect such people and property from a privately raised army who stood, armed, in defiance of a government decision. Their strategy was non-intervention as opposed to intervention. In effect, they sided with

the private army rather than with the government they were meant
to serve. An interesting aside is that the leadership of the mutiny held
very selective views as to who were fellow nationals and who were not.
Irish soldiers stationed on the border from the 1970s and through to
the 1990s never contemplated not following orders, and although it
seems inevitable that some of them from that locality may have held
nationalist views, there was no orchestrated effort to intervene and try
to change government policy. The only suggestions of mutiny came
from certain officers and some NCOs who maintained that people
who were seeking the right of association were somehow mutinous.
Although there was a type of collective action among soldiers who
were serving on the border at that time in trying to establish representative bodies, this bore no resemblance to the actions contemplated
by British military personnel at the Curragh in 1913.

Given the jurisdictional difference between Northern Ireland and
the Republic, the border itself became a very strategic location for
paramilitary activity. There were security requirements by both jurisdictions to secure the border and prevent its exploitation by groups
seeking to move across and back, thereby avoiding detection in one
area for crimes committed in another. Explosives, bomb-making
materials, arms and ammunition were often moved by paramilitaries
from the South of Ireland to the North and vice versa. The border
does not follow any particular geophysical or manmade feature
such as a road or a river, and in many locations it goes right through
property owned by a single individual. It straddles farms, mountains
and lakes. Observation and control of sections of the border can
be challenging in sometimes rugged terrain. Complete security is
virtually impossible. To this end, the Irish authorities established a
series of strategic checkpoints along the border through the 1970s
and 1980s. While the Gardaí manned the checkpoints to stop and
search vehicles, the Defence Forces provided armed support. There
had to be close co-operation and consultation between these two
security arms of the State. Working in such close proximity for
extended periods of time made it clear to soldiers that there were
several distinctive differences between how they were remunerated
compared to the Gardaí. In 1988, policemen who were manning the
checkpoints were deployed on an eight-hour shift basis. They were
given expenses for food and incidentals and received overtime in
addition to their usual weekly pay. In contrast, soldiers manned the

same checkpoints for periods of twenty-four hours at a time. This was not unusual in the sense that all branches of the Defence Forces undertook a whole variety of duties of that duration. In barracks all over Ireland, on ships of the State at home or abroad, on UN missions, anywhere around the world, men and women did twenty-four-hour duties, usually necessitated by security and/or safety. In most cases personnel who undertook such duties were compensated by way of a payment known as 'security duty allowance'. Depending on their rank, service or mission, personnel could find themselves 'detailed' or rostered for duty on any day of the year. In Ireland, the nature of paramilitary activity dictated the operational responses required by the security forces in the area. Kidnappings, abandoned murder victims, roadside bombs and the uncovering of arms dumps meant that the armed forces could be called out at any time of the day or night, 365 days per year. In the case of the personnel stationed in or near border counties, a special allowance had been created in 1972 known as 'border allowance'. It was designed to compensate personnel for living in what was effectively an operational zone that lacked the predictability of many of the barracks and military installations in the more peaceful southern part of the country. The allowance did have some disadvantages. All personnel in receipt of it lost their entitlement to security-duty allowance. This could mean that a soldier could be deployed in 'on the ground' military security operations at a moment's notice and several times in any given week. Because they were in receipt of a semi-permanent 'border allowance' as an addendum to their weekly pay, they did not receive any additional remuneration for the twenty-four-hour duty. Up to the end of 1988, when an increase of 77 per cent was made, the allowance stood at less than £3 per day.[36] This seemed to be inequitable to some who saw soldiers involved in barrack duties getting paid the same as those who had to operate in the unpredictable and uncomfortable environment of the border. Whether a soldier was on duty in the comfort of a barracks in Dundalk or Castleblayney or deployed in a roadside ditch providing 'cover' for a checkpoint made no difference to their pay. The border allowance for those personnel who were in 'operational' units seemed poor compensation when compared with those who did not have to deploy 'on the ground'. In many instances 'on the ground' meant literally on the ground. Troops were often required to lie in ditches for hours at a time to provide field of fire cover for police checkpoints. All armies in any operational theatre must have the capacity to feed their troops and in some cases very efficient field kitchens were deployed on the border to do so. In many other instances, however, food was prepared in the distant barracks and transported to soldiers near the checkpoints for consumption in position. When this method was used, complaints were often received from personnel who found the food was cold or had not travelled so well in the special thermal containers which were being used. In contrast, the Gardaí were relieved from their posts by their colleagues and went to the nearest hotel for meals. The armed soldiers saw their civilian counterparts rotating three personnel to complete the twenty-four-hour duty that just one soldier was expected to do. Comparisons were inevitably drawn. John Wolfe was an early activist in the pursuit of representative associations. He had met and spoken to many of the soldiers deployed on the border and raised the issue of their plight when he became a member of the Gleeson submission team for NCOs. John was among the original soldiers of the Eastern Command who founded the fledgling group that was to become PDFORRA. As a squadron quartermaster sergeant in the army he was very aware of the methodology and quality of rationing supplies and feeding the troops. He complained that conditions on the border were horrendous:

> The police were getting 3 and 4 times the money the lads were getting. They were being picked up and brought to hotels for lunch and soldiers had to wait, sometimes for hours to get fed. They were really pissed off up there and they wanted to try and do something about it.[37]

Conor Brady in his study of the Gardaí noted that 'It is remarkable that Ireland pays its police officers better than its teachers, its nurses and the bulk of its civil servants'.[38] Suspicions developed among soldiers that the police were in receipt of much better remuneration, for much less time, when deployed in the exact same location. Additionally, from the soldiers' point of view, it was felt that if any trouble did arise they would be the first target as, being armed, they posed the biggest threat to potential assailants in such a situation. In the subsequent claim by the NCOs team to the Gleeson Commission, the Gardaí were chosen as an analogue for determining new rates of pay. It was pointed out in their submission that in 1974 an army sergeant earned 10.5 per cent more than a garda, but by 1989, the garda was earning 20 per cent more than the army sergeant.[39] Charts were also compiled to show discrepancies in end-of-service gratuities.[40] In another series of ATCP operations soldiers were again to witness what they felt was inequitable treatment. Sgt Gerry Rooney, during his service in the army, was attached to St Bricin's Military Hospital in Dublin. Despite being a highly qualified technician, he was deployed on numerous occasions in ATCP operations, including on two occasions when prison officers and ambulance drivers were on strike. He became general secretary of PDFORRA and recalls soldiers getting to see how prisoners were treated in terms of the food that was available. Apparently, the food was better in Dublin's Mountjoy Prison than what some soldiers were receiving from the army.[41]

Because of the general security situation, the ATCP operations also included countrywide cash escorts where armed soldiers assisted the Gardaí in the transfer of cash to and from banks by civilian commercial-security vehicles. These 'cash escort' duties were also a source of dissatisfaction for the soldiers, who often had to remain on guard outside hotels while the civilian van drivers and Gardaí stopped for lunch. Escorts and armed cover were also provided to the prison service and Gardaí when paramilitary trials were taking place at Green Street, Dublin. The rising frequency and incidence of duty for ordinary soldiers as a result of the deteriorating internal security situation in Ireland began to encroach on the part-time civilian jobs that were held down by members of the Defence Forces. These, they argued, were necessary to make ends meet. Richard (Dick) Dillon was the founding chairman of PDFORRA and formerly a member of the 5th Battalion, Dublin. He was posted to an active operational battalion for his entire career. With a wife and family, with his experience and service overseas, in Portlaoise and on the border, he was well positioned to understand the difficulties encountered by soldiers in their multiple workplaces. He recalled:

> When you were doing the part time work you could get along reasonably okay. But when that started to be eaten away with the extra hours for aid to the civil power, people got really tired of it and the women began to talk about it.[42]

Soldiers also began to discuss what they saw as the noticeable difference between the treatment of the personnel of the uniformed services and that reserved to other sections of society. John Wolfe, a founding member of the representative association, recalled comparing himself at the time with others who were in receipt of social-welfare benefit:

I saw people around me during that particular recessionary time who were drawing the dole (unemployment benefit) and with similar family numbers to myself, similar age to myself, nixering like mad,[43] driving better cars, going on two holidays a year with their families, having more to spend, more disposable income and here was I with my role in my family as being provider, and I couldn't understand why I wasn't as successful as these people were and yet they were not technically working. So I realised that the army was not providing for me or the needs of my family. So I began to play with the notion of what to do.[44]

It was not so much that soldiers begrudged the conditions enjoyed by the Gardaí or the prison service who were deployed in the same situation as they were, but they wondered if having a representative body would make a difference in the State's approach to the different services. Various internal committees and groups had been set up to address pay problems in the army but, according to Richard Dillon, 'there was a great deal of cynicism about them and they were only seen as tinkering around the edges of the pay problems'.[45] He recalls that during this period, a debate emerged on a radio talk show about alleged incidences in which Irish soldiers serving in Lebanon had been briefed to shoot stray dogs because of the danger, in the Middle East, of rabies. In the ensuing discussion one caller suggested there was more concern about the treatment of dogs than there was about the treatment of soldiers. It would appear that this particular debate prompted a number of soldiers' wives from the border regions to begin to raise awareness in the media about just how bad conditions were for serving soldiers in the army.

Despite the feelings among many military personnel that they alone were poorly paid, the Department of Defence and its officials were conscious at that time of the broader picture of public-pay policy. Michael Howard, Secretary General in 2010, was also serving in the department in the late 1980s, and recalls that the economy was in a desperate condition and that financial control was very 'tight'.[46] Even if the Department of Defence had wanted to increase pay levels, government fiscal policy would not have permitted it. At the time, pay rates among different parts of the public service were effected through a system of 'grades'. These grades determined the rate at which people were paid, whether they were civilians in the Department of Finance, postmen in a general post office or nurses in a hospital. The problem was that an increase in pay in one sector had a knock-on effect of increases throughout the public service. An additional difficulty was that if one grade increased, then the differential in pay between it and the next one up the line had to be maintained. With such a system in place, the Department of Defence was restrained in making any improvements whatsoever in pay. The size of the combined services of the PDF at that time numbered about 12,500. Apart from the cost of raising wages for such a large group, the knock-on effect was the biggest fear among those responsible for maintaining pay restraint across the entire public service. In presenting the budget in Dáil Eireann in January 1988, the Minister for Finance, Ray McSharry, was conscious of the preceding years of industrial relations conflict and its cost, attributable in part to the absence of national pay agreements after the collapse in 1982 of the National Understanding Agreement.[47] He set out the financial difficulties of the country that would necessitate pay restraint, particularly in the public sector:

> The approach for 1988 remains unchanged. There is no choice but to continue to reduce dependence on borrowing. The main emphasis must be on reducing public expenditure and already Government policy on this has been clarified. The only other course would be to increase taxation substantially but this is not a practical option.[48]

One of the minister's key strategies in maintaining a firm managerial grip on the country's finances was a return to a national wage agreement involving all the social partners. The broad-based agreement, signed in October 1987, was known as the Programme for National Recovery (PNR) and it sought to ensure some form of industrial-relations peace in return for which there were guaranteed, albeit modest, increases for those in the public sector. Over 2 million working days had been lost through disputes from 1982 to 1987.[49] The minister noted the budget was possible as a result of the three-year agreement with the public service unions as part of the PNR that would contribute to orderly conduct in industrial relations.[50] The social partnership model was a revisit to earlier arrangements that had broken down in 1982. Gunnigle, McMahon and Fitzgerald contend that the temporary demise of the consensus approach during the 1980s is attributable to the change in government from Fianna Fáil to the Fine Gael/Labour coalition. They credit the 1987 Fiánna Fail government with the resurgence of the social partnership approach. In the case of the unions, the diminutive increases in pay were traded off against a new input into a 'wider economic and social agenda'. [51]

For members of the Defence Forces who were outside of the industrial-relations process, these strategies left little room for any realistic hope of an increase in pay. The increases secured by the unions and other social partners were very modest, and anybody getting anything beyond what was agreed would probably result in wide-scale industrial unrest. Even the improvements in social legislation didn't particularly benefit military personnel. There was, more often than not, derogation for the application of measures to members of the Defence Forces, such as in the Employment Equality Act, 1977 and the Unfair Dismissals Act, 1977. [52] Hillery's detailed surveys show that at the time when this progressive legislation was being enacted, the civilian workforce unions had no fewer than sixty-six full-time national trade-union officials and ninety-four full-time branch secretaries working on their behalf. [53] In contrast, soldiers had no representative officials or associations acting directly in their interests. In the absence of such representation, others tried to highlight the problems. It was not just opposition politicians in the Dáil or NASA who were complaining about conditions for soldiers in the army. In a lengthy emotional appeal, the head chaplain of the Defence Forces wrote to the Chief of Staff on 27 April 1988. In a three-page letter, Right Reverend Monsignor Dunne, on behalf of all chaplains throughout the country, outlined what he reported was deep concern about the low state of morale, brought on by poor pay and extensive financial hardship. The monsignor claimed that marital breakdown, material depriva-tion and mental stress were at levels that made soldiers vulnerable to influence from subversives and moneylenders. The letter pleaded with the Chief of Staff to represent the interests of the members of the PDF by making a special case to the government. [54]

A defence-policy review had been initiated in 1987 by government, but this was to examine the structure, strengths, roles and procurement procedures in the forces. Given that its primary purpose was cost-saving, the possibilities of pay increases at the time were even more unlikely. An Inter-Departmental Committee on pay was set up in June 1988 but it would report back in the context of the national strategy. [55] Despite these restrictions, the personnel at the Department of Defence who were responsible for the administration of pay sympathised with soldiers regarding low wages, but they still enjoyed a unique situation whereby they did not have to deal with unions or representative associations for the army. Every other department, when considering the imposition of pay policy, had to engage with the public-service trade unions or associations. Because the military up to that point had never had a representative body or a union, the department could implement policy in these matters in isolation and as they saw fit. A cursory examination of soldiers' pay rates in 1990, after the Inter-Departmental Committee had reported and their findings had been implemented, would appear to compare similarly to other sectors of the civilian population in average earnings on a weekly basis. Factory workers' earnings averaged £221.71 per week compared to a three-star private at £215.10, clerical workers at £248.97 compared to NCO quartermasters at £254.36, managerial staff at £396.38 compared to an Irish Army commandant at £398.[56] However, soldiers would argue that comparison with factory workers, who had the certainty of just forty hours per week, was unfair, due to the high incidence of twenty-four hour duties, and the danger and uncertain nature of military life. When public criticism by the spouses of soldiers arose in mid-1988, many of the issues they raised were about poor treatment of soldiers and matters other than pay.[57] In some respects the department was demonised by military commanders who blamed all of the ills of poor pay, lack of promotion and bad conditions on them.

A National Executive for Soldiers, a National Army Spouses Association (NASA) and a General Election

These aforementioned issues were a matter of discussion throughout 1988, not just among soldiers, but with their wives and families when they got home. The sense of inequity felt by them resulted in growing frustration, but there was no way in which soldiers could publicly articulate their grievances. Many noted that An Garda Síochána had three representative associations for their different ranks with elected officials who could speak on their behalf about problems in an industrial relations-type arrangement.[1] These associations had replaced an earlier one that rank-and-file Gardaí believed had failed them in their pay claims in the mid-1970s. The origin of the new representative associations had necessitated members of the force initially meeting in breach of regulations.[2]

Serving soldiers in Ireland at this time had no representative association and military regulations prohibited them from speaking to the media.[3] The growing feeling of frustration about the perceived inequity led to soldiers and their wives believing that the lack of access to the media and the absence of any representative association were the main reasons for the situation in which they found themselves. James Martin, an Air Corps flight sergeant, and John Wolfe, a squadron quartermaster sergeant, were both PDFORRA activists who had been members of the same Gleeson submission team. They held strong views about an internal association:

Without a representative body that had access to the media we would have been a toothless and silent organisation, suffering internally from the indifference of a management regime that hadn't the nuts to take on the establishment in the first place. What good would their designed structures be to us?[4]

Although never serious, the joking in the mess about a coup was an indication of the real frustration that people felt at that time, and when I was contacted to meet some lads to talk about an association I went.[5]

There were also many other issues perceived to be wrong for those who served in the Defence Forces. These included matters such as low pay, substandard living accommodation, poor promotional prospects through the ranks, lack of family-support mechanisms and restrictions on career-advancement training and educational opportunities among enlisted personnel. Flight Sergeant James Martin served most of his career in the Air Corps, he was the NCO representative for the Air Corps on the Gleeson submission team and through his deliberations was conscious of the many perceived shortcomings of the military structure in addressing problems for personnel. He and the NCOs team maintained that: 'It is considered by most NCOs and men that their views and needs cannot be adequately met within the present structures in the Defence Forces.'[6]

Representative associations and unions were not alien to Ireland. In the late 1980s most segments of the workforce and the professions enjoyed the right of association. Trade unions and representative bodies of one sort or another had existed in Ireland since the nineteenth century and before. Although not always accepted or recognised by employers, these bodies had become an integral part of the industrial relations landscape in Ireland. The Irish Trades Union Congress (ITUC) was established in 1894 in Dublin and represented a mixture of unskilled labourers and craft-and-trade unions. The Irish Transport and General Workers' Union (ITGWU), representing an even broader base of workers, became the largest union of congress soon after its establishment in 1908.[7] The Irish National Teachers Organisation (INTO), though founded in 1868, became affiliated to the TUC in 1918.[8] By 1936 there were forty-nine unions affiliated to congress, which by 1939 represented 172,000 affiliated workers, about a quarter of the workforce at large.[9] Despite the recovery of falling numbers of members in the early years after the foundation of the State, Professor Jack Lynch contended that continuing difficulties into the 1940s 'caused by the multiplicity of unions' saw unity being restored by the formation of the Irish Congress of Trade Unions (ICTU) in 1959,[10] by which time there were sixty-eight unions representing 409,000 members. During the 1970s, discussions between ICTU and the government underlined a willingness by both parties to engage with each other. The idea of workforce representation was elevated to the highest level of social acceptability in the emergence of 'social partnership'. Negotiated deals between the trade unions, agricultural and business sectors and the government led to initiatives such as the 'Programme for National Economic Recovery' in which unions promised industrial-relations stability in return for modest wage increases, improvements in conditions and social policy input. By the 1990s there were 682,000 workers represented formally by affiliated unions of the ICTU. However, the ICTU did not represent all employees of the State. There were numerous other bodies such as the Gardaí associations, the Irish Bank Officials Association (IBOA) and others that had representative bodies but were not affiliated to the ICTU.

In mid-1988, knowing that the serving Defence Force personnel could not engage with the media to highlight these issues, a number of soldiers' spouses in the Dundalk and Dublin areas began to meet and founded what they eventually called the National Army Spouses Association (NASA). The stated aims of this group were very specific:

2. Aims.
The aims and objectives of the association shall be:-

a. To seek and improve the pay, allowances and conditions of single and married male and female members of the permanent Defence Forces.
b. To develop a mutual comradeship between the families of serving and ex-serving members of the Permanent Defence Forces.
c. To organise effective methods of setting up a modern military welfare service for serving members of the Permanent Defence Forces and their families.
d. The setting up of a lawfully constituted representative body for members of the Permanent Defence Forces.
e. To achieve all the above aims and objectives through peaceful and legitimate means.
f. The association shall be strictly non-political and non-sectarian and shall not have any affiliation with any political party.[11]

The constitution was eventually adopted in June 1989, by which time there were branches and committees in Ballyshannon, Longford, Mullingar, Dublin, Kildare, and Dundalk. The women of this association conducted a very public campaign that high-lighted the grievances of the Defence Force personnel. They held their first press conference in Dublin on 26 October 1988.[12] Their stated aims were to improve the pay and conditions of their spouses and to seek the establishment of representative structures for army personnel similar to the Gardaí's. The Irish media found this hugely newsworthy. Previously, most of the information about life in the Defence Forces came from official military or departmental sources. Not surprisingly this resulted in a very one-sided portrayal of military life in Ireland. NASA attracted extensive media attention as it was highly critical of both the Minister for Defence and the army hierarchy itself. For the first time in Ireland, television news showed women and children picketing outside army barracks with placards and posters, protesting about the treatment of soldiers by their military bosses. On 3 November 1988 NASA marshalled hundreds of women to protest at the Dáil and called for the sacking of the incumbent Minister for Defence, Michael Noonan:

> Several hundred army wives, members of the National Army Spouses Association marched on Leinster House yesterday to intensify their campaign for improved pay and conditions for members of the Defence Forces. At Leinster House the women shouted slogans calling for the dismissal of the Minister for Defence, Mr Noonan who has refused so far to meet them.[13]

This campaign was the subject of even more interest when the women claimed that their husbands were being intimidated by their commanding officers because of their spouses' involvement.[14] The matter was raised in Dáil Éireann by Deputies Clohessy and Gregory who asked the Minister of Defence if he was concerned about the allegations of threats in Cathal Brugha Barracks, St Bricin's Military Hospital and Baldonnel.[15] Deputy Michael Noonan, Minister for Defence, denied being aware of any such activities and asked if evidence did exist that it be brought to him.[16]

THE 'ARMY CRISIS' OF THE 1980S

From late 1987, the government were being questioned on the level of morale in the Defence Forces. In that year alone, thirty-five officers had retired, an increase of ten over the previous year.[17] Typical questions of the period were posed by Deputy Molloy when he asked Deputy Michael Noonan, then Minister for Defence, if he was concerned about the low level of morale in the forces and reports that the General Staff were telling middle-ranking officers that they would be better off seeking employment outside.[18] Minister Noonan strongly refuted these suggestions at the time, but such questions continued and became focused on a variety of ailments across the Defence Forces. Deputy Molloy enquired about manning levels and lower numbers impacting on morale because of increasing incidence of duties.[19] The minister did not agree that morale was poor. By March 1988 questions were being posed regarding the fact that numerous soldiers were eligible for Family Income Supplement (FIS) from social welfare. The minister played down the query saying that a small number of the 11,700 members of the PDF were in receipt of it. Deputy Patterson remarked:

> Is the Minister not aware that the FIS was brought in to help people on the lowest wages, and is it not of concern to him to find that members of the Defence Forces qualify for such assistance? By direct implication it says that the level of earnings is among the lowest in the country.[20]

The public activities of NASA in September of 1988 also influenced the body politic and gave the opposition parties in Dáil Eireann additional material with which to criticise the government of the day. Much of the critical debate in 1988 had focused on pay and the long-awaited report of the Inter-Departmental Committee. The idea put forward by the women that a representative body should be established was immediately criticised by government and others. Minister for Defence Michael Noonan was asked directly in December 1988 about the possibility of permitting the formation of representative associations in the Defence Forces. He replied that such bodies were 'incompatible' with the system of command and policy:

> I am advised that the formation by members of the Defence Forces of associations or unions having a system of organisation and control

separate from that of the Defence Forces, would be incompatible with the system of command essential in any defence or military force contemplated by Article 13 and 15 of the Constitution and provided for in the Defence Acts and the regulations made under those Acts. Apart from objections based on the legal considerations involved there would be fundamental policy objections to any development towards the creation of unions or associations in the Defence Forces.[21]

Colonel E.D. Doyle, writing in a national newspaper, in considering the call for representative bodies in the army, raised the prospect of a pressure group with access to guns. He highlighted the difference between other pressure groups in the State and a proposed one in the army, pointing out that 'the people represented will have arms in their hands'.[22] The pressure they could apply as a group might become threatening when the State had a 'weak or divided government'. He maintained that a democracy such as Ireland, which had a 'flickering subversive threat', needed 'loyal Defence Forces with good morale'. These views were emphasising the perceived link between the idea of a representative body and disloyalty. Doyle addressed the necessity of obedience and the requirement that an army be 'a flexible tool in the hands of all lawfully elected governments'.

Commander McNamara of the Irish Navy believed in the late 1980s that the introduction of representation would have a severely negative impact on the professionalism of the Defence Forces. He believed that a country such as Ireland in 1990, which had 'significant subversion, deserves of its military professionals, total commitment to the security of the State in every sense. The State requires a bottom line, a body of defenders who are totally committed to that State'. McNamara quoted the introduction of 'uncertified sick leave' being granted to members of the force as an example of a development that was detrimental to the exercise of command:

> If the decision to come to work or get up in the morning is being left to the individual rather than the military commander, then command itself is diminished. He suggested that none of the 'real' armies such as the British and American, i.e armies that win wars [sic], would contemplate representation for five seconds.[23]

Aside from the total rejection of the idea of a representative body, the political leadership of the day placed much emphasis on the forthcoming report of the Inter-Departmental Committee. Set up in June 1988 with a view to examining army pay, the committee was headed by Minister of State Vincent Brady. The Chief of Staff, Lt General T. O'Neil, had, in the early discussions about the forming of this group, managed to have the scope of their deliberations widened to include the pay of enlisted personnel.[24] The deliberations and recommendations of this group were eagerly awaited in the Defence Forces. As the months leading up to autumn and Christmas passed, speculation began about the size of the award that might be recommended. The opposition spokespeople in the Dáil articulated their views about the pay increase percentage that was desirable. Deputy Connaughton of Fine Gael suggested that 18 to 25 per cent would be appropriate. Cautious government responses did little to quell expectations in the public domain. There was, however, an overriding feeling among officers that despite the tight public finances and government pay policy, that in the end, they would be 'looked after' once the Brady Committee reported. Lt Col Ryan was told as much: 'We understood a special pay award was going to come. General Officers Commanding (GOCs) briefed the officer bodies of their commands twice, advising them that this was the case.'[25]

Percentages of the magnitude suggested by Deputy Connaughton and others continued to circulate while the public awaited the report of the committee. As the year closed and Christmas beckoned, opposition parties and soldiers' wives campaigning for better pay and conditions increased calls on the government to finalise the Brady report and announce its findings. Reports began to emerge that the committee had presented their findings to the Department of Finance which had rejected the magnitude of the recommendations and approved considerably lower amounts. Finally, on 22 December 1988, the committee made its recommendations public. An announcement was made that an increase of 12 per cent had been recommended. There was little reaction in the Defence Forces over the Christmas holiday period, but word began to circulate in early January that the award announced was the same one that applied to the public service anyway, that it was to be paid in instalments, the first of which was not due for another six months. The National Army Spouses Association and members of the Dáil opposition parties reacted strongly:

As anger and discontent grows, the National Association of Army
Spouses said they intended to mount another protest campaign with
pickets at army HQ in Dublin every Wednesday, which is pay day. And
as army Chief of Staff Tadgh O'Neill considered what response to make
to the government on the pay issue after officers and other ranks made
known their anger at the pay offer, Defence Minister Michael Noonan
faces a political row when the Dáil resumes this month.[26]

The political fallout following the announcement of the Inter-
Departmental Committee recommendations was extensive. There were
a number of deep criticisms. Firstly, the amount of the award was seen
as small at 12 per cent, particularly as there had been speculation that
it could be as much as 20 per cent. Secondly, it transpired that it was
not a special pay award at all and was in fact in line with the intended
increases right across the public service. This meant that the perceived
gap between army personnel and other similar employments was not
going to close at all. Thirdly, there was to be no immediate payment
because the first round under the national agreement was not due to
begin until June: this left six months to wait before any increase took
effect. Again there had also been speculation that the award would be
made before Christmas. Fourthly, it was discovered that the 12 per cent
was to be distributed in phases over the following eighteen months.
Finally, in what was seen by many as the ultimate insult, the timing
of the announcement just before the Christmas holidays appeared to
be deliberate, as that way personnel would not get an opportunity to
question it until the new year. NASA, who had been given the chance
to make a submission to the committee during its deliberations, was
incensed. Army officers, NCOs and privates were livid:

> It was a right kick in the teeth. We had been led a merry dance for
> months on end, made believe that a special look was being taken at us.
> Duped into believing that our just cause would reap an honest response,
> only to have our hopes dashed in the dawn of another new year of
> struggle on low pay.[27]

Much of the criticism and blame was placed on Deputy Michael Noonan,
who was the incumbent Minister for Defence serving for the first time
as a minister. He was reported to have made a number of promotions
in the army to offset the morale crisis, but national newspapers reported

numerous reactions by those in the forces. Unimpressed army sources
said there were still 300 vacancies left to be filled. Thirty promotions
in one week brought the total in January to sixty-five, but NASA
continued to picket Defence Force Headquarters, soldiers continued
to seek permission to retire and the system whereby they could previously buy themselves out of the army was made far more difficult in the
review by bumping up the cost to the applicant.[28]

NASA produced a report that showed soldiers' pay as much as
£100 per week behind that of the Gardaí for similar hours and duties.[29]
The manner in which the government report had been announced,
the lack of any great improvement in its recommendations and the
continuing difficulties being articulated about the army heralded
the beginning of 1989, which was to witness many developments in
Ireland's military, political and departmental domains. The call made
by the women for a representative association for soldiers was about to
be echoed and made by the soldiers themselves.

SOLDIERS CONSIDER REPRESENTATION

In September 1988 at a fundraising evening for NASA in 'The 79
Inn' in Ballyfermot, Dublin, two serving army sergeants, Richard
Dillon and Michael Murphy, discussed the campaign being waged
by NASA. Dillon recalled that they concluded that evening that
the women's campaign would only get so far and that at some point
the soldiers would have to do something themselves, and relates the
following sequence of events.

Both men decided to speak to other colleagues in the army and
find out whether anybody might be interested in looking to form
some sort of an association to try to improve their pay and conditions. They set about speaking to their own peers and found there
was a lot of support for the idea of an association. Not everybody was
convinced it was the right way to go and some of their colleagues
were fearful of the consequences of seeking such an association in
the army. Some feared for their careers. Nevertheless, a core of eleven
serving personnel began to meet on a regular basis to discuss the
idea of a representative body. Between January and July 1989, secret
meetings were arranged in a public bar called 'The Twelfth Lock'.
This establishment was chosen for its quiet, almost remote location

in Lucan; moreover, the manager of the bar was a former soldier and friend of Richard Dillon. The meetings took place every two weeks and the participants explored ways in which they could set up an association. Although fairly secretive in their deliberations, Richard Dillon claims that all the individuals in that group were 'pro-government'. They first met with representatives of the Garda Representative Association (GRA) and later the Prison Officers Association (POA). The rulebooks of these associations were scrutinised and eventually used as templates to write a constitution for an association for soldiers. Different sections of the GRA rulebook would be discussed each week with a view to reshaping the format to suit the structures of the army. When the first constitution for PDFORRA had been written in this way, the advice of a solicitor was sought and it was decided that everybody should write to their commanding officers and send them a copy of the constitution with a carefully worded letter explaining what they wanted to set up.[30] The first of these letters were dated 4 July 1989 (see Appendix 1). In order to garner publicity for the events, the group gave an interview to the media and told them that a number of sergeants were taking pre-discharge leave at the same time to highlight the problems that existed with army pay and conditions.[31]

This was to attract considerable media attention. Soldiers with more than twelve years' service at that time were entitled to indicate their decision to retire from the Defence Forces. When this was done, the accumulated annual leave or holidays remaining to the soldier, together with a special 'pre-discharge' leave that was granted before retirement, were calculated and could often be as much as ten or twelve weeks. The date for actual discharge was then taken to be the day following the end of the leave period. During this period of pre-discharge leave, intending retirees remained officially members of the Defence Forces and could withdraw their intention to retire if they so wished, to continue their career as before. Combined leave like this was very often used by serving soldiers to experiment and see what it was like to work in a civilian context and community. If employment prospects were poor or if they found that civilian life did not suit them, they had the safety net of continued service once they returned to barracks before the discharge date. Taking this pre-discharge leave was not unusual or illegal, but when fifteen sergeants in the Eastern Command decided to take it together, it indicated some sort of collective action which could be construed as being inconsistent with military discipline. News of this action reached the newspapers and the wider Defence Force community. Prior to and after these events, the core of eleven soldiers had begun speaking to their colleagues about the need for a representative association. The template letter was copied, as was the draft constitution, and both were circulated to encourage others to write to the minister seeking permission to set up PDFORRA. The core group began to travel to different parts of Ireland to tell other soldiers of their ideas. They visited and held information meetings in places like Monaghan, Galway, Cork, Athlone and Donegal. It was at such a meeting in Cork that the author first heard about and then became active in the campaign for military representation. Eventually they organised a meeting for personnel from all command areas of the Defence Forces to gather together.

The emergence of the debate on representative structures on the naval base on Haulbowline typifies the way in which the word was spread. Senior Petty Officer (SPO) Sam Fealy was the army equivalent of a quartermaster. Whether Irish Army, Navy or Air Corps, all potential quartermasters had to have completed a 'QMs' course in order to be qualified to do the job. This course was usually conducted at the Curragh Training Camp in County Kildare and had a typical duration of about four months. People who did such courses together often established friendships and contacts that would last throughout their service. On his qualifying QMs course, SPO Noel (Sam) Fealy had met and become friendly with Squadron Quartermaster Sergeant John Wolfe, and remembers being contacted by him:

> I got a phone call one day from John who was one of the army lads who had been complaining about the conditions on the border and their pay. He told me that a group of them had met in Dublin to discuss the problems and see what could be done. The soldiers asked each other whether they knew anybody in other commands so that the word could be spread. John had said he knew me and had undertaken to contact me. I thought he had a very valid point. It seemed there was an amount of frustration felt by soldiers from the border.[32]

SPO Fealy thought it was a great idea but decided he would have to be very careful about who he would speak to on the naval base. He contacted three friends of different ranks and divisions in the navy and invited them to a meeting in Dublin where there was supposed to be military personnel coming from all over the country. He said, 'there was a fair bit of excitement about the possibilities of an association but there was also a lot of fear. It was people's livelihoods at stake and they were fearful for themselves and their wives'.

In July 1989, personnel who continued to organise themselves around the country contacted each other, and over the following three weeks organised a large meeting with representatives from all six operational command areas of the Defence Forces. These were the Eastern Command, the Curragh Command, the Naval Service, the Western Command, the Air Corps and the Southern Command. On 26 August 1989, in a parish hall in Prussia Street, Dublin, two representatives from each of these areas were elected from among members drawn from all commands to a twelve-man 'national executive'. This was an historic meeting and had been arranged and overseen by a group of soldiers from the Eastern Command who up to that point were the founding advocates of representation for military personnel in Ireland. Five or six of them remained on in an advisory capacity to the national executive that had been formed. This meeting was held in secret and without the permission of the military authorities. Thus their status as a national executive remained ignored and unrecognised by both the government and the military leadership. In this sense, it was described as an 'ad hoc' national executive, but its members now felt they had a legitimate mandate from soldiers from all around the country to speak on their behalf.

Richard Dillon was elected as chairman of the new executive. As he was one of the founding fathers this seemed an appropriate choice. I, a warrant officer of the navy at the time, was elected secretary/public relations officer (PRO). This position was later to prove pivotal in the whole strategic approach to a legal case that ensued. The author was the public relations officer of a group that was not permitted by regulations to speak to the press. Because of these restrictions on the right of serving personnel to speak to the media, no public announcement was made about the formation of the executive that day. Nevertheless, a local solicitor had advised that there was a legal argument that all citizens had the right of association under Ireland's Constitution. The implication was that if one has the right to associate, one also has the right to act as a spokesperson for an association. This concept was to form the basis of the constitutional case that was to occur later. The formation of the 'ad hoc' national executive facilitated discussion among enlisted personnel from all sections of the Defence Forces. In the three months between

May and August 1989, when the ad hoc national executive was formed, there were numerous major developments that were to impact on the emerging campaign for the 'right of association'. NASA had entered the political fray, soldiers had sent their first letters to the minister requesting permission to establish an association, a general election had taken place and major announcements had been made about the Defence Forces by a new Minister for Defence. The details of that general election are worthy of note.

GENERAL ELECTION 1989

While the serving personnel of the Irish Army, Navy and Air Corps were organising themselves around the country, the women of NASA were about to embark in a new direction. The highlight of the women's campaign came about as a result of their decision to run a number of candidates in the general election of 1989. These included June Kiernan from Mullingar, Carol Tiernan from Dublin and Margaret Kiernan from Monaghan. The election campaign was launched in Dublin on 30 May 1989 and Carol Tiernan was chosen as their spokesperson. She reported that if any of the three candidates found themselves in the position of 'power broker' in the new Dáil, they were prepared to negotiate with whatever leader would provide the best deal for the army.[33] The electoral policy of the candidates was outlined in a circular compiled by Mullingar NASA (undated):

1. An elected representative association for all ranks
2. Equal pay with other members of State security within five years
3. Health, education, unemployment and environment
4. Appoint an experienced Minister who is sympathetic to the Defence Forces and understands military affairs

A special note stated:

> This is the first time serving and retired members of the Permanent Defence Force and their families have had a legitimate opportunity to express the manner in which they have been treated by the present government and past governments. The candidates were themselves described thus:

June Kiernan, Mullingar Army Wife

Full time housewife, married seventeen years. Five children ages between six and sixteen years. Former member of parent/teachers council, involved in community games and youth work. Former chairperson, PRO and delegate, NASA Mullingar.

Carol Tiernan, Dublin Army Wife

Part time nurse. Married ten years. Four children four to eight years. Course in youth training. Involved in summer community project. Former PRO executive committee NASA.

Margaret Kiernan, Monaghan Army Wife

Full time housewife married eight years. Five children two to fifteen years. Teaches French, for a period studied accountancy, involved in Credit Union, community games, youth work. Former secretary executive committee NASA.[34]

Each of the women was described in her 'former' role in NASA to comply with the provisions of their own constitution at paragraph 2f, which stated *inter alia*, 'the association shall be non-political'.[35] The spokesperson for the three women, Carol Tiernan, said 'we're confident we'll get elected and even if we don't, we'll have highlighted the army conditions. We hope too that even if Fianna Fáil return to office that we won't have the same Defence Minister'. Minister for Defence Michael Noonan accused the women of intimidating the military vote and called on Defence Force personnel to stay 'aloof'.[36] The women felt that a potential 8,000 votes could be gleaned from the military, if every soldier got ten votes out.

Despite the extensive coverage received by NASA in the media, and the airing of the problems in the military, the mainstream parties did not provide the Defence Forces with any great priority in their respective manifestos, and only in one case was a representative association mentioned. Fine Gael accused the government of callousness in their dealings with the forces and suggested that the problems with morale should be dealt with urgently, the Progressive Democrats mentioned pay being linked to the average industrial wage, but it was the Workers' Party who openly called for the establishment of representative bodies for the Defence Forces.[37] This is probably no surprise as Pat McCartan of the party had been a strong advocate of the idea. He had personally attended the meeting for the launching of NASA in Mullingar in February and was reported to have spoken 'very enthusiastically about the army in general and NASA's efforts to improve the conditions of serving personnel.' Described as a very impressive speaker, he promised to raise army matters as often as possible in the Dáil. It was reported that at the same meeting, a very negative response was received from Fianna Fáil 'in general', and councillor Glynn in particular. Henry Abbott, TD, a government elected representative, was not very helpful or enthusiastic.[38]

Newspapers profiled the three 'army wives', and the media attention they had received around the country in the preceding six months was probably going to be a help to them on election day. When on 22 February 1989 NASA in Mullingar placed their first picket outside the gates of Columb Army Barracks, all local newspapers covered it. Three days later there was a national protest outside the Royal Dublin Society (RDS). There was a simultaneous protest outside Collins Barracks in Dublin when the minister came to officially close it down. The ministerial car turned back twice during the afternoon and would not pass through the picket. On 11 April a protest by the women forced the minister to use the back gate of McKee Barracks, where he had come to officially review the new battalion about to deploy on a peacekeeping mission as part of the United Nations Interim Force in Lebanon.[39] Fianna Fáil party workers in the Cavan–Monaghan, Kildare and Longford–Westmeath constituencies expressed concern that the emergence of candidates from the army wives could damage the party.[40] Their fears were somewhat realised and the fact that none of the candidates gained a seat there was perceived to be political damage to the party.

Margaret Kiernan ran in the Cavan–Monaghan electoral area and polled 1,069 first-preference votes.[41] This was 2.01 per cent of the total poll, and while it was not enough to recover her deposit, it represented half the percentage drop in the Fianna Fáil vote for that area since the previous election. From the 1987 to the 1989 election that party's support dropped from 54 per cent to 49 per cent. Carol Tiernan ran in the Kildare constituency, where many soldiers and their families were stationed in the numerous military establishments of the Curragh Camp. Although there was no discernible effect on the existing seats in the outcome, she did poll

2,690 first-preference votes.[42] Despite the fact that a seat was not won, it was felt by those involved in the NASA campaign that it was a great moral victory. They believed at that time that when lobbying the government for anything, the only effective currency was votes. June Kiernan ran for election in the constituency of Longford–Westmeath. Like Kildare, this constituency contained heavy concentrations of soldiers and their families based in the large military barracks in Athlone, but also in the barracks at Longford and Mullingar. June polled 3,207 first-preference votes, the highest number of the NASA candidates. Her story adds greatly to the understanding of the motivation, drive and determination of these women in pursuit of their aims.

June Kiernan and her husband Jack, a corporal mechanic in Mullingar Barracks, contemplated at the outset that she would run for election. Neither had any political party experience nor had ever conducted a political campaign. Despite their inexperience, their subsequent efforts shook the political establishment in Ireland and were probably the most significant factor in persuading the government to begin to consider the whole idea of representative bodies in the Defence Forces. The story of how this came about is crucial to the understanding of how a previously apolitical group were motivated and empowered by what they saw as unacceptable treatment at the hands of the army hierarchy and the government. It goes some way towards answering the question posed by Finer in his consideration of the role of the military in politics, which suggests that 'we don't know how politics gets into the military and establishes itself there'. June recalled how she became involved:

> I first heard about the idea of a representative body for the soldiers on the news. Carol Tiernan of NASA was on the television. I talked to Jack about it. In the following months, because he travelled a lot with the army around the border area, he heard about the women's group and what they were trying to achieve.[43]

Jack was also impressed with the notion of representation, and he too was exposed to newspapers, television reports and what he heard in the workplace. He remembers his reaction: 'The whole thing was a fantastic idea. Myself and my friend Pat Lynch, who himself had been a quartermaster sergeant in the army talked a lot about it and decided to support the women if they were going to get involved.'[44]

June and her close friend Ita decided after many discussions that they
were going to see if there was any support locally for the setting up
of a branch of NASA in Mullingar. Jack got a telephone number of a
founding member in Monaghan, Margaret Kiernan (no relation), who
told him there was a committee up and running in Athlone. Contact
was made by June and Ita, who sought advice and information from
them. They spoke with Joan Carney from the committee there and
decided to organise a Mullingar meeting to see if there was sufficient
interest locally. At the first meeting held in February 1989 in what was
then Broder's Hotel, about twenty women turned up. June recalls:

> We were at the top table, Ita and I, never having run a meeting before.
> It was a very hard meeting with all the women talking about their husbands'
> problems. I never realised there was so much difference in people's pay and
> the number of different jobs that people did in the army. A committee was
> elected but with difficulty because people were terrified of getting involved
> on it. The fear was that it would have a negative effect on promotion for
> their husbands and they would get dirty duties and such.[45]

As elected members, June and Ita went to Athlone to meet with other
NASA committees. They were made very welcome and aims were
discussed. June Kiernan said, 'The way I felt about it was that soldiers
were defending everyone else's democracy but nobody was defending
theirs'. The reference to democracy and democratic rights was increasingly used, not just by the women's group, but later by the soldiers
themselves. When exposed to the other associations of the European
Organisation of Military Associations (EUROMIL) later, this idea
of a soldier being a citizen in uniform found easy passage in Ireland.
Jack Kiernan, having been a mechanic in civilian life, did not see why
there should be 'so much of a difference being a mechanic in another
garage or one who had a uniform on'.[46] The aim of the women at the
Athlone meeting was to have the soldiers get their own representative association. In pursuit of that objective, June Kiernan and many
other women juggled children, home and husbands with a whirlwind
of meetings, discussion and protests up and down the country. June
herself owed a debt of gratitude to her mother, Mary Doyle, who
'took the kids, made dinners and was an integral support to what
I was doing.'[47] The Mullingar branch of NASA looked to meet the
Minister for Defence and asked their local representatives to take their

case to the Dáil for them. Together with the national committee they undertook interviews, wrote letters and conducted a very effective countrywide campaign that raised awareness of the low morale in the Defence Forces and the bad pay and poor conditions. Michael Howard suggests that, while pay levels were always a concern of senior military personnel, a lot of the protest was about how soldiers were treated, and the issues pursued by NASA and PDFORRA differed from those pursued by the military in this regard.[48]

In order to fund the activities of the women, collections were made at every meeting from the women who attended. They also assembled in groups using buckets which they placed outside of barracks on pay day. On these occasions the women were always treated very well. In March 1989, June Kiernan recalls the weather being very inclement, with wind, rain and cold buffeting them outside the barracks gate. NCOs brought them into the mess and gave them tea and sandwiches, encouraging them in the work they were doing. It was felt by the women that the politicians, by comparison, did not respond to their complaints and efforts to rectify the problems in the army. June Kiernan maintained that although Fianna Fáil had always traditionally got the army vote, their sitting TD Henry Abbot would not meet them. In looking back at the period, June Kiernan maintains, 'I would never have run as a candidate for election if Henry Abbot had just met us'.[49] According to Jack Kiernan, the idea to run as a candidate and to field a number of NASA women nationally was born in Jack and June's living room. 'Pat Lynch and I were sitting down one evening, talking as we did every night about the NASA campaign and its progress. We both came to the conclusion that if the politicians were not willing to help in the whole process, we should try and have the women run against them'. When they asked June she said she could run, but had absolutely no experience in the whole political field and feared that, if she was to actually acquire a seat in the Dáil, she would not know what to do. She was reassured, however, by family and friends, who asked her: what do the politicians at the moment know about life in the army, what are they doing about it? 'When I thought about it,' June said, 'I realised they were only knowledgeable about whatever issue they were running under too'. Jack and Pat became the *de facto* 'directors of elections' and set about orchestrating what became a very effective campaign.

Having decided that this might be a good strategy nationally, the Mullingar committee proposed at a meeting of the NASA national committee in Athlone that a number of candidates, in the areas where troops and their families were concentrated, should be run. This was adopted, and, in keeping with the NASA constitution, it was a condition that anybody running would have to relinquish membership of the association. During the campaign for election, the women of Mullingar had occasion to knock on doors seeking votes. They came across many army officers and their wives and got a great supportive response from them both in terms of money and moral support. On one occasion, while they were in the home of a senior ranking officer, speaking to his wife, the officer popped his head in the room, went to make tea for the NASA women, came back and said 'I won't stay to hear your conversation but the best of luck'. These instances of widespread silent support from serving officers were countrywide, and were augmented by many retired officers who openly sent letters encouraging the women in their efforts. Retired Col Jim Fagan pledged support and enclosed a £5 contribution to June's electoral campaign, writing, 'Best of luck in the elections. You have my full support and we will vote for you on the 15th … keep up the fight because it will be a long battle'.[50]

Military and Political Responses

Serving officers often felt that, while they were very supportive, they could not articulate that support openly. Lt Gen. Gerry McMahon was a career officer with distinguished service. He served as a company commander in Ireland, a battalion commander at home and abroad and enjoyed the distinction of having missed completely the controversial events of 1988 and early 1989 regarding representative associations. At the time he was the Irish military adviser to the United Nations Headquarters in New York and was domiciled there. On his return, he was projected into the centre of the deliberations representing the military authorities and became familiar with the context of discussions with the newly elected representatives of PDFORRA. He remembers thinking, when he heard the wives were running for election, 'With all that is going on I am glad that somebody is taking up the cause of the Defence Forces'.[1]

The eventual results of the election were a political shock for the government. While June Kiernan did not win a seat, it is widely held that the votes she attracted prevented the return of Fianna Fáil's sitting TD. In the previous 1987 election, Fianna Fáil had held three of the four seats in the Longford–Westmeath constituency with Fine Gael holding one. The 1989 election saw one of them losing a seat. Fianna Fáil's Henry Abbot, who had received 8,037 first-preference votes in 1987, only got 6,733 in 1989. The poll of 3,207 votes by June Kiernan was thought to have directly led to the loss of this seat. It was all the more frustrating for the government because they now had two Fine Gael seats where they previously had only one, and both of them had polled less first-preference votes than Abbot.[2] The early responses of Fianna Fáil to the emerging NASA appeared to be a factor in the diminishing confidence in the party in Mullingar and Athlone. During their campaign, NASA did not withhold the dissatisfaction they felt at Henry Abbot for his claiming he had to 'toe the party line'. They were also disappointed with the contention by another prominent Fianna Fail TD that she had not received a registered letter sent by the association to Dáil Éireann, for which they later unearthed a signed receipt proving it had been delivered. At the time, these and other issues were made known to the military voting community, which was not just confined to existing service personnel. In March 1989, the Organisation of National Ex-Service Men in Mullingar had also pledged support to the women. In a letter from the secretary dated 3 March, members had congratulated NASA on their formation and pledged the help of seven or eight men for the upcoming Flag Day.[3]

Fianna Fáil lost their overall majority in the 1989 election and single-party government for them, at time of writing, remains an elusive aspiration. Long after their attempts at the ballot box, NASA remained a formidable and active group. On 31 December 1989 they held a very visible protest march at the opening celebration of Ireland's presidency of the European Council of Ministers. In Dublin, government leader and Taoiseach Mr Haughey had his brief speech partially drowned out by banner-waving members of NASA.[4] Jack Kiernan recalled: 'It was a fantastic protest; we got a load of placards made up in different languages because we knew all the European press would be there. Loads of them came over to us as we were the only ones there that were newsworthy.'[5]

June Kiernan believed that this was a turning point in the attitude of the government towards the whole issue of a soldiers' association. Mr Haughey, as president of the council, was to be questioned within six weeks by a Danish parliamentarian regarding Ireland's treatment of members of the Defence Forces seeking the right of association. Member of the European Parliament (MEP) Jensen wrote: 'I have asked the Irish presidency about PDFORRA – an Irish soldier association, its status vis-á-vis the Irish Constitution, its possibility to work unhindered and the recent imprisonment of persons affiliated to PDFORRA.'[6]

This letter was prompted by members of EUROMIL who had become aware of the PDFORRA and their efforts to get representation. The NASA media campaign and their arrival on the political landscape was one of the essential ingredients that led to the formation and public acceptance of a representative body for members of the armed forces. The Irish Times remarked of them: 'In recent months

NASA has enjoyed great success in highlighting what they believe are appalling levels of pay in the army and a general crisis in morale, which has been sapped by the virtual ban on promotion and recruitment.'[7]

Michael Gannon, an Irish commandant doing his military masters degree in 1992, said of NASA:

> In highlighting their situation NASA lobbied politicians, arranged protest marches to Dáil Eireann, and picketed both the Dáil and selected barracks throughout the country. In this way it became a formidable pressure group, forcefully articulating the feelings and frustrations of non commissioned personnel in particular, who under military law could not do so.

Michael Gannon also suggested it was the success of their campaign that inspired enlisted personnel to establish PDFORRA: 'the non commissioned ranks, seeing the success of NASA, then set about organising their own association immediately after the general election.'[8]

In fact, the soldiers had been organising long before the elections, and from as early as September 1988, a full nine months before the summer elections of June 1989, soldiers of the Eastern Command were meeting fortnightly to formulate a strategy to establish an association, produce a draft constitution and set about garnering countrywide support from their colleagues throughout the Irish Army, Navy, and Air Corps. What the women did was to provide a platform from which to highlight the prevailing conditions in the forces, and they did that very well. The women were speaking a language that the public understood. They talked about trying to make ends meet, about the absence of their husbands on long hours of duty. A lot of public and political sympathy was created. But the group did not serve merely to highlight problems, a crucial part of their message was that their husbands needed representation in order to resolve their difficulties with army pay and conditions. The only regret that June Kiernan had about her whole experience was that Henry Abbot had lost his seat as a result of the whole thing.

ELECTION AFTERMATH

The incoming government of 1989 would have been acutely aware of the impact of the NASA political campaign and the loss of their seat in Longford–Westmeath. Over the previous eighteen months they had witnessed a concerted opposition that had raised the temperature of public debate about the army crisis; they had suffered politically at the hands of NASA and were now struggling to form a coalition government from among former opponents. Given that the national highlighting of the need for improvements in pay and conditions in the PDF and the calls for representative bodies for serving soldiers showed no signs of abating, once established, the government moved very quickly to placate the whole question of problems in the Defence Forces.

It was against this background that, on 27 July 1989, a week after the Dáil rose for summer recess, it was widely reported that a new approach was to be taken in relation to army pay. That morning the newspapers reported an imminent announcement from the Taoiseach and the Minister for Defence. Reports suggested that following a meeting of the cabinet the previous Tuesday and in response to the loss of vital votes in the general election, the much-criticised timing of the pay award for the Defence Forces was to be brought forward.[9] This speculation was not entirely accurate. The announcement, when it came that day, was much broader and was to have far-reaching consequences for the improvement in pay and conditions in the Defence Forces and the establishment of a representative association. Firstly, an independent commission, chaired by Senior Counsel Dermot Gleeson, was to be set up to examine, report, and make recommendations regarding remuneration and conditions of service in the Defence Forces. Secondly, new structures were to be set up to provide 'ongoing consultation' on conditions. Acknowledging that the previous review committee's recommendations did not 'meet the situation', Taoiseach Charles Haughey said: 'We know there is a problem, that morale is low and are anxious to solve it as quickly as possible. The fairest and most equitable way is to set up this commission which is what the members of the Defence Forces have been seeking.'[10]

In the case of the commission, the members were named and were given their terms of reference that day, which included 'carrying out a major review of the remuneration and conditions of service of the Defence Forces having regard to their separate and distinct role and organisation, and make recommendations'.[11] In addition, the Minister for Defence, after consulting with him, instructed the Chief of Staff to appoint three teams, one for privates, one for NCOs and one for officers. Each team was expected to present a case to the commission on behalf of their particular group. In the new government, Deputy Michael Noonan, who had been the Minister for Defence in the previous Dáil, was replaced by Deputy Brian Lenihan. This was seen in a very positive light among serving personnel in the forces. Brian Lenihan was a formidable, experienced politician and a very senior member of Fianna Fáil. As deputy leader of the party he was appointed also as Tánaiste, deputy leader of government. This was the first time in a number of years that a minister of such high standing was appointed to the Department of Defence. Mr Lenihan was also a very amicable man, known in political circles as being a 'fixer' but a tough negotiator should the need arise. In the middle of 1989 his appointment as Minister for Defence was an exciting development in the new Haughey administration. The announcements were greeted with enthusiasm by many and it seemed as if the problems in the Defence Forces regarding pay and conditions of service were to be given serious and unprecedented attention. After seemingly ignoring the letters of military personnel, at last the government seemed willing to respond to the demands for a representative association and better pay.

These developments appeared to herald a major breakthrough, given previous emphatic government opposition to such measures in the recent past. They were welcomed in some quarters. NASA, however, only afforded them a cautious welcome, saying they would give a more detailed response when they received further information.[12] The serving military personnel who had been meeting up and down the country in preparation for forming an association were silent on the news. It later transpired that there had been no consultation with any of the personnel prior to the public announcements. In an unprecedented communication from the Chief of Staff, a letter dated 27 July 1989, addressed to 'each officer, non-commissioned officer and private in the Defence Forces', the chief advised personnel of the creation of the commission and of the instructions he had received from the minister to set up a new system in the Defence Forces for consultation and information on pay and conditions. The letter caused doubts to arise immediately on the type and extent of consultation that was envisaged. The last paragraph was widely perceived as a threat among the enlisted personnel. It read:

This will ensure that your views at unit level will be taken into account on an ongoing basis. I strongly recommend this new system. I am confident with your participation and support these new arrangements will work to the satisfaction of all ranks, thereby rendering your membership of any other organisation unnecessary and divisive.[13]

Although it was not understood by the general public until sometime
later, it was here that a fundamental difference of approach and
ideology was to emerge between what the Defence Force authorities and the government wanted on one side and those seeking the
formal recognition of PDFORRA wanted on the other. The government had instructed the Chief of Staff to look at the introduction
'of some form of representative body *within* the Defence Forces for
ongoing consultation on pay and other matters'. This was welcomed
by many, including NASA, who were reported as expressing delight.[14]
The opposition spokesman on defence, Deputy Ted Nealon, who had
been campaigning for a representative association, also welcomed
the move.[15] However, it was not welcomed by the members of the
ad hoc PDFORRA. As the NCOs team submission to the Gleeson
Commission reflected, they wanted an organisation that would operate
outside of, and independently from, the military chain of command.
The difference in emphasis was a crucial point of principle, although
this did not become immediately apparent to the media or the public
at large. Despite the instructions by the minister to the chief to look
at structures and to consult with other armies, the chief chose not to
consult with the enlisted personnel in his own army. Requests by the
Gleeson Commission NCOs team to meet and make recommendations for the chief's 'structures' were denied. The letters that had been
sent via the chief to the minister remained unanswered. Despite this
dilemma, those who were involved in seeking a representative body
adopted a wait-and-see approach to the Gleeson Commission and the
arrangements that were to be made for the submission of cases to it.

It had been decided by the government that all personnel of the
Defence Forces would get an opportunity to make recommendations
to the Gleeson Commission. General submissions were to be made
by representative teams, each comprising of six personnel who would
reflect the views of their colleagues at a particular rank. These representative teams were drawn from the three strata of the Defence Force
rank, those of privates, NCOs and officers. Of the six members of
each team there had to be one from each of the six commands. Each
Command was to select a person of each rank from among them to
go forward. This elective approach was unusual for the military.

What was noteworthy about the NCOs and the privates' teams was
that most of those selected, albeit through the military system, were
organising members of PDFORRA and supporters of the view that a

representative association was needed. When personnel were selected, they were instructed in August 1989 to report to the Planning and Research Department (P&R) of Defence Force Headquarters (DFHQ) in Dublin. The teams would meet there on a daily basis over the following months to compile their submission to the commission. One member of each team was elected as a spokesperson for his teammates. Each of the three teams was also provided with at least three staff officers, supposedly to assist in the better formulation of the cases to be made to Gleeson in both an administrative and 'advisory' capacity. James Martin of the NCOs team thought they had a different function. He said of them:

> Although they were presented as being at the disposal of the teams, they sat in on discussions and engaged in debate often trying to persuade the teams to take a slightly different approach. In our team it often led to accusations that these officers were trying to influence the cases we were making so that the army wouldn't be seen in a negative light.[16]

Prior to embarking on their work, the teams were instructed to attend an official 'briefing' by senior officers of DFHQ. Although it had been inferred in various briefings that each team could submit any claim or suggestion to the commission regarding pay and conditions, it was strongly recommended that each submission confine itself to the issue of basic pay. This, according to senior military officers, is what mattered to most people across all ranks of the Defence Forces. It was also emphasised that time was short as all submissions had to be in by the end of September, and since there was so much to do, the subject of pay should take priority. During the wrap-up question time, I, as the spokesperson for the NCOs group, asked if there was any problem in making a case to the commission about representative associations. The reply from the military hierarchy was that this fell outside of the remit of the commission and it was not permitted. He sought clarification asking 'are we being ordered not to make any submission regarding representation?' 'You are', was the response.[17]

Soon after the teams commenced work, they were invited to meet with Mr Gleeson at Government Buildings.[18] Although he met the three teams individually, each of them was accompanied by the assigned staff officers and in the case of the NCOs team by the assistant Chief of Staff. Having briefed the team on the aims of the commission and the modus operandi, Mr Gleeson asked if there were any questions. John Wolfe recalls:

> Our spokesperson, Michael Martin told Mr Gleeson that the team had been anxious to present a case in their submission for the introduction of a representative association but that their superior officers had told them they could not do so. Gleeson did not comment about the rights or wrongs of who said what or merits or otherwise of representation. He simply said that he wanted to hear everything they had to say and did not want to find himself in a position, in a number of months' time, having published a report only to discover there were other matters that had not been aired.[19]

From this point onwards, the NCOs and by precedent the privates' team could officially formulate a case to the commission on the right of association for members of the Defence Forces. Very soon after this meeting, the NCOs team sought a meeting with the General Staff to discuss this matter. It did not materialise and was refused until it was the subject of a complaint to the minister by the team. Now that Gleeson had cleared the way for a submission on representative associations, the teams were not just free to submit their case but they also had the administrative and logistical resources of the Planning and Research staff officers to help them do so. This was utilised when the NCOs team sought their help in acquiring the contact names, addresses and telephone numbers of all legitimate representative associations in Europe. The subsequent contacts that were made played a crucial role in later developments. Civil–military relations in Ireland were about to change at this point. The military hierarchy had lost a seemingly small element of control over their subordinates and the change had been precipitated by actions made on behalf of the civil authority. A new relationship was emerging whereby all matters of a military nature, previously raised solely by the military hierarchy, would now come within the remit of another segment of the military – those who had been charged with representing enlisted personnel. This new segment, comprising of unfiltered views of enlisted personnel, quickly brought external views to bear on their new relationship with the government. These were European views that had not been previously aired much in Ireland, particularly during the debates on representative associations.

EUROMIL AND THE INTERNATIONAL DIMENSION

With clearance from Gleeson on the issue of making a case for representation to the commission, the NCOs team requested assistance from their assigned staff officers at P&R. They gathered the contact details of all European representative associations. A number of countries in Europe at this time had some sort of military representative bodies. Well-established associations from Germany, the Netherlands, Belgium, Denmark and Austria were all members of the European Organisation of Military Associations (EUROMIL). This association, based in Bonn,[20] had consultative status with the Council of Europe and was influential in the adoption by both the Council and the European Parliament of resolutions that called for all member States to afford their military personnel the right of association in peacetime.[21] EUROMIL was established in 1972 with eight military representative associations from Belgium, Germany, Denmark and the Netherlands. The stated objects were to:

> Encourage understanding and friendship among peoples, to encourage regular exchange of experience between the individual member associations, to promote general, ideal, social and career interests of soldiers and to represent member associations vis-à-vis supranational organisations.[22]

This was an organisation that existed for the purpose of encouraging the right of association in any country where it did not already exist. Members of the Irish armed forces who were seeking this right were to benefit greatly from engaging with such a group. Immediately after being provided with the relevant information by P&R staff, I, as the spokesperson for the NCOs group (I was also secretary/PRO for the national executive of PDFORRA), contacted EUROMIL and established a rapport with them, gaining insight into the type of associations that existed elsewhere, how they operated and how effective or ineffective they were in pursuing the interests of their members. Following these exchanges, an invitation was extended to the ad hoc PDFORRA group to attend the quarterly conference of the EUROMIL Presidium in Ringkøbing, Denmark, that was to take place in February 1990. In the meantime, the Chief of Staff pressed ahead with the task of establishing representative structures as instructed by the government, but no invitation came to the Gleeson teams to elicit their views on the matter. The submission that was made by the NCOs' team and the privates' team to the commission in November 1989 included a request for a representative association and contained the same constitution that had accompanied the original letter sent by thousands to the minister through the chain of command. There were at least two important additions inserted by the Gleeson submission teams. These were independent access to the media and independent financing.[23]

In the last quarter of 1989, there were numerous strands of activity being conducted by the various stakeholders that could be collectively called the constituent parts of the 'Defence Community'. The government were involved in facilitating the operation of the Gleeson Commission and were awaiting their conclusions. The Department of Defence, parliamentary draughtsmen and the minister were busy preparing framework legislation to introduce new representative structures for members of the Defence Forces. The Chief of Staff was busy having structures designed, at the minister's request, that would provide a consultative framework in the Defence Forces. The Gleeson teams were compiling the cases that would make up the Defence Forces submission to the commission. Ad hoc PDFORRA continued to encourage members of the PDF to join their association and send their individual applications to the minister through the chain of command to seek approval for their representative association. Activists for the establishment of PDFORRA claimed in February 1990 to represent 8,000 members based on the sending of these letters.[24] Unhappy that the chief's structures were not the subject of consultation, the ad hoc PDFORRA announced on 11 November 1989 that they had established their association under the Constitution of Ireland. The group had met that day in St Colman's parish hall in Cobh, County Cork. This was to be the first press release issued by the fledgling association that had not yet been recognised or acknowledged by the government or the army. There was lengthy discussion about the release, with many of the ad hoc national executive expressing concern about the consequences of 'going public'. This concern was valid in light of the fact that engagement with the media was still prohibited by military regulations. The announcement was sent by the secretary/PRO via fax machine to various national newspapers and radio stations.

CONSTITUTIONAL PROVISIONS AND THE MEDIA

The idea that members of the Irish armed forces may have had a consti-tutional right to form representative associations was first explored in early 1989 by the group of Eastern Command soldiers who initially led the campaign for the foundation of PDFORRA. Legal opinion was sought from a solicitor who engaged Senior Counsel (subsequently Justice) Frank Clarke.[25] His opinion reassured soldiers that there were grounds for an argument under the Constitution that soldiers had a right to associate. On 11 November 1989, when a meeting of the ad hoc PDFORRA national executive decided to issue a press release announcing that they had exercised their right under the Constitution to form an association, they did so anonymously.[26] The constitutional section that they referred to was under article 40.6.1° (iii) of the Constitution of Ireland. This article states:

6. The State guarantees liberty for the exercise of the following rights, subject to public order and morality:

(iii)   The right of the citizens to form associations and unions. Laws, however, may be enacted for the regulation and control in the public interest of the exercise of the foregoing right.

The legal advice had been that although the Constitution provides for the control and regulation of the right, significantly, it does not state it can be prohibited. The press release sought an early meeting with the minister who indicated there was no prospect for such an event.[27]

Minister for Defence Brian Lenihan 'ruled out any negotiations between the army authorities and the unofficial representative group …'[28] He later argued he could not meet any group who had set them-selves up without proper election, and announced that he had instructed the Chief of Staff to investigate structures that could be established in the Defence Forces to represent the views of personnel, looking at other models in Europe. His refusal to meet led to the new group releasing a second press statement calling on the Taoiseach to recognise them officially and take cognisance of European resolutions advocating the extension of this provision in peacetime to all members of the armed forces.[29] The call on the Taoiseach was particularly significant as Deputy Haughey was due to take over the European presidency in January 1990.

Subsequent requests for meetings with the minister, the Chief of
Staff and the government went unheeded. During this period, close
contact was also maintained with EUROMIL. As the eventful year of
1989 came to a close for the armed forces, the contrasting demands by
members of PDFORRA and the Department of Defence, including
the military authorities, became polarised. This was evident in both the
questions posed to the Minister for Defence by opposition deputies and
his answers. Repeatedly he was asked whether he would not recognise
and engage with PDFORRA, and repeatedly he responded by referring
to the internal structures on which the Chief of Staff was working.[30]
Political pressure continued to be applied to the minister and the
government for what was referred to as the 'crisis in the Defence Forces';
questions on the pay problem and the recognition of PDFORRA
were now augmented by queries regarding the findings of the Gleeson
Commission, with criticism being levelled about the delay in reporting
their findings. Ad hoc PDFORRA were still not revealing the identity
of their spokesperson at this point as military regulations prohibited
them doing so. Nevertheless they continued to seek a meeting with the
government, to no avail.

No name appeared on the press release regarding the formation
of the association on 11 November. In this action and in speaking to
journalists whom they met secretly, members of the ad hoc PDFORRA
were in breach of military regulations. The solicitor the soldiers had
engaged for the initial advices at that point disengaged himself as legal
adviser for the group. Due to their precarious position in relation to the
law, the members of PDFORRA sought advice from another source
(a solicitor in Galway) regarding the way in which a perceived 'constitutional' right could be established to ensure that any dealings between
the press and the association would not result in the penalisation of its
members. The original idea among soldiers had been that perhaps a
collective action could be taken by members to establish the right of
association if it became necessary. The legal advice suggested this was
not possible. By late 1989 it was becoming evident that the government
were determined in their plans to establish internal representative structures for the Defence Forces, but without the input of enlisted personnel.
This would mean that the ad hoc PDFORRA would perhaps continue
to exist but would be ignored in favour of an official grouping set up
by the minister and the Chief of Staff under new legislation. As there
was no apparent way of stopping the minister from setting this up,

the question of legal action became more urgent. The advice suggested that while it might not be possible to initiate a collective action, the best route to take would be (where an individual felt their constitutional rights were being infringed) to seek a ruling in the High Court. In such circumstances, the High Court had a duty to establish whether or not an infringement on a person's constitutional rights had occurred. Although the government and military authorities had not officially taken any action against those who had sought representation, none of them had apparently broken the law either.

The position was to change radically as a result of a radio interview given from Denmark by me, the secretary/PRO of the association. In early February 1990, I and Richard Dillon, the ad hoc PDFORRA chairman, travelled to Ringkøbing in Denmark to attend the EUROMIL conference to which PDFORRA had been invited. Over three days, all the participating countries of EUROMIL were briefed on the situation in Ireland. They pledged their support to the efforts being made by PDFORRA. Dick Dillon recalls:

> I remember reading about Euromil in a book somewhere, I showed the article to people at a meeting and I think you were there. I thought we should meet these people. They were a help but not as much a help as they believed themselves to be. They had representation and it worked, but what we had turned out to be superior. They still have not managed to advance the cause of the Portuguese association after all this time.[31]

On 6 February, while we were still in Denmark, announcements were made in Ireland by the Minister for Defence that legislation was to be rushed through the Dáil to set up the new structures designed by the Chief of Staff.[32] Despite the fact that these structures were for the use of enlisted personnel, no privates or NCOs had been consulted on them or asked for any opinion, contribution or suggestion. Crucially, the minister also announced that elections were to be held for representatives into the structure recommended by the Chief of Staff. A circular had been distributed to all members of the Defence Forces outlining a broad internal structure.

As secretary and PRO for the, as yet, unrecognised association I gave a radio interview on 6 February on the *Morning Ireland* show on the national radio station RTÉ Radio 1, regarding the impending legislation and the constitutional rights of members.

This was the first time that a serving member of the Defence Forces had spoken out on national media about military matters. I was now in a precarious position. The Constitution appeared to offer protection to anybody forming an association. But this had not been tested. Military regulations on the other hand were very definitive about members of the armed forces being prohibited from communicating with the media. Back in Ireland there was a widespread media response to the interview, with speculation mounting about what military sanctions would be brought against the interviewee. It was thought this was a very important development in bringing the whole matter into sharper focus. Not everybody was convinced, however. Richard Condron, who was serving on the national executive at that time, felt aggrieved that the interview had taken place. He said of it:

> First of all, it should not have happened. The national executive knew nothing about it. I think that an element of it was Michael Martin was going for the job of General Secretary. There was concern after it, like there had been before when we gave in our letters [sic] as to what would happen next. In terms of its importance, it made a point about us as a representative association but Brian Lenihan told me it was because of NASA and their showing in the elections that they eventually came to the table.[33]

Two days after the interview from Denmark, I flew back into Dublin Airport to a huge media presence, and the subsequent press conference got extensive primary coverage. Tom McCaughran, an experienced and well-known journalist at the time, was the RTÉ television news security correspondent. He covered numerous controversial interviews but later commented on the enormity of a serving member of the Defence Forces defying regulations to pursue a right, and said 'we made history that day in the airport'.[34] One of the fears at the time was that I would be arrested at the airport by military police for having given an interview, or to prevent more. The newfound EUROMIL colleagues in Denmark and Bauke Snoep of the Dutch military representative associations had promised to watch closely what happened at Dublin Airport with a view to encouraging the Dutch ambassador to raise objection if I was detained. On the home front, my navy colleague and close friend John Lucey was the second navy representative on the national executive. He alone was prepared to step into my shoes if an arrest took place. He was willing to speak to the media in my place if I was silenced and detained. John recalled to me a few days later, 'No need to thank me Michael, I was just as scared as you were for my job and future. The reality is I would have done it if you were arrested but I am glad you weren't.'[35]

The national executive met in Limerick the next day and were briefed by the chairman, Richard Dillon, and me as secretary. I outlined the reasons for 'going public'. The PDFORRA minute books records:

> On receiving information with regard to the Minister's Statement in the Dáil and the often varying and ambiguous press reports, the secretary discussed with the chairman, the issues involved and reached a decision there and then to go public ... The general consensus at the end of the address was that the Euromil trip had been very beneficial and that from a public relations aspect it was far better than any advertisements in the press or radio and TV.[36]

Despite his recollection quoted above, there is no record in the minutes of any objections by Richard Condron about the interview or any adverse comments by anybody at the meeting regarding the EUROMIL trip and the interviews to the media. Within days of the meeting, I returned to duty at the naval base. I was immediately notified by my commander that I was to be charged in military law under article 27 of the military regulations A7.

This was a serious offence. I was one of the most senior-ranking non-commissioned officers in the navy. There were only six warrant officers throughout the whole Defence Forces altogether, and my technical skills and rank placed me in a position of great trust and importance. It was highly irregular and unusual that such a senior-ranking NCO would be charged under military regulations. Such charges could impact in a very negative way on career prospects such as advancement or promotion. Although the possibility of being charged had existed from the moment I gave the radio interview, I had hoped at the time that the government or the military would not go through with it. It seemed irrational that they were supposedly setting up representative bodies for serving personnel and yet were now prepared to penalise one of them who spoke with a mandate on behalf of others.

As had been advised by legal counsel, and despite the fear of expensive litigation and possible dismissal from the Defence Forces, there now existed a situation whereby military regulations could be challenged in a court of law. Although this course of action had been discussed with legal counsel and PDFORRA activists on numerous occasions, I also discussed this scenario with my wife, Geraldine. I told her that in the event of a High Court challenge failing, I could be discharged and lose my military career in the navy. I articulated my fear about the possibility that I might never get a government or public-service job anywhere thereafter. This was a serious and frightening time. The family already suspected that their phone was being tapped and fellow military colleagues had suggested to me that I was being followed in both Ireland and Europe by military intelligence officers. Against this background of fear and uncertainty, my wife supported me in the same way that the army wives had supported their husbands from the outset, and told me that I had her blessing.

Before the military charges were enacted at the naval base, I made my way to the High Court in Dublin with lawyers provided by PDFORRA. On 13 February I made an application for an interim injunction to restrain the State and the military from hearing charges against me on the basis that I had been exercising my constitutional right to associate under article 40, while acting as public relations officer for a legitimate association. The case was listed as Martin vs the Minister for Defence, Commander Eoin McNamara, the attorney general and the people of Ireland. Legal representation was provided by Frank Clarke SC and Eamon Leahy BL. The initial case was heard in front of Justice Hamilton, who was then president of the High Court. What was being sought from the court was a restraining order that punitive actions against me, including the charges that had been drafted by the military, would be held in abeyance until such time as evidence could be presented that there was a constitutional case to be answered. If this was granted, the military charges would not be permitted to proceed until a date for a hearing (provided by the court), at which point an interlocutory injunction could be sought to keep the status quo (the prevention of me being charged) for the duration of further proceedings where the question of constitution-ality of the regulations could be presented to the High Court. Such an order, if granted at that later point, would protect me for the duration of the constitutional case and until the court reached a decision as to whether military regulations were in breach of the Constitution. My legal counsel was set to argue that the military regulations that forbade members of the Defence Forces from dealing with the media were 'ultra vires', or outside of constitutional provisions under Article 40.

Members of the national executive accompanied me to the High Court, where Justice Hamilton considered the application. He concluded:

> The application is based on the alleged constitutional right of Mr Martin to join an association of his choice and the right to exercise freedom of speech guaranteed in the constitution. This claim raises serious issues. I would normally be slow to interfere with a Defence Forces Disciplinary matter but as guardian of Mr Martin's constitutional rights and having regard to the serious issues raised, I believe it in the best interest of all that the State be restrained from proceeding with the disciplinary hearing.[37]

The justice ordered the court to reconvene on the matter two weeks later. The challenge for me and PDFORRA was that the government were already rushing through legislation to enact their own style of representative structures even as the court hearing was taking place. If the case was to falter, the undoubted result would be the imposition of the Chief of Staff/government-structured representative body that would be internal, ineffective and with no access to the media. If I was successfully silenced now, either by the courts or military charges or sanctions, PDFORRA would have no means of articulating their opposition to what was being forced upon them. Despite the political success of NASA, despite the promises of the Taoiseach, despite the Chief of Staff's research and consultation with everybody except his own enlisted personnel, the group calling themselves PDFORRA were still not recognised by the government and their thousands of letters to the Minister for Defence for a structure of their own remained unanswered.

One thing was certain, however, and that was that a constitutional case was now about to take place. A justice of the High Court had said that he was a guardian of my constitutional rights. It was no longer a commanding officer telling me I had committed an offence or a government deciding on whether soldiers were within their rights to form an association; this was the highest court in the land about to make its own decision about an important constitutional and human-rights issue. The Irish judicial system is independent of the government and it would decide on the issue regardless of government policy or attitudes. The next immediate question to be resolved was whether or not I would be given the protection of the courts for the duration of the constitutional case, but whether I received that or not, the case was set to proceed. In Cobh, Geraldine and I were greatly relieved by the judge's comments. Geraldine recalled:

> It was so reassuring to hear a Judge say that he and the court had a duty as a guardian of Michael's constitutional rights. We were both greatly relieved. Even if he ended up being charged by the navy, his case would still be heard by an independent judiciary that would not be swayed by politics or military commanders.[38]

Justice Hamilton set the date for the next hearing to take place the following Monday week.

The parties reassembled at the High Court in Dublin on 5 March 1990. Mr Harry Whelehan SC representing the State argued that I had given an interview in contravention of regulations and that he was not prepared to give an undertaking to desist from further breach of regulations pending the final determination of the representation matter.[39]

With the final arrangements now being put in place to introduce the (unwanted) Chief of Staff's representative structure, it was imperative that I continue to articulate PDFORRA's opposition to it. For their part, the military authorities and the State were anxious to silence me and prevent PDFORRA and me from taking to the airwaves to explain that the legislation about to be put in place would ignore PDFORRA and impose an internal structure.

Despite Whelehan's contention for the State that I was in breach of regulations and further arguments he made, Justice Barron said he required more information from the State before he would lift the protective order. He adjourned the application for three weeks on the basis that there would be no breach of regulations by me and no disciplinary actions taken against me by the authorities.[40]

What was really crucial at this juncture was that, despite the military authorities making a definitive statement that I was in breach of regulations and should be charged, the court was not sufficiently convinced to lift the order and was still willing to protect me on the basis that it was the guardian of my constitutional rights. If there had never been any hint of it before, there was now a clear indication that this was going to be a full, lengthy constitutional case that could end up with the government having charged me in a way that might prove to be unconstitutional. If I at this point spoke again to the media, the authorities were free to charge me, but that could still be deemed at a later date to have been unconstitutional. The dilemma was that, if the government now went ahead with their representative structures and subsequently lost the case, there was a possibility that everything may have to be deconstructed or dissolved.

Constitutional Challenge

The stage was now set for a full constitutional hearing. As in all countries, the constitution is the framework under which all legislation is made. Legal acts and regulations made under them must be compliant with the Constitution. In the forthcoming High Court case, I was planning to argue that if the Constitution stated that all citizens had the 'right of association', then military regulations (specifically those outlined in section A7, which forbade any member of the Defence Forces from dealing with the media) were in breach of the written Constitution.

At this point, the Dáil was processing the legislation that was to become the framework under which the 'Chief of Staff's representative structure' would be enacted. Most enlisted personnel of the Defence Forces did not want to be forced to accept the limited options that the chief's structure offered. In fact, thousands of them had written to the minister, advising him of their desire to set up their own association known as PDFORRA. In the chief's structure, there was no access for the association to the media, no independent means of raising finance, no option to have meetings outside of barracks and no direct contact with the minister or his officials in the Department of Defence or any other government department. If the framework legislation that was being rushed through by the government was passed, PDFORRA as envisioned by its members would be rendered useless and probably illegal. The only thing that now stood between the Chief of Staff's structure being forced upon enlisted personnel and their clear desire for their own independent association was the impending constitutional challenge. The monumental efforts that had been made by NASA over the previous two years, the extraordinary work of the Eastern Command soldiers led by Dick Dillon and his colleagues, the selfless endeavours of thousands of committed activists in every barracks and command around the country would all have been in vain if the chief's structure had been enacted under the planned legislation.

Crucially, despite all they had done to ignore PDFORRA and put their own structure into place, neither the army nor the government were empowered to stop the judicial process that had begun with my constitutional challenge in the High Court. The government were now left in the dilemma whereby it was the High Court, not them, that would effectively decide whether an independent PDFORRA could be permitted to exist. A legal and strategic stalemate had now arisen for the government and military authorities. Would they go ahead with the legislation to enact the chief's structure without the consent or the agreement of enlisted personnel, thereby risking being found to have acted unconstitutionally in charging me? Or would they take a gamble and hope that the court would come down in their favour? PDFORRA had nothing to lose in awaiting the outcome. The charges were already drafted against mr, the efforts of the enlisted personnel had already been ignored and the High Court might find in their favour. If I lost the court case, there were very serious implications for me. A crushing legal bill, possible dismissal from the Defence Forces, possible banning of access to any other public-service employment and perhaps the loss of my home. If the government lost the case there would certainly be a loss of face, as they had acted unconstitutionally, but what they feared the most was that, if they did lose, they would possibly have little or no control over the shape and make of any future representative association for military personnel. It was a question now of who blinked first. In the end it was the government.

ENGAGEMENT AT LAST

The first indication that came to the members of the ad hoc PDFORRA that the government had decided to speak to them was relayed by a phone call to the chairman of the national executive, Richard Dillon, in mid-March 1990. An army officer telephoned some of the Eastern Command soldiers with whom he had served to relay the message. The minute book of the national executive committee records: 'An approach was made to the Chairman and through an intermediary as to whether there was room for discussion.'[1]

This was a major breakthrough. The government had never spoken to PDFORRA before. Up to this point the only communication received officially from the government to members of PDFORRA had been a simple flat acknowledgement of the letter that members had sent individually to the minister requesting endorsement for the forming of the association.

A meeting was arranged for the two sides at 5 p.m. in the Ashling Hotel Dublin on 21 March. Members of the national executive convened from various parts of the country. The government was represented by parliamentarians Dr Brian Hillery TD and Tom Kitt TD. Hillery was a skilled negotiator with an academic background in industrial relations and dispute resolution. He recalls the background to the meeting:

> I was requested by the then Minister for Defence Brian Lenihan to meet the group who at that stage were already calling themselves PDFORRA and to meet with the leading light of that group who was deemed to be Michael Martin. I had been aware of the spouses' associations especially in the Midlands and knew that the Gardaí had long since established a representative body which enabled them, on a limited basis to conduct negotiations on behalf of their members, albeit in a manner somewhat less than that of the usual industrial relations sense.[2]

This was the first occasion on which the committee claiming to represent a sizable body of personnel in the Defence Forces would interface with emissaries of the government. It was a significant development. Even during the deliberations of the Gleeson submission teams in the preceding months, enlisted personnel had never been afforded the opportunity to meet with members of the commission on their own. Although the commission had visited many barracks and spoken to many people about the problems in the Defence Forces, these encounters had taken place in a very controlled environment with all the necessary clearings and briefings that the army provided for those who might end up engaging with the commission members. In the Ashling Hotel on that first evening, it was enlisted personnel of the ad hoc association who themselves decided on who should or should not be there.

At this point in the evolving events, the government had commenced the passage of legislation through the Dáil. It was envisaged that this legislation would be a framework under which the structures that had been recommended by the Chief of Staff would be enacted. As stated previously, the organisation proposed by the chief comprised of three groups or bodies, one each for the commissioned officers, the NCOs and the privates. There had been little or no consultation between the military authorities and the various ranks. PDFORRA had complained to the Minister for Defence, as had the NCOs team of the Gleeson submission team, that the chief and his staff were setting about recommending structures for the provision of a representative association for people whom they had not bothered to consult. Richie Condron recalls strong opposition to the idea: 'Those structures, known as the white book had been rejected by everyone. We had our own constitution and people were not going to be swayed into the army one which was all about them and how they could control us.'[3]

The chief's structures were being forced upon enlisted personnel who were told that interest in any other organisation was being viewed as 'divisive'. Even though members of the Defence Forces did not want this body, the chief went ahead and organised elections for it anyway.

In what was seen at the time as a very undesirable development, PDFORRA threatened that if the chief's structures were to be enacted under the legislation, their members, who they said comprised of 80 per cent of the enlisted ranks, would not participate in any elections for them. They claimed that if such associations were formed, nobody would take up membership. To emphasise their point further, PDFORRA called their own national elections for candidates to fill their existing ad hoc organisation. Advertisements for these appeared in the national press.[4] This action by PDFORRA defied the Chief of Staff's plans and resonated deeply with government. According to Dr Hillery, the calling of any kind of public elections for members of the armed forces was of great concern to the government:

There was concern at official and political level due to the unofficial nature of the elections. The immediate target was to meet with PDFORRA with a view to calling off the elections that were scheduled for Easter time but also to listen to the concerns of PDFORRA. I was to be a conduit with my colleague Tom Kitt and on the night Michael Martin and his colleagues had an agenda on a range of items. I had been given a briefing but in trying to capture the general tenor of the period there was a willingness to resolve the issues.[5]

The Ashling Hotel discussions went on for over eleven hours. PDFORRA had come to the meeting with a very specific set of aims. These were the same aims that had been proposed to the Gleeson Commission. They were handwritten and brought to the discussions on the day.[6] Specifically, there were three areas that PDFORRA identified as being crucial to the success of any representative body, and eight other matters that they set out as being necessary for any agreement. The specific matters included:

Name of the association to remain as PDFORRA
Total control of own finance to be raised by subscription
Deduction of subscriptions at source from army payroll facility
Full independent access to the media
Affiliation to EUROMIL
Conciliation and arbitration scheme
Officials of the association to be seconded from military duties
Elected members elsewhere facilitated with time off
Consultative status at all levels of the military chain of command
Financial assistance with provision of outside PDFORRA HQ
A memorandum of understanding

The government were concerned that the elections that were to take place would be seen as being the official elections rather than the decision of a break-off group of military personnel acting independently of command. Up to the meeting at the Ashling, it had appeared to the public that soldiers wanted a representative body and the government were taking steps to provide it with the assistance of the army. What was lost on many was that the representative body proposed by the Chief of Staff was seen by the soldiers themselves as an ineffective solution that would still have to contend with all the existing restrictions featured by an internal army system. The NCOs group, in their submission to Gleeson, had rejected the chief's proposed structures, which, when eventually circulated, had offered the following:

Private and NCO groups at barrack, command and DFHQ levels
Provision to make proposals that would not be altered
Process of adjudication (not specified)
Provision for a review of structures
Provision for the dissemination of progress on the proposals

These outlines of the chief's structures were circulated to all commands in January 1990. They were seen to fall far short of what was being sought by the soldiers.[7]

The meeting that evening went back and forth through the night, with many issues being raised and discussed. There were many breaks and often disagreements and numerous times when one side or the other had to check back with political or legal advisers. PDFORRA had legal counsel available on the night and were in telephone communication with their legal teams in Galway and Dublin to get advice on any matters that arose. Brian Hillery was also in regular telephone contact with a very senior member of the Department of Defence, most likely the Secretary of the Department of Defence and the minister. As the discussions proceeded, items that were agreed were ticked off. Eventually, to everyone's relief, an agreement was made. Members of the PDFORRA executive had drawn up a list of their demands, and those of them that were agreed upon were printed and signed by members present, but also by Dr Hillery and Tom Kitt.[8] Both parties seemed to have satisfied themselves that they had achieved enough to change the positions slightly. In the case of PDFORRA, they had compromised on two issues, the cancelling of their planned elections and the cessation of the court case. On the government side, they compromised on the crucial issue of abandoning the Chief of Staff's structure and providing, under the impending legislation, PDFORRA as an outside independent body with access to the media. The resultant impact of this agreement was that the new legislation formulated to accommodate the chief's structure was now going to be the same framework that would bring PDFORRA into legal statutory existence. It would be known as the Defence Amendment Act, 1990.

Dr Hillery had been aware of political concern at the highest level of government, and when he arrived into the Dáil the next morning he was summoned by the Taoiseach of the day, Mr Charles Haughey, who he recalls was relieved that matters had been resolved.[9] That same morning of 22 March 1990, when Brian Hillery was at the Dáil, I was giving a radio interview to the radio programme *Morning Ireland*. The presenter, David Hanley, described me as being 'very fresh' in view of the fact that I had been up all night negotiating. In that interview, speaking on behalf of PDFORRA, I reported that a breakthrough had occurred and that progress would now be made on establishing proposed independent structures through which negotiations on pay, allowances and other matters could be made.

Brian Hillery felt that there had been a strong case for a representative body and that there were many issues that needed to be addressed. The signatories that night on the document included myself, Michael Murphy, Richard Dillon and Richard Condron. This document would be subsequently held aloft as if it was a sacred covenant and a visible form of evidence that the agreement was solid. It has been photocopied many times and would be considered a physical manifestation of the first agreement reached between members of the, up to then, unrecognised PDFORRA and the organs of the State. The interesting aspect of this episode was that the military authorities were completely excluded from the deliberations. This was later to become a subject of complaint by the General Staff. In the immediate wake of the agreement, provisions were made to involve the Department of Environment, who were responsible for the organisation of State elections, in whatever arrangements needed to be made in order to elect candidates for the new structures about to be enacted by the introduction of the Defence Amendment Act, 1990. There was to be no prohibition on any personnel who had previously been involved in ad hoc PDFORRA to offer themselves for election into the new structure, which, as had been agreed, would be also named PDFORRA.

The Ashling Hotel agreement signified the beginning of the acceptance of PDFORRA by the civil authority. In excluding the military hierarchy from the negotiations that night, an altogether new dimension of civil–military relations was enacted. Technically, the government were about to do as they always said they would do, introduce framework legislation for representative structures, but significantly the structures that would be legitimised under the legislation were the same structures that the chief had warned would be divisive. Furthermore, the structures he had framed were now to be abandoned.

As expected, most of the activists that had been part of what was called ad hoc PDFORRA were returned in the State-sponsored elections and became the de facto representatives for the new structure. One factor that had been crucial in the discussions with the Department of the Environment was the type of electoral system that would be used. In the initial phases of the pursuit of the right of association, soldiers from the Eastern Command led by Dick Dillon and others had compiled a draft constitution that became known later as the 'Blue Book'. This was seen as a crucial first step in seeking the right of association; however, once a national executive had been formed from among the rest of the country, a decision was made to update the book and create a new constitution. It differed from the original in that it had a system of barrack-level, command-level, Defence Force HQ-level and government-level representation as a matter of right. The earlier book had been based only on a command structure. A subcommittee led by the late John Lucey was set up, and a more streamlined, appropriate constitution was framed and adopted at the first annual delegate conference. The electoral system agreed with the department that it was known as a 'list system'. This enabled those voting to choose their preference for an entire committee. One issue about internal representation became a regular point of debate around different parts of the country as the association was formed and indeed thereafter. It was the issue of the 'block system'. The Defence Forces in Ireland at that time were comprised of four army commands, with the Naval Service and Air Corps making up another two. Numerically, the army commands membership was much greater than the other two. However, at the annual delegate conference, voting rights were equal for all commands. This meant that the Navy and the Air Corps had the same delegate mandate as each of the other commands. From time to time over the years there were proposals to have this changed, but they were never successful. Advocates of the system at the time would argue that if equal representation of the commands were not advanced to the smaller ones, they might break off and form their own associations. That never happened.

FIRST FORMAL DISCUSSIONS

In the new environment of co-operation, the Minister for Defence Brian Lenihan TD invited the newly elected representatives to a press launch in the army headquarters in Dublin. It was a most unusual press conference in that the speeches were held in-camera. Despite the presence of the national media in the building, when it came to the minister making his speech to officials, General Staff, the newly elected representatives and the Chief of Staff, the cameras and the journalists were excluded from the room. The minister gave his speech to an assembly of representatives and senior military authorities who up to this point had had completely different views

on the whole issue of representation. The military were whole-
heartedly against the idea of any sort of independent representative
group and had even been accused of using intimidating tactics to
discourage enlisted personnel from pursuing their aims. It had been
suggested to sailors and soldiers that they were engaging in mutiny;
I suspected and was subsequently told that intelligence officers had
been following me. There had been claims made by NASA that
their husbands had been overlooked for promotion because of their
involvement in PDFORRA, and subtle threats that felt like intimi-
dation had been made.

LEGITIMATE ELECTIONS

The elections that had been agreed between ad hoc PDFORRA and
the government TDs, Dr Brian Hillery and Tom Kitt resulted in most
of the former activists being returned. These were now recognised
officially as the new legitimate representatives of enlisted personnel.
The intention was that these representatives would engage with the
Department of Defence in order to formulate and agree a new set of
regulations that would take account of the 1990 Defence Amendment
Act, which provided for the existence and operation of new representative structures in the PDF. The date for the first meeting was
set for 10 July 1990. This encounter was the first of its kind where
members of the enlisted ranks of the armed forces were present in
their own right to engage with, and make representations to, the civil
authority, which was itself being represented by the Department of
Defence with appointees from both the civil and military branches.

A fundamental shift occurred here in the context of civil–military
relations in Ireland. Legally and in a forum approved by the government, a group of enlisted personnel sat with a legitimate mandate to
engage with officials of a State department. All were there to create
a set of regulations that would enshrine the way in which relations
between the State and a large section of the armed forces would be
conducted from then on. This first encounter was precipitated by
legislation that could be argued came from a form of intervention
by military personnel. Michael Howard, who, serving as Department
of Defence Press Officer in 1989 and 1990, was at the centre of the
events, maintained in 2010 that:

I think you would have to say objectively that intervention took place. The settled policy position was that there should not be a representative association. The decision that there would be a system of representation was a political one. Like all political decisions it had come about because influence had been brought to bear. Governments in all democratic societies respond to pressures and influences. That influence was fostered by serving military personnel by a variety of means.[10]

This intervention began with political agitation by NASA, who were not members of the armed forces, but it was continued through the media and the courts by serving members, all of whom were enlisted personnel. It has to be noted here that Huntington's contention that enlisted personnel had no role in civil–military relations is no longer sustainable. Up to this meeting, there had been a share of aggravation, disappointment and fear among personnel on both divides of the military establishment regarding the aims and methods of soldiers who were seeking the right of association. In addition, the government itself had been forced to contend with protests, opposition attacks and public criticism. In this first set of discussions, people who had been vehemently opposed to each other's aims were finally meeting to try to reach agreement on matters of great importance. Some fundamental principles regarding the exercise of command were challenged and scrutinised in these discussions, the relationship between the military authorities and State was brought to a straining point and the demands of enlisted personnel were, perhaps for the first time, thrown centre stage in the consideration of a State's civil–military relations.

Although the official departmental side chose to ignore it for the purposes of these discussions, the elected representatives were fulfilling a dual role in that they were also members of the national executive of ad hoc PDFORRA. On this first occasion, the representative delegation comprised of the whole national executive, while in subsequent meetings a smaller number attended. Present were:

- Richard Dillon, national chairman of the association and also a company sergeant of the army in the Eastern Command
- Michael Martin (author), national secretary and a warrant officer in the navy
- Irvine Ferris, national executive and flight sergeant, Air Corps

- Denis Whelan, national executive and sergeant, Curragh Command
- John Lucey, national executive and chief petty officer of the navy
- Louis Parminter, national executive and an acting corporal, Curragh Command
- Donal Coakley, national executive and company sergeant of the Western Command
- Richard Condron, national executive and company sergeant of the Eastern Command
- Harry Higgins, national executive and sergeant of the Air Corps
- Geoff Keating, national executive and private/signalman in the Southern Command
- Jack Kiernan, national executive and corporal in the Western Command
- Joe Power, national executive and company quartermaster sergeant in the Southern Command

On the departmental side, the two branches were represented by the following:

- S. O'Brosnachain, secretary Department of Defence
- T. Conway, Department of Defence
- P. Kelly, Department of Defence
- P. Hammond, Department of Defence
- Brigadier General M. Downing
- Colonel W. Phillips
- Lieutenant Colonel P. Nowlan
- Commandant M. Baynes[11]

Richard Dillon, the founding chairman of ad hoc PDFORRA and the one who had been campaigning longer than anybody else for the right of association, had mixed feelings that day:

> I certainly felt a sense of achievement on behalf of all those who had been involved in looking for representation all along. I also thought that day and for a long time after that the military side in particular were going to use every opportunity to delay the process.[12]

Richard Condron, who was subsequently to become part of the representative-side negotiating team, felt that:

Attending that meeting that day meant that everything had been achieved. The military that were present were part of a group that had told us representation couldn't happen, they had said no to it. Now we were sitting down with them and doing what they said was impossible, that is negotiating about pay and conditions of our members.[13]

This first meeting dealt with general operating arrangements regarding the conduct of the discussions and negotiations that would follow. These included areas such as the preparation of minutes, the compilation of the agenda, the size and location of the meetings, time off and travel arrangements, office accommodation and liaison between the two groups. It was also confirmed at this time that the new regulations that were to govern the operation of the representative associations would be a self contained Defence Force Regulation (DFR). The draft minute stated in paragraph 8: 'The regulations which will be drafted by the Department will be completed in consultation with the representative's side.'[14]

When the minutes were presented at the next meeting three days later, there were a number of amendments sought by the representatives' side. They did not accept the wording of paragraph 8 and successfully had it amended and adapted to read the following: 'The regulations will be drafted by the Department in consultation with the representative's side.'

Although the change seemed minor, it is clear that the representative side did not want drafting of the regulations to be undertaken by the departmental side alone. There was another problem with the minutes that day. This too seemed at first to be of little consequence, but the reality was that it was to become one of the major issues of contention between the military and the representative side, and later between the military authorities and the government. The representative side rejected the record of attendance at the previous meeting because they had been referred to with their rank. Thus Richard Dillon was documented as Coy Sgt Dillon. They proposed an amendment to delete the references to rank in the attendance appendix A and argued:

The use of rank and uniform in discussions with their military superiors would place them at a psychological disadvantage; would inhibit them in the discharge of the representative role and could lead to an undesirable impact on discipline if that role was not clearly distinguished from their military duties. Precedents in relation to other military associations abroad and Garda representative associations were cited and given as examples by PDFORRA.[15]

The departmental side responded by arguing that:

> The question appeared to be an issue because it was being made into an issue; ranks were laid down in the Defence Act and it would be a pretence (and possibly contrary to the provisions of the Act) to set ranks aside from a military standpoint. What was proposed would be at variance to military life as we know it in this country. In practice the special position of representatives in the representation forum would be recognised.

The appendix to the minute was therefore not agreed. Apart from these matters, a discussion document on the items to be addressed in talks was considered. The document contained headings that were felt could be used to formulate the items that needed to be discussed in the attempts to create new regulations. Headings included the official name for the association, cognisance of the fact that the elected representatives were also association representatives and that the terminology the association used should be adopted, membership of the association and subscriptions and facilities. There were also a number of headings that the representative side wanted included in the document for discussion. These were:

- A memorandum of understanding
- Affiliation to outside organisations
- Channels of communication with the department and the military authorities
- Access to official noticeboards
- Inclusion on distribution list for routine orders
- Provision of two sets of DFRs
- Arrangements for movement of elected representatives at national level between commands and the facility to have expert advice at meetings.[16]

These and subsequent exchanges in the early meetings were to form the basis of creating the new regulations. They represented an interface between certain members of the armed forces and the State itself. In the only real area of disagreement, concerning the use of rank, the discussion went back and forth for one-and-a-half hours of a four-hour meeting.[17] It was agreed that a statement of positions would be outlined in documents to be compiled by both sides and presented for the next meeting on 20 July 1990. The arguments that were subsequently presented go to the heart of relationships between military personnel and military service, but also between military personnel and the State.

The military authorities and the representatives of PDFORRA both presented documents as agreed. In a ten-paragraph position paper, the military authorities set out the importance of rank and uniform. They opposed any circumstances in which the wearing of uniform and the use of rank would be discarded. From the first paragraph, the document set out the overarching consideration of the issue and the contention that practices were legally grounded and strategically necessary:

> The use of military rank coupled with the wearing of military uniform is inseparably tied to the exercise of command and authority in the Defence Forces upon which the structures of control, organisation and discipline are based ... it is the assessment of the military authorities that any derogation from such customary military law will have a deleterious effect on the exercise of command and discipline ... having regard to the present security commitments of the Defence Forces the mere possibility of such a development must not be allowed.

The document went on to acknowledge the concerns outlined in the representative-side arguments and promised to take cognisance of them, but suggested that: '... everyone in military life should have a rank and there is no provision for the dropping of rank.' It finished by suggesting that the legal responsibilities of the military authorities merited their position to be the most important in these matters:

> The misgivings about setting aside ranks/uniforms impinge particularly on the area of responsibility of the military authorities. While all ranks have a deep interest and concern in the maintenance of military discipline and control, the military authorities have the statutory responsibility in this area and, having regard to the position stated, their judgement in this matter ought to be paramount.[18]

The paper set out very clearly the crucial nature of rank and uniform to discipline, and implied a heightened importance, given the security situation that prevailed in Ireland at the time. It suggested that those who were subject to the Defence Act, 1954 were bound to their rank as a consequence of their military life. There was no contemplation of any other 'life' other than a military one, at least during membership of the Defence Forces. This perspective provides an insight into one concept of military service. Does arguing that there is but a single identity recognised by rank and regardless of activity portray a belief in a single-dimensional existence? Is the idea that, once a person is conferred with a rank under military law, there are no apparent circumstances in which that rank may be ignored? One can certainly understand the merit of institutional ranking; it defines relationships, establishes hierarchy and, in many cases, identifies skills sets. In the context of any institution, these are useful attributes, but how far beyond the barracks gates do modern military personnel consider themselves soldiers in peacetime?

If ormulated a response for the representative side, which submitted a five-part paper under the headings: 'Representation as a military issue', 'Effect of the uniformed revolving door role', 'Psychological disadvantage', 'A new forum' and 'Historical policy'. This paper set out the argument that soldiers are no longer engaged in total service and that they have another life outside of the constraints of the barracks. It also acknowledged the arguments made by the military of the importance of rank and uniform in the military context. The points made in my paper clearly envisaged a co-existence in addition to 'military life' during activities that would be considered as being outside of military life and outside of the barracks. The paper rejected the idea of 'total service':

> The concept of total service is as misplaced in peacetime as it is necessary in times of conflict and emergency ... the reality today is that a soldier enjoys another alternative type of existence outside of, and independent to, the military chain of command and the duties and life of that discipline ...[19]

While the military authorities argued that the endowment of rank and the wearing of uniform in themselves played a central role in the efficient operation of military discipline and command and stated that any change would undermine it, the representative side referred to the importance of training during the 'transition' from one element of their lives to the other and spoke of some limitations of the military chain of command:

> This transition can be effected with ease and speed as a result of sound training and the influence of the military ethos, the wearing of uniforms and the relationships between ranks greatly assists in this transition. The military chain of command by its very nature cannot possibly hope to deal with many of the issues that impact on the soldier's 'other' existence.[20]

From the opposing papers it can be seen that the military authorities and the representatives of the enlisted personnel had very different perspectives on the operation of authority and its 'jurisdiction'. It would appear that the Irish model of military authority was grounded in a requirement for immediate, militarily disciplined responses to orders that are crucial for the successful fulfilment of any military operation. On the field of battle such requirements are self-evident, but do such models of authority have a place in peacetime? In his examination of military hierarchy and authority, Janowitz recognises that the type of authority may change as a consequence of changing circumstances:

> In the past authority in the military profession has been rooted in custom, tradition, law and heroic achievement. To understand the changing patterns of authority in the military establishment, the sociologist directs attention to the changes in the skill and rank structure, the status system and the techniques of discipline.

He contends that the mission of the military in particular in relation to preparing for war, as opposed to deterring wars, plays an important role in determining which type of authority is appropriate: 'If the military is forced to think about deterring wars rather than fighting wars, the traditions of the "military mind" based on the inevitability of hostilities, must change and military authority must undergo transformation as well.'[21]

A question arises as to whether, in 1990, the concentration by the military leadership in Ireland on the physical trappings of authority in the form of rank and uniform was appropriate for an army which was not at war, at least not in the conventional sense. The representative side, it seems, were at pains to explain that the formal military hierarchal system of obedience was appropriate in the full military context but perhaps not in matters that they claimed were outside of the realm of military life. They also articulated recognition of the methodology used to maintain a skill or a managerial distance between officers and enlisted ranks in order to attempt to better effect their authority:

> Discouraging of any social contact or relationships between them, the setting aside of any humanitarian qualities and the reliance on the influence of rank alone and not the professional ability or leadership suitability in order to exact the desired response from the subordinate.[22]

The representative side sought to separate the representative activities and divorce them from the normal trappings of authority. They argued that, contrary to the fears expressed by the military, such a separation would in fact help discipline rather than hinder it. Neither side accepted the argument of the other. The military paper had emphasised in its title that it was referring to barracks and posts; however, its content seemed to go beyond these workplaces to extend to a military 'life'. The representatives of enlisted personnel appeared to accept the need for strict enforcement of rank and uniform tradition in all things military, but saw military life in peacetime as being only one aspect of their lives in which, they intimated, the military authorities had no expertise or authority.

One of the more interesting contexts of this debate was that a seemingly internal set of core values for the military, usually dealt with by them and them alone, was now being articulated and argued in the presence of the representatives of the civil authority, and while they may have had no real input into the finer points of the debate itself, they were a witness to it and would become the eventual arbiters. In this instance the relationship between the civil authorities and the institutions of the military was altered or at least re-enforced. This was an early impact on civil–military relations that went almost unnoticed by those engaged in the debate. Despite the unique skills of the army profession, as has been pointed out, military personnel are still subject to civil authority. This does not prevent the internalisation of standards and rules within the corporate identity of the army. Various definitions of professional identity suggest that the training, skills and standards are internally upheld and maintained, even when the skills themselves are provided as a service to a client. In his consideration of the military profession, Talcott Parsons contends that: 'Professional training requires the maintenance of reasonable standards according to the rules of the profession, exercised either by the concerted opinion of its peers or the organisation that patronises the profession.'[23]

The professional body that was the Irish Army in 1990 was having its own professional standards and procedures questioned. Matters that had been taken as normal internal corporate rules were under scrutiny and being challenged by the new elected representatives who, unlike the client State, claimed knowledge of the internal workings. It was a challenge from within. In addressing the claims of the representative side, the professionals had to justify long-standing practices not just to the representatives of their own enlisted personnel but also to representatives of the State. Prior to these encounters, the professional qualifications of the military authorities over their civilian counterparts might have been sufficient to allay any challenge of the rights and wrongs of any internal queries. However, there was now a questioning of what had been considered fundamental parameters in which the military had previously operated.

The contents of the representative side paper also provide a rare insight into the mind of military subordinates and their perspective in relation to superiors. Although provided for the purpose of arguing against the wearing of uniforms during representative business, they shed light on the special relationship between subordinate and superior. In the section of their position paper entitled, 'Effect of the uniformed revolving door role', the representative side argued:

> The military chain of command quite rightly dictates the manner in which we speak and respond to our superior officers ... The representative forum must be divorced from all other military roles and relationships and clearly defined as something outside of the military chain of command.[24]

In the subsequent minutes of the meeting in which this paper was presented, it was noted that the representative side stated that the division of roles was acknowledged by the Tánaiste and Minister for Defence on 6 July 1990.[25]

The debate on rank and uniform was to be a continuing source of disagreement for the duration of the talks and it escalated as a result of another issue relating to the posting of information bulletins in army barracks by the representative side. Despite the lack of agreement

on the issue of rank and uniform, there were many other items that
had to be addressed in order to set up the structures, practices and
regulations that would constitute the means by which the associations and the Department of Defence would engage with each other.
Defence officials suggested that non-contentious issues be dealt with
in parallel with the main issue to be resolved so that they could be
disposed of quickly to make 'tangible progress'.[26] Other items that
emerged for inclusion in subsequent talks included the Conciliation
and Arbitration Scheme, which was to be the dedicated industrial-
relations machinery that would deal with formal claims in relation
to pay and conditions of service. It was felt that the discussion on this
scheme would be best held off until all the regulatory matters under
other headings had been resolved.

During this period, it was still the case that the representative associations had not yet been officially set up. Regulations had not yet been
amended and therefore it was still an offence for enlisted personnel to
speak to the media. The departmental side at the meeting of 24 July
appeared to give permission for the representative side to make public
comments on the findings of the report of the Gleeson Commission,
stating that it was expected that 'informed media comment' would be
made. The rather testy response of the representative side was that they
'reserved the right to respond to media enquiries without prejudice
to the ongoing discussions'.[27] In a legal sense, the public statements
made by me as secretary/PRO could have again resulted in military
charges. That this did not happen at this point displayed a new environment of co-operation if not understanding between the two sides.
It also inferred an independent association was already operative.

Having considered the papers submitted by both sides in relation to
the rank and uniform issue, the parties met again on 27 July 1990 to
discuss them. The departmental side comprising, as usual, of military
and Department of Defence officials, stated that, given the fact that the
system was not yet up and running, and that it was to be a completely
new environment, they felt it was 'not valid in the absence of actual
experience to predict the interface between commanding officers
and elected representatives would be made difficult by the wearing of
uniform and the use of rank'. The views of the representative side were
reiterated and they gave the example of discussions on 'matters dealing
with family issues, on which they represented their members, were
not military in nature and could not be dealt with on that basis, i.e. as

subordinates to superiors'. The departmental side, in their response, also acknowledged that a 'process of education would be required on all sides in order to fulfil the new role'.[28] At the next meeting the issue arose again and on this occasion the representative side summarised their reservations thus:

- Wearing of uniform inhibits proper responses.
- Wearing of uniform sets up certain behaviour patterns.
- Wearing of uniform enshrines the superior/subordinate role.
- Wearing of uniform is inappropriate where the relationship may involve heated debate.
- Removal of uniform and the dropping of rank would encapsulate the representative function and set it apart.
- Removal of uniform and dropping of rank in the representative role would maintain the command and control relationship in the military role.
- Removal of uniform and the dropping of rank are necessary for the full discharge of the new representative role by the representative side.
- There are precedents in many other countries which can be drawn on to illustrate arguments made.[29]

Following the presentation of the summarised version of their views, the representative side, who had refused to discuss any other matters until the issue of rank and uniform was resolved, agreed to consult with their national executive to enquire as to whether they might be mandated to discuss other issues.

8

Military Ethos Critically Examined

Apart from the views expressed by the military authorities in relation to the rank and uniform issue at meetings, they eventually made a robust written response to the representative side's paper, taking paragraph by paragraph the points made and commenting on them to reach a conclusion that regarding the chapter entitled 'Representation as a military issue', there were falsehood, fabrication, undue influence by personal notions, failure to distinguish a full-time liability to military law from one's personal life and incorrect interpretation of the scope of representation under the Defence Acts. The response to the second part of the representative paper entitled 'Effect of the uniformed revolving door role', made the point that all ranks were part of the chain of command, that existing courtesy between ranks was being ignored, that the permanency of rank was misunderstood and that it was a contradiction to suggest that issues within the scope of representation were non-military and at the same time wished to raise matters with military superiors. On the chapter entitled 'Psychological disadvantage', it was stated that it was absurd to assume that the mere wearing of uniform would reverse the quality of good relationships. It contended that this chapter was aggressive and confrontational and illustrated an antipathy towards authority rather than a quibble over the outward display of rank and uniforms. The general conclusion that was reached in this response to the representative-side paper was stated as:

> Even with the making of allowance for such inaccurate expression and partisan views, the proposal in relation to rank and uniform is far from convincing and no apparent justification exists for such a far reaching departure from the norms of military life.[1]

In his examination of the military establishment as a social system, Janowitz reflects on the wholeness of the job and the assimilation necessary for one to be absorbed into the military system. In other works, he had suggested the military is among a few groups that place so much emphasis on it:

> Assimilation involves the ongoing process of recruitment, selection, training and career development. Not only must the new recruit, officer, enlisted man learn a complex set of technical skills, he is also expected to master an elaborate code of professional behaviour and etiquette, since membership in the military means participation in an organisational community which regulates behaviour both on and off the 'job'.[2]

This view would be consistent with the expressed position of the military authorities in Ireland at the time. Not only are there certain patterns of behaviour expected in the military but it would appear that these were also expected 'off the job'. In this respect, the PDFORRA position was at variance with what was considered normal not only by those inside the command structure of the army, but also by a noted sociologist. The representative side and the official side nonetheless both held very strong views and continued to address this as an issue of extreme importance.

At the seventh and eighth meetings between the departmental side and the representative sides, held on 31 July 1990 and 7 August 1990 respectively, the only items on the agenda, apart from minutes and 'any other business' (AOB), was the question of rank and uniform in the representative role. In an effort to deal with the stalemate, at the eighth meeting the representative side suggested that they could meet in the current forum with the General Staff to discuss the question of rank and uniform without the presence of the civilian side of the Department of Defence. They felt that the military representatives present at the talks did not have the required negotiating flexibility on the matter. The departmental side suggested consideration be also given to the idea of meeting with the General Staff in McKee Barracks, in uniform. Both parties agreed to consider the two suggestions. With this temporary deferring of the rank and uniform issue, it was agreed that the matter of establishing a definitive list for inclusion in the 'scope of representation' could be advanced.[3]

At the next meeting, the representative side requested permission for the use of noticeboards in military installations to convey information to their members. The departmental side agreed to consider this matter. The meeting turned to the items for inclusion in the scope of representation. Under the Defence Amendment Act, the representative bodies were being established for the purpose of making representations on behalf of their members on matters that came within the 'scope of representation'. The detail of this was not specified in the legislation. The idea had been that the scope of matters that came within the remit of the associations to discuss would be laid down in regulations having regard to the main provisions of the Act. The representative side put forward the following twenty-two headings that they wanted included:

- The scope of representation and its concept. Independence from the chain of command. The manner in which members overseas would be represented
- Access to the media
- Posting of materials on noticeboards
- The principles governing conduct of association affairs within military installations
- Release/secondment of personnel
- Claims regarding pay, allowances, and other emoluments in cash or in kind
- The principles governing hours of duty
- The principles governing the allocation and standards of accommodation officially provided
- Pensions/superannuation
- The principles governing the granting of annual, special and sick leave, including uncertified sick leave
- The principles governing recruitment and training
- The principles governing promotions
- The principles governing discipline
- The principles governing transfers and postings
- Finance and financial independence
- Welfare of association members and dependents, including medical benefit schemes, assistance funds, recreational facilities, education, civilian employment adjustment courses, dependents' assistance, credit unions and contact with other welfare bodies, including those of the military authorities

- Conditions in the workplace including occupational safety
- Conciliation and arbitration system
- Suggestions of general application promoting the efficiency of the Defence Forces
- The making of regulations and the implementation of reports that impact on members
- Affiliation to external bodies
- A provision to give consideration to as of yet unspecified matters which may arise in light of experience as a consequence of the evolution of representation or the non-acceptance of the concept of representation through word or deed by any of the partici-pating partners[4]

It emerged at the tenth meeting of the sides that, out of the twenty-two headings submitted by the representative side, the departmental side had no difficulty with half of them (items 2, 3, 5, 6, 9, 10, 15, 16, 17, 18 and 21), but there were reservations about the rest. The expression of these reservations and objections again throws light on the perceptions of both sides on the operation of the relationship between the civil authority and the military. The departmental side asked for further elaboration on the headings dealing with hours of duty, and on principles governing discipline, promotions, recruitment and training. With regard to accom-modation, the side agreed in principle about standards but not allocation. They contended that the principles governing discipline were excluded by Section 2 of the Defence Act, 1954. The minutes of the meeting stated: 'In general the authorities were prepared to discuss a wide range of items through representation but would not countenance an asso-ciation's resort to the media to publicise matters which were intimately concerned with army command, discipline etc.'[5]

Defining the scope of representation was an extremely important exercise for all parties to the discussions. From the civil-authority point of view, the government responsibility for the raising and commanding of an army could not be diminished in any way. They were also acutely aware of the power of the media in influencing public opinion, which they had already seen utilised as pressure brought to bear on politicians. From the military-authority point of view, the exercise of command and discipline went to the heart of the operational efficiency of the army as a military force. Any interference in this area would be seen as dangerous in light of the role of the military in any State, as they are the last line of defence in the protection of the country and its citizens. How or if these matters were to be discussed or excluded was very relevant. From the perspective of the representatives, the application or the effect of some of these issues went beyond the mere right of the government or the army to do as they must do. They made clear that they agreed with the need for discipline and the exercise of command and that full unambiguous power was legitimate, but, where such decisions in these contexts impacted on their members, they felt the necessity to be able to represent their interests. In realistic terms, the representatives saw no role in the command decisions that would, for example, decide to deploy troops on an operation in Ireland or overseas, but they held it quite legitimate to negotiate and have input regarding the effect of such deployments or operations. So if the army decided to plan and undertake an operation that resulted in soldiers needing special medical attention, special allowances or arrangements for family contact, the representative body should be entitled, they felt, to negotiate on such matters.

In a discussion about the implementation of the Gleeson report it was agreed by the Department that all matters that came within the scope of representation would be the subject of consultation before any implementation. In effect, it was at this point that the elected representatives acquired the right to be consulted as a matter of course, and have an input into matters that would have an impact on their members. In many respects, elements of responsibility to soldiers that had previously been within the remit of the officer body were removed and passed on to the new group. In a purely industrial-relations sense it was a significant advance in that the 'right' of consultation about certain matters had now been agreed. There was, however, a little caveat in that the Department still maintained the right to elicit views from within the military chain of command. Their position was recorded in the minutes:

> The Departmental side stated that it was their intention that the
> elected representatives would be consulted on matters which would fall
> within the scope of representation but that, in relation to the Gleeson
> Commission Report, and indeed any other matters affecting the
> management and control of the Defence Forces, there will continue
> to be the normal eliciting of views and examination of proposals etc.,
> within the command structure.[6]

In September 1990 another important concession was wrought by the elected representatives from the official side. They had previously requested access to noticeboards in military installations. It was agreed that notices addressing the following matters could be posted up by representatives: 'Times and dates of committee meetings, details of fundraising events, results of fundraising draws.'[7]

Though these headings seemed quite restrictive, the first notice presented to the military was a four-page information sheet that covered numerous issues beyond what was agreed at the meeting. In a circular out to the commands, it was stated that the Chief of Staff had agreed to the posting of a PDFORRA information sheet on all barracks noticeboards. Petty Officer Jim Halligan, who had been passionately involved in seeking recognition for PDFORRA, had vivid recollections of seeing the notices up for the first time:

> I remember seeing our PDFORRA information sheet on the notice board at the Naval Base as if it was yesterday. Our logo and our name not just posted up but referred to properly in the accompanying instruction. It was a great day for all the efforts made by all the people who had had to hide the name PDFORRA and their involvement in it for so long. Despite the content of the sheet which was important in itself, for me the posting of it on the official Naval Base noticeboard symbolised legitimacy of our organisation and a visible manifestation of it at long last.[8]

The circular stated, 'This information sheet is somewhat lengthy but permission for its display is being granted as it contains important details on the progress of negotiations. Any future information will be shorter'.[9] The undated information sheet comprised of four pages, and although unsigned it was presented on PDFORRA-headed paper.[10] It had numerous paragraphs dealing with matters of importance to the organisation. Committees around the country were to be tasked with studying the report of the Gleeson Commission so, when the time came to negotiate its provisions, there would be a considered position from which to start. It referred to the ongoing negotiations to create new DFRs for the operation of the association on a statutory footing and described them as 'painstakingly slow'. It listed some of the topics then under discussion and progress where it had been made. There was confirmation that the association was to retain its name and that district committees had been allocated an hour per fortnight during

working hours in which they could meet in barracks. In an interesting
paragraph entitled 'EUROMIL', it referred to political developments
throughout Europe that had far-reaching implications for the welfare
of European soldiers. Reports from East Germany suggested that as
many as 40,000 soldiers were to be discharged and they were not sure
if any welfare payments or assistance would be paid to them. The final
paragraph contained the news that the practice of soldiers who were
being deployed overseas paying for their kit bags was to discontinue.

The information sheet was an important document in that
PDFORRA was being permitted to transmit information through
the official channels of the army. That this was being done prior to
the implementation of new regulations was significant and, on the
face of it, showed goodwill. The matters that were outlined were of
particular interest to enlisted personnel and indicated progress in the
lengthy timeframe it was taking to draft the regulations. The mention of
EUROMIL was also significant, and two members of PDFORRA went
on to attend a EUROMIL meeting in Leipzig, East Germany on 3 and
4 October 1990, the day of East and West German reunification. Despite
these seemingly positive developments, the issue of noticeboards was set
to become a main point of contention, not just between the army and
the association, but also between the military and the civil authorities.
Difficulties arose when military commanders insisted that the local
notices were to be signed, but with the rank of the representatives to be
included. A request for an urgent meeting was sent to the Minister for
Defence and An Tánaiste Mr Brian Lenihan by Richard Condron, who
signed it as a member of the national executive of PDFORRA. [11]

When a delegation from PDFORRA met with the minister less
than a week later, they brought up the issue of noticeboards and the
problems they were experiencing because of the rank and uniform
issue. In a memorandum that was circulated on 10 October, the minister's private secretary advised:

> Following his discussion of the matter with representatives of NCOs
> and privates and having considered the views expressed by the Chief
> of Staff, An Tánaiste has concluded that pending resolution of the
> question of the use of rank and the wearing of uniforms by personnel
> engaged in representative business he will not object to the posting
> of newsletters containing references to elected representatives without
> use of their ranks on official noticeboards. This interim arrangement

is without prejudice to the decision to be taken in due course on the ranks and uniform question.[12]

The minister had an understanding of the views of the Chief of Staff at this point – the memorandum acknowledges this. In what could be regarded as an internal military issue, the minister had sided with the representative association. Given that the interpretation of the professional corporate wisdom usually rests with the officer corps, by any standards, this was a significant decision. On the lowest level it meant that decisions arrived at by commanding officers in not allowing the notices be displayed would be reversed. Whatever impact this would have on the exercise of command and discipline would not become immediately apparent. The impact, however, on the authority or influence of PDFORRA, the new association, was significant. Because this issue had been one deemed to be of crucial importance by the military authorities, it was they who reacted most strongly to the minister's decision. Unbeknown to the representative association, the Chief of Staff and the General Staff had indicated to the minister that the very future of the Defence Forces was at stake. They reiterated their arguments regarding the essential link between the use of ranks and the wearing of uniform being inextricably linked to the exercise of command and discipline. They had advanced many arguments, ranging from public order to political and subversive infiltration possibilities, in the earlier requests for the associations to conduct meetings outside of barracks. Now they turned to the internal detrimental impact that notices not carrying the rank of their authors would have. Deterioration in morale, discipline, and the security of the State was advanced as a consequence if the minister instructed the military authorities to allow the notices, despite their trenchant opposition to them. It was suggested in one communication with the minister that such an initiative was illegal.[13]

Members of the representative body PDFORRA were impressed, and they felt that Brian Lenihan was of sufficient stature to 'take on' the generals:

> I believe without exception every member serving in the Defence Forces at the time welcomed the idea of Brian Lenihan becoming Minister for Defence. Some even thought it raised the profile of the Department of Defence which was seen up to then as being perceived as a backwater position.[14]

For the army, however, the decision by the minister to allow the dropping of the ranks, even on a temporary basis, was catastrophic. The fundamental operation of command and discipline was linked to rank and uniform. External tools such as rank markings define the authority and status of the superior. Janowitz argues:

> The military exhibits extreme status sensitivity … It is not surprising that the military establishment has evolved an elaborate basis for according its limited supply of status and prestige to its own members. Most pervasive is the criterion which is applied universally through the services, the distinction between the officers and the enlisted men.[15]

Within the hierarchal confines of the army, nobody could have ignored the wishes and orders of the General Staff. Authority was singular in its direction from top to bottom; in this new situation, enlisted personnel had not only bypassed the command structure, but had been backed by the only external authority that could overrule the Chief of Staff. Had this been on a minor issue, perhaps the military authorities could have accepted it more easily. Because the issue was deemed to be fundamental to the exercise of control of the army itself, letters were sent first pleading and then in the strongest possible language. It is ironic that in 2010 nobody interviewed in the Department of Defence can remember the last time that rank and uniform was an issue. The best guess was from Secretary General Michael Howard, who thought it had been fifteen or sixteen years since he had heard it mentioned: 'I remember that being an extremely controversial issue. The fact is that the culture in the Defence Forces seemed to have been much more flexible and adaptable than what people had expected it could be.'[16]

What had arisen was a situation where the views of the ultimate authority of the Defence Forces in command of the Irish Army, Navy and Air Corps, in relation to rank and uniform, were now at variance with those of the Minister for Defence, a respected and powerful member of government. In addition, the minister was issuing instructions to the army, which they clearly felt was not in the best interests of the army or the State. The military authorities would also have felt that this area was clearly one in which they had professional experience, and that their views were paramount in this regard. They were, after all, the military experts. The divergence in views about the matter was indicative of the different perspectives of the parties involved.

The PDFORRA representative side perceived their work as falling into the category of industrial relations: they held a simplistic view that, as soldiers, they were military personnel, but areas and activities that were not operational were open for negotiation and debate. The military authorities, on the other hand, saw all activities of all military personnel at all times being 'military' and subject to the regulations, tradition and practice of the Defence Forces. The government, it would appear, saw both sides at once: 'There had always been and there still is a great respect in government for the army. It is widely recognised that they play an essential role. At that time the government was really geared towards providing solutions and advancing matters.'[17]

Despite the respect the government had for the army and its hierarchy, the rank and uniform issue and, in particular, that of the noticeboards that were to contain their names or ranks, resulted in the government acting against the wishes of the military authority of the day. A letter from the office of the Chief of Staff to the Tánaiste dated 17 October outlined the chief's grave reservations regarding the posting of newsletters without the use of rank by members of the PDF. It went so far as to suggest that:

> The surrender to PDFORRA on every major issue to date has progressively undermined the status, function and delegated responsibilities of the General Staff and of the prescribed functions of GOCs and Unit Commanders. The future wellbeing of the Defence Forces is at stake. The question of the use of ranks and uniform is a basic issue on which the military feel obliged to take a firm position. The noticeboard decision is seen as a serious erosion of the authority of military commanders at all levels. It is my view as Chief of Staff, fully supported by the General Staff that any matter which adversely impinges directly or indirectly on the prescribed and exclusive military responsibility and prerogative of the exercise of command and discipline of troops is not only inimical to the exercise of that command but is also in essence, illegal.[18]

This letter from the most senior military figure of the State to the second most senior figure of government in the country clearly outlines the way in which the military authorities viewed the various agreed provisions being made to the associations by the Department of Defence and the minister. In addition to seeing them as detrimental to the command system, the military also deemed them to be illegal.

The question arises here as to whether the chief and his staff felt that the security of the State was at risk, and if so what they were prepared to do about it. It is difficult to find an example of such a strained relationship between the offices of the Chief of Staff and of the Minister of Defence since the antagonism between General Mulcahy and the government of 1924. The General Staff at that time acted in what they believed was the best interest of the State and the army, and were politically isolated and forced into retirement for their stand. Mulcahy resigned as a result; however, there was little comparison between the two periods and what prompted the incidents. In one instance the posting of notices and, in the other, the interception of armed men planning a mutiny. There were no resignations by anybody in 1990, but nevertheless civil–military relations were going through a difficult time.

The formalities and otherwise that had existed up to then, the systems of contact and the assumption of professional competence in the military and civil sides in their dealings with each other were now being called into question. It is at this interface between the civil authority of the country and the military that civil–military relations are determined and operated. Like any two groups that operate in a system of clientship or management together, there are assumptions made about each one's competency and legitimacy. When these are clear and accepted, both can get on with the job of fulfilling their respective roles. If two groups have a system of interaction, if they have a clear sense of the other's role and a knowledge of the other's right to be there, work can be done.

In Ireland, it had long been established that the military were subject to the control of the civil authority. The Department of Defence was the government agency to whom the military body reported. The government and the Department were and are the senior partners in the relationship between the two. For both, there was an assumption of professional competence. The Department was responsible to the minister and the government for the running of the Defence budget, the creation of regulations, the organisation of staff and procurement of equipment. The military on the other hand would have been adjudged to have competence in the area of security risks and requirements, manning levels applicable, military-equipment needs and operations. They would have been deemed to have exclusive competence in such areas. In the normal course of events, the civil servants of the Department of Defence would not have served in the military themselves. There was no such requirement. The matters of allocation of government budgets, administration of pay and pensions do not in themselves require military knowledge, and therefore it would be unlikely that they could question the competence of military officers when being told what was required or acceptable in military operational matters.

The internal area of professional normalities portrayed by the military to the civil department had not ordinarily been called into question. Now with PDFORRA in the environment, some of the accepted practices and etiquette were being questioned. These working meetings now meant there was a third party in the room. Being a part of the discussions, the civilian side were now present to hear the challenges on what had been previously presented by the military authorities as normal and acceptable. They would later be led into a situation where they had to either defend or condemn a position that they might not yet be familiar with or competent in, relying on the military officers' competence to maintain a position. Prior to these meetings, enlisted personnel had not interfaced officially with the Department. All matters dealing with pay and allowances were processed by the military authorities who did not deploy any enlisted personnel to deal with them. It was a new departure to have enlisted personnel deal directly with civilian public servants and to hear on some occasions a completely different perspective on matters relating to the army. The fact that they were also military personnel and that they had an entitlement to be there challenged the exclusivity of competence previously enjoyed by the officer corps alone. There were new ideas on what constituted priority. There were also new criticisms of some of the internal actions of the management in the PDF. Such matters would not have been previously conveyed by officers who were themselves responsible for the practices that were being objected to.

Where this would really portray itself was in the discussions and argument that were not exclusively operational or military in nature. If the enlisted personnel were forwarding an argument that was non-military, in the sense that it dealt with an issue like pay or allowances or the impact of welfare schemes on their families, there was a view that they were in a better position to describe and explain the impact on their families than the officer corps were. This implied that the enlisted personnel were more competent to deal with requests and demands arising from them. This did not detract from the very real duty of care felt by most military commanders to their subordinates.

Even in purely military terms, where issues like rank and uniform arose, the Department and the minister were now being exposed to an alternative perspective, and whether or not they agreed with the sentiment, the right of the enlisted personnel to be there conferred on them a right to be heard and considered. In the context then of the relationship between the military and the civil authority, this meant major change. As a consequence, there evolved a situation where the supremacy of the military authorities in purely military matters had been diminished. This was because the minister now became the final arbiter in cases where the officers of the official side and the enlisted personnel could not agree. Although the noticeboard issue seems in retrospect to be a minor or even petty argument, the reality is that issues such as competence, professionalism, supremacy of decision-making and the nature and shape of civil–military relations were about to change.

It was against this background that the Chief of Staff and the General Staff felt obliged to adopt a firm position. In a broader question, if one genuinely felt that the interests of the State were at risk, was there a moral obligation to do as much as one could to prevent events or developments that might worsen the situation? In the days prior to the calls for the right of association, the General Staff had been frustrated by their inability to convince the Department of the need to improve pay. In some respects, this was easier to swallow: after all the Department, on behalf of the government, would claim exclusive competency in the area of public finances and pay. The chief's arguments at the time may have included purely military considerations such as morale, but superior competence in the area of public finance would place the Department in the dominant position for that debate. What hurt the most about the issue of the noticeboards was that the Department were arbitrating in an area that the chief believed was exclusively military, and so his position should have been the dominant one. But that was not how it was unfolding. If the chief and his staff felt a wind of change, they were correct: the absolutism of previous relations between subordinates and superiors was about to change. Janowitz suggests that changes in the style and type of military command can be altered in light of change, particularly technological change. Some of what he holds may have relevance in the new environment of there being representative bodies in the Defence Forces. He suggests that: 'Military authority must shift from reliance on practices based on domination to a wider utilisation of manipulation. Traditional or ascriptive authority relies heavily on domination, while manipulation is more appropriate for authority based on achievement.'[19]

His description of dominant authority certainly fits into the model usually found in the army. In previous times, the case of noticeboards or any other issue on which a superior declared a position would be deemed to be an instruction, an order to follow. Now for the first time such instructions or stated desires were to be challenged by virtue of the presence of a new forum in which matters were to be debated and negotiated. In this sense the arrival of the representative associations may have altered the type of authority that had been utilised up to then. Unfortunately, as can been seen in the military position, such changes were seen more as a diminution of authority rather than a change in type of authority. The difficulty with this view was that it was not in line with government or departmental thinking. In the civilian side of the Department, the whole question of engaging with the associations appeared to be approached from an industrial-relations perspective. In the initial approaches made by government to the representative associations, the emissary was Dr Brian Hillery, a Professor at University College Dublin, lecturing in the field of industrial relations. This gives some indication of how the government categorised the army. The chief was very clear in his letter that there was no place for comparison to An Gardaí or industrial-relations-type relationships in the military:

> There is a fundamental difference between the role, function, organi-sation and modus operandi of the Defence Forces and the Gardaí. Comparing the two forces in terms of the scope of representation or other aspects of association is invalid. The general application of trade union and industrial relations principles and practices to military repre-sentative associations is, in the military view, equally invalid.[20]

These different perspectives caused difficulties. In a simplistic sense, the 'official side' that would in the future negotiate with the associations was to comprise of members of the military branch and the civilian branch. If both these groups who were on the same side had different views about the fundamental nature of what they were supposed to be doing there, it couldn't but lead to difficulties. One of the tenets of successful negotiations is the requirement to have a unified party at the table. In the ground-breaking environment of

creating a new system without any previous precedent, and in regard
to a field that was State-sensitive, every inflection, tone and interpretation could be fraught with misunderstanding. To begin with, some
of the relationships lacked the sort of trust that could only develop
in the fullness of time. There were also suspicions about motive and
intent, and very real fears about State security among senior military
chiefs. There was also a sense of deep frustration felt about what
PDFORRA claimed was years of neglect. These all added to a variety
of challenges that had to be surmounted before businesslike work
could be effectively conducted at the negotiating table. The series
of first discussions and the potency of arguments regarding issues
such as the noticeboards reflected this mix. There was a real belief,
outlined by the Chief of Staff, that the very basis upon which military
command operated was to be undermined. The fact that this did not
transpire subsequently would have provided little comfort to a force
that, in the 1980s, was contending with internal security threats from
subversive organisations north and south of the border with Northern
Ireland. It would ordinarily be the case that the military maintained
exclusive competence in assessing the military threat despite the fact
that deployments were usually in response to requests for aid to the
civil power. The military would have felt that, in the particular security
environment of the time, there was a real security threat. If the army
were to aid the civil power with their military expertise, with what
Huntington describes as their application of violence, it is understandable there would be fears regarding the undermining of the exercise
of command and discipline in the force. It is very evident from the
aforementioned letter that there was frustration among the military
authorities, who sincerely believed they were being undermined not
just in the exercise of their roles but also in their wider responsibilities
to the security of the State. When it was agreed to advance the items
under discussion for future meetings, the issue of rank and uniform
was set aside in order for other matters to be addressed.

The first formal discussions had been set up to decide on the new
regulations that would effectively become the basis on which the associations would operate. These were to be denoted as Defence Force
Regulation S6 or DFR S6. They would also provide the necessary
restrictions required to maintain the security of the State, while at
the same time allowing for the meaningful pursuit of claims by representatives. Given that the military authorities were opposed to the

introduction of representative bodies in the first place, perhaps it was inevitable that difficulties would emerge, but, as can be seen by the foregoing, many fundamental principles had to be discussed.

Once the issue of rank and uniform had been temporarily set aside, the focus returned to the operating parameters and the necessity of agreeing regulations and arrangements. However, during these discussions, a number of issues in which the representative side had a keen interest emerged. Although the associations were not fully up and operating within the new regulations, these issues would be typically found under any new scheme. They included matters such as the implementation of the Gleeson Commission report and the introduction a new Health and Safety at Work Act. The discussions forum on regulations provided an opportunity for the association to make representations on behalf of their members. And although the regulations were not yet signed and the new associations not yet legally established, the Department of Defence accepted the representative side tabling proposals on these matters. This did not mean that they conceded any points or automatically agreed with what was being said, but the fact that they were prepared to consider them marked the beginning of a new relationship between members of the military and the operative organs of the State. Though it may not have been perceived in those terms at the time, the fact was that matters that were of concern to ordinary soldiers could be raised and dealt with by their representatives at the highest level of the civil authority.

9

New Statutory Engagement and Residual Matters

In a prime example, the Gleeson Commission report had made certain recommendations on the payment of security duty allowance (SDA). Prior to the report, SDA was paid for a listed number of duties performed by military personnel in a rostered arrangement. The type of activity and the duration of duties that attracted SDA varied greatly across the Defence Forces. Proposals had been made by the NCOs team that additional allowances for duties should be time-based. They had pointed out anomalies whereby some duties only required the presence of an individual for a couple of hours, and in such cases this person received the same rate of SDA as a soldier who performed a twenty-four-hour guard duty. They proposed that payment be made based on time rather than military classification. The Gleeson report recommended this new system; however, there were a very small number of personnel who were then in receipt of the allowance and would now suffer a loss under the new arrangement. The representatives involved in the discussions raised this issue and pointed out that they should be consulted on how this recommendation was to be implemented. The immediate response of the Department was that this was a government directive and they were set to implement it. The representative side felt obliged to appeal to the Minister for Defence,' stating that people were about to lose money as a result of the implementation by the Department of Defence of the Gleeson report, the original intention of which was to improve pay, not diminish it. When eventually the new rates were published, the memorandum contained an important note:

Following the introduction of the new system of SDA any serving non-commissioned personnel who wish to continue to receive payment of SDA under the old system will be permitted to opt accordingly as a once off arrangement. The old rates will be frozen at their current level on a 'mark time' basis by reference to the rates under the new scheme.[1]

This proved to be one of the first practical representations made by the association on behalf of its membership. Although they would have seen this as a natural element of representing their members, the military authorities had very different views on the nature of what representation meant. Their interpretation of what the function of the association should be was connected to the statutory description of the association. The adjutant general outlined the views of the military and provided a memo from the office of the deputy judge advocate general (DJAG):

> … the reservations of the General Staff have, if anything, deepened and further considerations relating to the authorisation of 'other activities' of representative associations are contained in a memorandum prepared by the DJAG. The General Staff request that the attorney general be invited to review these considerations and to offer a formal opinion on the general advisability of including within a regulation, provisions dealing with 'other activities of an association' as proposed in the current draft of DFR S6.[2]

In the memorandum attached to the letter, the DJAG appears to suggest that the activities of the association be confined to the very narrow function of just making representations on behalf of its members:

> The statutory purpose of the association is that of representing members and not for the actual provision of services and benefits to the Defence Forces or a number of members thereof who may also be members of associations. The Minister's regulating power is limited to specifying the matters which are to be subject to representation and other matters which are 'ancillary, subsidiary and connected' with the establishment of representative associations … it appears therefore that it is not within the regulation making power of the Minister to expressly authorise activities on the part of the association which do not form part of the statutory purpose of such associations.[3]

The contents appear to attempt to row back on the general intention of
the activities of the association as understood by most people involved,
despite the fact that by December of 1990 the two parties had been
in discussion for over four-and-a-half months, in the course of which
they had participated in twenty-two formal meetings and numerous
informal talks. This position of the General Staff indicated an interpretation that the representative body should be confined to articulating the
views of their members in certain matters such as pay and remuneration.
A legalistic argument was made that suggested that the Defence Act,
1954 (the principal Act) already catered for the provision in DFR Q11
of schemes the object of which was to 'promote the moral, social and
material welfare of NCOs and privates', which in turn is inseparable
from legal duties and obligations relating to the maintenance, command
constitution and organisation of the Defence Forces. In tying these two
functions together, it could be argued that associations engaging in such
schemes were engaging in activities which the 1990 Act prohibited.
The point was made that:

> ... it is hardly consistent on the one hand for the Minister to engage in
> six months of consultations regarding the precise functions and proce-
> dures of an association and then on the other hand to give 'carte blanche'
> to the same association in respect of other activities which would not
> be the subject of supervision and safeguards otherwise required by the
> Minister for the good of the Defence Forces and the common good.[4]

The response of the Department reflected the more general view that
had prevailed around the table and in the public domain:

> ... If the difficulties now outlined as being in the way of participation by
> the associations in welfare activities are sustainable, those difficulties will,
> I consider, have to be overcome and the associations must be accorded
> a meaningful role; involvement in this area was seen as the acceptable
> face of association activities from an early stage – long before we came
> to terms with the substantial role which they are now being given.
> (Incidentally the draft regulation as presented to the elected representa-
> tives was apparently, as I understand it, an agreed official draft).[5]

This was another very firm example of a significant alteration in the
conduct of civil–military relations. The military authority's reservations

and their solid belief in the professional and legal folly of the emerging circumstances were not taken into account. The third party, in the form of the representative association, had in some respects diminished the position of the military in being the absolute authority on all military-related matters. This most certainly represented a diminution of influence and a strengthening of the supremacy of the civil power in the relationship between the State and its army. Another debate that became a matter of contention had to do with the provision of permission to have association meetings outside of military establishments. While members of the forces were coming together to discuss the whole idea of representation in the summer of 1989, large meetings of many soldiers had taken place in several locations around the country. Once, in a sports hall in Cork, a journalist had made her way into the gathering to listen to what was being said, but she was asked to leave. Despite the fact that the associations were now on the brink of coming into statutory existence, the military still had significant reservations regarding the gathering of soldiers outside barracks. While there was no objection to meetings of elected representatives outside barracks, the Chief of Staff stated that the General Staff were totally opposed to meetings of the general membership. He outlined many possible negative consequences that might come from this, including agitation in concert with trade-union groups or subversives, marches on the Dáil, infiltration by the media and the erosion of good order and discipline.[6]

Again, the civil authority did not concede to the recommendations of the military. In a note from the minister to the secretary of the department, copied to the Chief of Staff, it was made clear that the minister had considered the matter but was not prepared to entirely restrict meetings in the fashion requested by the army:

> Following consideration of the issues involved I have come to the conclusion that some arrangement should be worked out to permit meetings outside barracks by members of the association – over and above meetings of elected representatives as already agreed. I am aware of the potential problems which are visualised, but consider that it should be possible to provide for appropriate controls and safeguards.[7]

Proposals were presented to the representative side. An arrangement was agreed that enabled numerous meetings to take place, but some of these were only possible with the consent of the minister. The annual general meeting of the association takes place now every year and delegates numbering in excess of 250 gather in civilian attire. These meetings, since their inception, have been well organised and free from any of the scenarios presented by the chief in 1990. Despite the fact that his concerns seemed to have been about the possible consequences of outside meetings, the case made by the deputy adjutant general had been grounded more in the legal concept of command and control. He made the point that, regardless of the sort of activities in which the representative associations may eventually be engaged, their statutory existence could not be considered in isolation:

> When advancing reasons for restricting members of the representative associations from meeting as such outside military installations it must be borne in mind that while the Defence Act 1990 is the only act to provide for representation, it cannot be separated from the other Defence Acts in terms of its interpretation … Any activity of the association must be viewed in light of the role of the Defence Forces in the security of the State and the necessity in the furtherance of that role for the maintenance and good order, discipline and morale in the Defence Forces.[8]

The views expressed were similar to those that had arisen regarding the wearing of uniform. Neither the legalistic nor the purely militaristic arguments fully won the day, and when the discussion forum eventually agreed on a schedule to enable certain types of meetings of the association to take place there were elements of it that contravened the advice of the military. But the association did not have it all its own way either. There were to be certain restrictions, for example on the number of general meetings of the membership in barracks.

Before the last meeting of the negotiating groups had been held, the representative-side team met with the Minister for Defence and the Chief of Staff. At Dáil Eireann, on 24 April 1991, the Minister for Defence, the Secretary General of the department and the Chief of Staff met with me, CS Richard Dillon, CS Richard Condron and Sgt Harry Higgins. They were welcomed by the minister who 'expressed optimism for the future', and the Chief of Staff used the opportunity to state that he was 'very happy with the responsible attitude being adopted by PDFORRA and wished to thank them for the manner in which they were conducting their business'.[9] Numerous issues were discussed, the first of which was a requested meeting between the minister and the national executive. It was agreed that it should take place when the regulation was being signed. A serious issue regarding the Defence Force Widows' and Orphans' Pension Scheme was tabled by the representative side regarding their members' ability to opt into or out of the scheme, which had become mandatory from 1985. The minister thought that there might be a knock-on effect to other parts of the public service if any amendments were made. There was a pressing concern of the representative side regarding the provision of deductions of subscription at source for soldiers who wished to pay their association dues directly from their pay. The minister agreed to ensure the processing of this scheme within three or four weeks of the forms being submitted. This was a very working-style meeting between the minister and the representatives, and it established a good rapport for future relationships. Meanwhile, the business of finalising the broader negotiations continued. By late April of 1991 a formula had been almost agreed and was appended to the DFR S6. Meetings between committees of the associations were to be facilitated with suitable accommodation within barracks subject to the exigencies of the service. Meetings outside barracks were also permitted but not in uniform. The general meeting of the membership in barracks, though quite restrictive, was also agreed. Most types of meetings were specified, but there was a general clause that enabled the association, with the minister's permission, to organise meetings not specified in the list below:

a) An annual delegate conference
b) A meeting of the national executive
c) A meeting of command-level committee
d) A meeting of barracks-level committee
e) Meetings at barracks level involving no more than 50 per cent of the personnel in the barracks or post may be held with the permission of the officer commanding the barracks or post concerned.

Meetings other than those referred to at (a), (b), (c), (d) and (e) above shall not be held without the permission of the minister – the arrangements in this regard to be agreed between the minister and the association.[10]

From this set of discussions, structured arrangements were being put in place to enable the serving military personnel of the State to assemble and conduct the business of their associations.

This development displayed a measure of trust extended by the civilian government to a section of the military, despite the hierarchy having reservations. The finalising of the new regulation that would provide for the first representative bodies in the Irish armed forces was now virtually complete. The last matters to be negotiated and agreed for inclusion in the new statutory provisions were the agreed arrangements for funding, the deductions at source facility, the release on secondment of members of the national executive and a rewording of a provision to allow representative matters be raised by the association in respect of issues that might arise while personnel were serving overseas: 'Matters arising on overseas service which come within the areas specified in the second schedule to DFR S6 shall be dealt with at a National Level. Assistance may also be given in the dissemination of information in regard to representative matters to troops serving overseas.'[11]

The last meeting to conclude the first formal discussions took place on 2 May 1991, almost a year after they had first begun. Nobody could have foreseen the complexity of discussions that were held, for what some perceived as a simple exercise to authenticate an existing organisation and place it on a statutory footing. One huge effect of these discussions had been to raise many fundamental issues that went to the heart of military philosophy on service and duty. They questioned the extent to which rank and military service extended or intruded into the family and social life of soldiers. They challenged the accepted concepts regarding the exercise of command and discipline. They revealed the extent to which the internal security of Ireland featured in the thinking of those who initially opposed the idea of representative associations for the armed forces. Seemingly intractable problems had been resolved between bitter opponents. But like in most negotiations, there was a set of conclusions with no parties getting everything they wanted and all getting enough to proceed and endeavour to initiate a new way of conducting business for the betterment of everybody. At the thirty-sixth meeting of the group held in DFHQ in Dublin on Thursday 2 May 1991, the representative side requested their closing statement be reflected in the minute: 'As discussion and negotiation on Defence Force Regulations S6 were now completed they wished to record their congratulations to all concerned on the departmental side for the time and effort expended on the making of the regulations.'[12]

The departmental side also expressed thanks to the representative side for their help and co-operation during the discussions. It was noted that the following task would be the drawing-up of the Conciliation and Arbitration Scheme, or the C&A scheme as it would become known.

CONCILIATION AND ARBITRATION

After agreement had been reached on the formulation of the regulations that would take effect when the Defence Amendment Act, 1990 was enacted, the first priority was to introduce a Conciliation and Arbitration Scheme similar to many that operated in the public service and for An Garda Síochána. 'New arrangements' were also negotiated and agreed to provide practical direction in the day-to-day operation of the schemes at both military and national levels.

Under the new agreed arrangements for PDFORRA, elected representatives from among the enlisted ranks, chosen by secret ballot, would form committees at three levels of command – barracks level, brigade or command level and national or DFHQ level. These arrangements reflect the military chain of command and seek to highlight and resolve issues that come within the scope of representation at the lowest possible level. In negotiations that take place at these levels, there is the option of referring unsatisfactory outcomes upwards to a higher authority. So far these arrangements are not too dissimilar to the purely military system that was in place previously. There was, and still is, an option whereby a soldier may bring any matter to the attention of any superior at any level of the Defence Forces, provided that the addressee was preceded by all those in the various levels of command beneath. What is different in the agreed arrangements is that individuals do not make a case. PDFORRA pursue the principle of a case in a collective way. This methodology provides recourse to the higher civil authority. This is one of the ways in which the representative bodies give weight to the hierarchy of civil over military authority. Any issue begun at any level in the Defence Forces can now find itself the subject of consideration by the civil authority, which may exercise its right to overrule a decision arrived at by the military authority. In addition, there is a formal C&A scheme that in Ireland operates for the wider public service. This scheme is the negotiating forum where elected representatives of the soldiers deal directly with the representatives of the various State departments, but most importantly with the Department of Finance. The scheme has two features that would have been undesirable to the military authorities in the early 1990s. Firstly, it has a higher status than that of the senior military-authority level at Defence Force Headquarters; secondly, it is very much operated in the spirit of best 'industrial relations' practice and procedure. Despite reservations that may have been there at the time of the scheme's inception, there is now no doubt that the military authorities accept the manner of its operation.

RESIDUAL MATTERS ARISING

The emergence of the statutory representative association PDFORRA for the enlisted personnel came about as a result of a confluence of events, perspectives, actions and reactions of numerous interested parties that have been outlined in previous chapters. As was stated by Col Brian O'Keefe, prior to the introduction of the Defence Amendment Act, 1990, officers had never particularly seen representation as a means of resolving the issues of pay and conditions in the Defence Forces. The Representative Association for Commissioned Officers (RACO) was a feature of the new legislation that hadn't been sought by serving officers. Nevertheless, the government insisted on it and brought it formally into existence under the legislation. This is not to say that officers did not have grievances like the enlisted personnel, but their perceived resolution of these issues was very different to the resolution proposed by those who felt representation was the solution. Apart from the paternal concern for the welfare of their soldiers and the frustration they felt at their incapacity to do anything about it, officers did have their own problems with pay and conditions of service. During the 1980s it was felt by many of them that their pay and allowances had fallen behind those of others sections of the public service. When the initial announcement of 10 and 12½ per cent increases was made in December 1988, this was greeted with enthusiasm by officers. They believed that the special relationship of loyalty and service to the government had stood to them and had been taken into consideration in the granting of this unique award. When it emerged that the increase was not specific to the army but was to be part of a general increase across the public service and paid to everybody, officers everywhere were not only very disappointed but they felt they had been let down. Colonel Brian O'Keefe recalls: 'Officers felt absolute betrayal by the government, we were devastated. We had a tradition of complete and absolute loyalty, but loyalty is a two-way street. We expected perhaps naively that they would look after us.'[13]

The betrayal that officers felt was articulated in meetings held at command level, during which the same GOCs that had advised of an impending 'special pay award' now had to brief their officers that this was not the case. 'The exchanges were forthright and robust. People were annoyed and angry. They made known their views to the GOC'.[14]

Coincidently, while NASA were organising in Ireland, a very similar situation arose in Spain in 1989 with spouses of soldiers there establishing a campaign to seek better conditions for their partners in the military. The motivation of the Spanish women arose for different reasons, but nevertheless the mode of their campaign and the eventual calls for the right of association bore direct similarities to what had happened in Ireland. As was the case in Ireland, EUROMIL were contacted and the Spanish women received assistance and advice that culminated in them persuading their husbands that the right of association had to be pursued. I and other representatives of PDFORRA met the Spanish wives and soldiers at EUROMIL meetings across Europe and visited Spain. We shared with them our recent experiences from Ireland and offered advice on how best to approach their campaign. Knowledge of the approach that had been taken by Irish women and soldiers influenced the approach that the Spanish took to their perceived problems. The original initiatives by Spanish personnel, prompted by an internal grievance, led to the broadening of their efforts to address that grievance beyond the Spanish Army and Spain. It was the negative response they received that brought the argument further afield and onto the international stage. The same could be said about Ireland, and as former Company Sergeant Richard Condron, Commander Eoin McNamara and Lt General Gerry McMahon have suggested, had things been done better, had there been a more meaningful response to issues that were a source of grievance, maybe representation would not have evolved at all.

Civil–military relations have traditionally concerned themselves primarily with the special relationship that exists between the armed forces of a State and its civilian leadership. It is acknowledged by most that the relationship is a skewed one in the sense that every country assumes the need for the finality of the application of violence in its own defence or interests. The ultimate capacity of the army to deliver that force makes it theoretically capable of turning that violence on the government and becoming a threat to it and to the State it serves. In a sense it is probably understandable that an army or any identifiable element of it which challenges the government is in some way also a threat. Huntington, Finer and others speculate on the propensity, the motivation, the capacity and likelihood of military intervention in one armed force or another or in one type of a society or another.

That the Irish Government were subjected to a type of military intervention as currently defined is certain. This was preceded by normal civilian democratic intervention in the form of protests and lobbying of NASA. Their members were civilians, their actions were legitimate and, although novel because they were representing complaints about an organisation usually closed to wider society, their activities in themselves and the strategies they employed were nothing new. Whether NASA was a force in itself highlighting the inequities that impacted on army family life or simply the catalyst that prompted the pursuit of the right of association, or both, is an interesting aside. In any event they were a critical motivation for the soldiers themselves to take some form of action. But until soldiers did something themselves, military intervention could be said not to have taken place. Despite the existence and high profile of the activities of NASA, it was the first meeting of concerned soldiers to speak about what could be done that marked the beginning of military intervention in Ireland in 1988.

Upstanding, reputable and loyal soldiers such as Dick Dillon and Michael Murphy who first spoke about the need for a representative association were never going to be a threat to the security of the State, and neither of them would have abided or tolerated anybody or any actions that were. Nevertheless, the association that they helped to found was, for a long time, perceived as a threat, as evidenced by the written views of the General Staff, revealed in previous chapters.

Huntington defined the constituent parts of national security and the role of civil–military relations as being the principal components of military-security policy. It has been shown now that Ireland's civil–military relations underwent massive change as a result of the introduction of representative associations. Although these associations are excluded from the basic operational decision-making regarding where and when the military should be deployed, claims in relation to pay and allowances do impact on what Huntington termed 'the fundamental question of the proportion of State resources devoted to military needs'. In addition, the emergence of the associations raised concerns regarding internal security policy and, in at least one instance, the civil authority insisted on permission being given to the holding of meetings that the military authorities would have deemed a threat. Huntington's assertion that the status of an officer equates to that of a civilian profession such as surgeon is somewhat weakened by the exposition of the successful initiative taken by enlisted personnel in Ireland to address a matter that had clearly impacted on morale in the forces. Officers had tried and failed to address these issues and were led by enlisted personnel in this regard.

The army hierarchy in Ireland found itself in a situation where many of its decisions would eventually become subject to the need for agreement or consultation, largely as a result of their refusal to engage on a consultative level with their own soldiers even when there was an unique opportunity to do so (when they were asked to establish representative structures). This does not detract from the fact that they endeavoured in vain to improve the pay and conditions of their subordinates at a time when it was perceived by Defence Force personnel and their families that their pay and conditions were deteriorating.

Civil–military relations in Ireland were in a state of erosion in the late 1980s as evidenced by a number of factors outlined in this book. Among them, the frustration reportedly experienced by the incumbent Chief of Staff who felt that no one was listening to him regarding problems in the Defence Forces; the view held by senior personnel in the Department of Defence that the Chief of Staff was encouraging soldiers to be incensed by their situation, which led to political criticism and difficulties for the government; the dissatisfaction of the General Staff with the minister for defence and their suggestion that he was engaging in possible illegal initiatives regarding the introduction of elements of the representative structures and activities.

To what extent any members of the Irish officer corps influenced any part of the intervention and emergence of PDFORRA has yet to be revealed. No evidence has yet come to light. As has been shown, many officers agreed with the grievances articulated by NASA and were themselves frustrated by the perceived intransigence of the government in relation to pay and conditions, but the corporate officer body never intervened as a group to exert collective opinion or will upon the government. By Huntington's criteria, their professionalism would have made it unlikely anyway. They participated gladly in the Gleeson Commission submission teams and represented, as best as they could, the views of the corps in relation to pay and conditions, and although the commission could be said to have been brought about by intervention, participation in it was strictly in compliance with military and government wishes. It seems from this that the enlisted personnel of Ireland were involved in a form of intervention that excluded the officer corps, but contrary to Huntington's expectations they in fact led the officers in what became a very positive development for the overall welfare of the Irish Defence Forces. The developments that brought about change in civil–military relations in Ireland were led by enlisted personnel who have not generally been considered as having a role in the study of civil–military relations.

The regulation of the representative associations under the Irish Defence Amendment Act, 1990 provides a formal means in which members of the 'military' may interact with the government of the State at numerous levels. It is a means outside of the normal military 'chain of command' that establishes a relationship on matters other than the application of State violence. Up to now, civil–military relations had regularly considered the crucial relationship between the civil authority and the military body in terms of the latter's capacity or propensity for armed intervention or the threat of it. In the traditional coup d'état, soldiers take up arms against a government whom they believe are acting against their interests or the interests of the State. In Ireland the military's professional ability to access and use arms never emerged as a consideration in the pursuit of the right to associate. As has been outlined, it was always about what they considered to be a constitutional right. The fact that a constitutional case was initiated indicates that the ultimate weapon was the judicial process, not the use of weapons.

It has also been shown that the political persuasion, democratic lobbying and electoral endeavours by NASA achieved much and prompted a swift response by a new government, but in the case of representation only to the level of internal structures. These fell short of the demands of the soldiers who sought full independent representative associations. The imminent cancellation of what the government saw as 'unregulated elections' of a large body of military personnel and the withdrawal of a constitutional High Court case against the State were the concessions won by the government on the night of the Ashling Hotel agreement. In return, the soldiers got what they had been seeking all along.

The workings of the representative associations by their very nature defuse the propensity to intervene with force of arms. By way of traditional negotiation, matters that could develop into justification for intervention in some countries are aired and dealt with in a non-violent and non-threatening way. Even in situations where the officer body or enlisted ranks deem the actions of the government not to be in the interests of the State, there is a means to articulate those views and at least have them heard and perhaps acted upon.

The operation of formal representative bodies in Ireland underpins a relationship between the civil and the military which deliberately sets aside any propensity of violent intervention and confers a 'civilian' or 'democratic' identity on the soldier. The 'military' hitherto seen as a corporate entity has been recognised as having two dimensions, that of the soldier and that of the citizen. The existence of these associations gives daily weight to the fact that the relationship between the civil and military authorities is also hierarchal with the civil authority being the final arbiter. In this sense, countries that fear what the organisation of soldiers could lead to should take note.

The struggle to bring this state of affairs about included 'intervention' by Irish military personnel. Their very existence and operation separate and acknowledge a new perspective on civil–military relations. The military side of the equation can now be separated and seen to comprise of the usual military corporate identity plus the new social or industrial-relations identity that was thought by many to be incompatible with the exercise of command and discipline. The representative body for officers, RACO, and many individual officers including the Chief of Staff interviewed in Ireland during research for this book indicate that the associations have improved the exercise of command and the general conditions in the service. The style of 'democratic' intervention in Ireland such as the lobbying of politicians, the electioneering of the NASA group and the taking of the court case all demonstrate a type of 'intervention' that is primarily peaceful and within the bounds of the law. Even the instance when the association's public-relations officer breached military regulations by speaking to the media there was a constitutional doubt about whether such action breached the actual law of the land, and the Irish High Court was willing to hear it.

The needs of any modern army to manage complex organisational requirements such as procurement, technology, human-resource management and the required application of violence have now been added to by the advent of associations whose presence alter the relationship between the corporate affairs of the army and those of the civil authority. Decisions which had, in the past, been made solely by the army regarding the management of their personnel and their conditions of service can now be subject to alteration or rejection by a government. One of the areas that seems to be somewhat neglected in the consideration of civil–military relations is the fact that soldiers do have an outside life beyond the realm of the army. The fact that in many countries they are now fully integrated into mainstream society with full access to the political machinery of a country has not been taken into consideration.

There was clearly military intervention in politics in Ireland in the 1980s. It was not perpetrated by the military hierarchy, however, and this in itself is significant. The briefing by off-duty personnel of opposition-party spokesmen in Dáil Eireann itself testifies to that. In fact, representatives later said that they would see such off-duty intervention as part of their 'non-military' existence. Perhaps it was 'civilianised' intervention rather than military. New perspectives on what constitutes military intervention are needed. The soldier cannot continue to be seen as a single-faceted entity, a political eunuch. In the same way that the representative associations in the Irish armed forces have managed to separate the security issues from the non-security issues, so too can military intervention in the traditional sense be separated from legitimate political activity. If a soldier exercises his or her right to vote, they are already engaged in politics. Consideration should be extended to other non-threatening forms of political engagement. Certainly, if the perspective of the General Staff in the 1980s were to be considered, there would be no such thing as a civilian dimension to a soldier's life and therefore no legitimate entitlement to engage at any level of the political process other than by exercising the franchise to vote. Political intervention of enlisted personnel as seen in Ireland did not threaten civil–military relations. In some ways it became a safe staging area for traditional rivalries between the military hierarchy and the civil authority, but both sides gained and lost some of the issues that emerged and their respective power or hold over the majority of those serving was lessened. It changed the context of those relations but could not be said to have damaged them.

Military intervention can often be precipitated by a perception of poor pay and conditions or circumstances in which soldiers feel aggrieved at the civil authority. In such circumstances, representative associations certainly provide a mechanism for channelling those grievances into negotiation, and while other reasons for intervention may not be prevented by their existence there are a least some cases in which they can lessen the propensity for intervention and defuse an emerging deterioration of security.

As has been outlined, there have been incidences of military intervention in Ireland at the time of the so-called Curragh and 1924 mutinies. Neither of these events ranks with the emergence of representative associations with regard to the long-term impact on the structural operation of civil–military relations in Ireland. In the case of the former, there was an impediment created by the actions or inactions of the soldiers on a single albeit important military operation. In the second instance, in 1924, there was an important long-term effect that settled the hierarchy of the civil–military relationship, not as a result of the intervention of disgruntled military personnel but thanks to the voluntary extrication of Mulcahy, which settled the matter and preserved the integrity of the rest of the force. The emergence of the representative associations resulted in a fundamental change in the conduct of civil–military relations in Ireland. Among other results, new legislation was enacted, new formal institutions of negotiation were put in place, a new statutory presence was created in many arenas of Defence policy, the exercise of constitutional rights for military personnel was enabled and a powerful mechanism for the diffusion of conflict came into being.

These events also gave substance to the European resolutions and beliefs that soldiers are citizens in uniform and that in peacetime they should be afforded the same democratic rights they are expected to defend in times of conflict. The European Organisation of Military Associations helped clarify the aims of the Irish personnel involved in the 1980s, and they too have gained from their exposure to the Irish case. The Irish influenced other struggles, such as those described in Spain, emphasising that the pursuit of democratic rights in a peaceful way for a representative association was the key to resolving their particular problems.

What finally changed the government's mind and prompted them to eventually come to meet and speak to the ad hoc PDFORRA in March 1990 was not previously admitted. The electoral activity of

NASA certainly had a major influence in the introduction by the new government in mid-1989 of the Gleeson Commission and an announcement regarding representative structures, but despite this, for eight months after the announcements there was no move either to speak or to engage with the body calling itself PDFORRA, and in any event the chief was instructed to propose his own. In terms of the timing of the Ashling Hotel meeting, contact was made in the very narrow timeframe between the onset of the constitutional case that was then in the High Court, and the government timeline for the introduction of the new legislation. It is significant that, having granted most of what the representatives had asked for, the only request the government made that night was that the association elections be abandoned and the court case be 'discontinued'.

Ordinary soldiers during this period in Ireland sought to influence government policy. They succeeded, but not under the threat of arms. They relied instead on democratic political persuasion. The women's group and the very real mandate they achieved, the use of the open political system and the independent judicial system may only be adjudged as military intervention because soldiers participated in it. This does not take account of the civilian dimension of the soldier. If that were recognised, the activities themselves could hardly be construed as either threatening or damaging to society. The actions of members of the armed forces in Ireland during the struggle for and the emergence of representative bodies enhanced democracy rather than threatened it.

In considering the actions of soldiers in the British and Irish 'mutinies' in 1914 and 1924 in the context of what PDFORRA did, it can be clearly seen that the methodology of the army wives and the founding members of PDFORRA was not only less threatening to the State, but achieved far more in terms of the interests of the soldiers themselves. Unlike in the previous incidents, where the intention of the State and the safety of its government were inhibited, in the late 1980s Irish soldiers, despite the conservative reservations of the officer body, proved themselves worthy of trust and co-operation.

Huntington's preoccupation with the professionalism of the officer corps and his dismissal of enlisted ranks in the consideration of civil–military relations can be now seen as a serious omission in his work, characterised by the events and explanations of what happened in Ireland. NCOs, whose professionalism he did not consider, did not just lead events in Ireland but also ensured, by their attitudes and ethos, that the State would never be under threat either from force of arms or withdrawal of services. This marks a level of professionalism and loyalty to the State that is only superseded by the actuality of NCOs providing leadership and innovation in proffering a solution to the problems of pay and allowances that the military authorities had been grappling with for many years without success. Indeed, the acquisition of the 'right of association' for officers in Ireland only came about as a result of NCOs and their wives taking on the institutions of the State in the most democratic way possible. The subordinates led the superiors, and, in this field at least, rank markings, contrived 'tradition' and assumed professionalism by virtue of rank did not count for much. It was the courage, action, the risks, the organisational ability and the persuasiveness of enlisted personnel that resulted in great strides being made in Ireland for all military personnel in a way that was protective of democracy and the public safety it expects. This new development in the area of civil–military relations in Ireland may provide a framework from which to examine whether the consequent structures would be acceptable or would work for other armies in other countries.

Despite the initial robust resistance of the Irish government and the Army hierarchy, PDFORRA was established officially on 6 May 1991 under the Defence Amendment Act of 1990 and the newly negoti- ated Defence Force Regulation DFR S6. Since then their elected representatives have continued to independently negotiate better pay, conditions and human rights for their members, the enlisted personnel of the Irish Defence Forces. I was elected as their first General Secretary.

Appendix 1

Letter of Proposal to Form PDFORRA

TO   Minister for Defence

THROUGH Chief of Staff

SUBJECT   Proposed Formation Of The Permanent Defence Forces
                 "Other Ranks" Representative Association

Sir,

1. I No. _____ Rank _____ Name _____
of _____ am contemplating together with other
members of the Permanent Defence Forces the formation of a Representative Associati
in accordance with the enclosed Draft Constitution, Objects and Rules.

2. I have been advised that there is not any legal (whether Military or Civilian) barr
to the formation of such an Association.

3. I believe the Association would command the support of the overwhelming majority of
the "Other Ranks", members of the Permanent Defence Forces, however prior to taking
any steps towards the formation of such an Association, I would be anxious to recei
your views. I would of course be willing to consider any alterations which may see
to you to be appropriate.

4. I am satisfied that the formation of such an Association would be to the benefit of
the Permanent Defence Forces as a whole and would contribute substantially to the
enchancement of the welfare and morale of its members.

5. While I appreciate that the enclosed Draft will require consideration, I would be
greatly obliged for an early acknowledgement.

_____ Signed.

Source: PDFORRA Archive, Head Office, Benburb Street, Dublin.

Appendix 2

Letter from Chief of Staff to All Ranks

**Office of the Chief of Staff,
Army Headquarters,
Parkgate,
Dublin 8.**

27th July, 1989

<u>TO EACH OFFICER, NON COMMISSIONED OFFICER AND PRIVATE
IN THE DEFENCE FORCES</u>

Attached to this letter is a copy of the Government Statement
establishing an Independent Commission on Pay and Conditions of
Service in the Defence Forces. I consider that this is a major
step forward for the Defence Forces and one which will lead to a
fair and just resolution of our problems in these matters.

As you will see from the document, I have been instructed by
An Tanaiste and Minister for Defence to establish a new system in
the Defence Forces for consultation and information on Pay and
Conditions of Privates, Non Commissioned Officers and Officers.
This will ensure that your views at Unit level will be taken into
account on an ongoing basis.

I strongly recommend this new system. I am confident that with your
participation and support these new arrangements will work to the
satisfaction of all ranks, thereby rendering your membership of any
other organisation unnecessary and divisive.

T.M. O'NEILL
LIEUTENANT GENERAL
CHIEF OF STAFF

<u>Copy:-</u> Each serving member

Source: PDFORRA Archive, Head Office, Benburb Street, Dublin.

Appendix 3

Advertisement for
Notification of Elections

Source: PDFORRA Archive, Head Office, Benburb Street, Dublin.

Appendix 4

PDFORRA's First Press Release

16/11/89

The PERMANENT DEFENCE FORCES OTHER RANKS REPRESENTATIVE ASSOCIATION (PDFORRA) was formed under article 40.6.1 of the Constitution of Ireland, on Saturday the 11th of November 1989.

The objects of the association are as follows:-

To unite and organise enlisted personnel ("other ranks") of the Permanent Defence Forces and to provide a means for the expression of their collective opinion in relation to the seeking of:-

a. The right of consultation in matters relating to pay and allowances.
b. To make recommendations for the improvement of conditions of enlisted personnel of the Permanent Defence Forces (PDF), through the already established chain of command.
c. To afford, assist and advise members on all welfare matters.
d. To promote the interests of and to strive for the raising of the educational efficiency and professional standards of enlisted personnel of the PDF.
e. To establish and administer a fund or funds for the purpose of providing assistance to members and their dependants in accordance with the Rules.
f. To organise, promote and control members' interests in an Enlisted Personnel

Source: PDFORRA Archive, Head Office, Benburb Street, Dublin.

Appendix 5

Letter from MEP Jensen Regarding PDFORRA

Kirsten JENSEN
Medlem
af Europa-Parlamentet

Den Socialdemokratiske Gruppe
i EF-Parlamentet
Thorvaldsensvej 2
DK-1998 Frederiksberg C
Tlf: 31 39 15 22; Fax: 31 39 40 30

European Parliament
Att. MEP, Barry DESMOND
79-113, rue Belliard
B-1040 Bruxelles
Belgien

7th March 1990
kj/kij

Dear Barry.

I have asked the Irish presidency about PDFORRA - an Irish solider association, its status vis-à-vis the Irish Constitution, its possibility to work unhindered and the recent imprisonment of persons affiliated to PDFORRA.

I am sorry not to have informed you at the moment I made the inquiry (19th February 1990) in order to seek your advice. I hope for your understanding and forward you a copy - in Danish - of my question to the presidency.

Best wishes,

Kirsten Jensen

Kirsten Jensen

Source: PDFORRA Archive, Head Office, Benburb Street, Dublin.

Appendix 6

List of Demands
Ashling Hotel Agreement

1. NAME OF ASSOCIATION.
   To be PDFORRA.
2. FINANCE.
   Total control of own finance raised by subscription.
3. DEDUCTIONS AT SOURCE.
   To commence from date of election, if not before.
4. ACCESS TO MEDIA.
   Fully independent. Regulation after consultation.
5. ADDILLIATION EUROMIL.
   As it will already be in place it must be approved.
6. CONCILLIATION + ARBITRATION.
   Very broad scheme necessary to offset disadvantage of no industrial action and to ensure every issue has recourse to arbitration
   and that arbitration is on demand.
7. SECONDING OF PERSONNEL.
   As with GRA, POA etc.
8. RELEASE FROM DUTIES.
   400 man days per regional co.
9. CONSULTATIVE STATUS.
   At all levels indicated in structures.
10. HEADQUARTERS.
    Financial commitment from govt, as with GRA, POA etc.
11. MEMORANDUM OF UNDERSTANDING.
    Agreed upon by elections.

All of these to be guaranteed in writing prior to ELECTIONS.

Source: PDFORRA Archive, Head Office, Benburb Street, Dublin.

Appendix 7

Signed Document of Ashling Hotel Agreement

- command level
  The GOC of the Command, the Brigade Commander and/or officers nominated by them.

- baracks level
  The OC of the barracks, Unit Commanders and/or officers nominated by them.

11. __Memorandum of Understanding__

As in the case of regulations, a memorandum of understanding may, if such is considered to be necessary, be drawn up in consultation with the representatives who emerge from the first elections.

THIS IS THE SIGNATURE OF A GOVT. DEPUTY!

Signed: Brian Hillery TD John M L

Michael Martin

22/5/90.

Source: PDFORRA Archive, Head Office, Benburb Street, Dublin.

Appendix 8

Cover Letter for
Chief of Staff Structures

Naval Base
Haulbowline
Co Cork

NSB/A.GEN/1

To Distribution:

All Members of the Naval Service and Attached Army Personnel

PROPOSED STRUCTURES WITHIN THE PERMANENT
DEFENCE FORCE FOR CONSULTATION AND
INFORMATION ON PAY AND CONDITIONS OF SERVICE

1. The briefing notes attached which have been approved by
An Tanaiste are released for the information of all members of the
Permanent Defence Force.

2. The purpose of these notes are to provide information on, and clarification of, the various aspects of the proposed representational structure.

3. Any member of the Permanent Defence Force who wishes to
comment on the proposals outlined should do so. The comments
should be forwarded through the usual channels to reach us before
19 January 1990.

JA DEASY

Captain (NS)

COMMANDING NAVAL BASE AND DOCKYARD

Cc

File

JC/CC

Source: PDFORRA Archive, Head Office, Benburb Street, Dublin.

Appendix 9

Comparative Bar Graph for Soldiers and Gardaí Gratuities

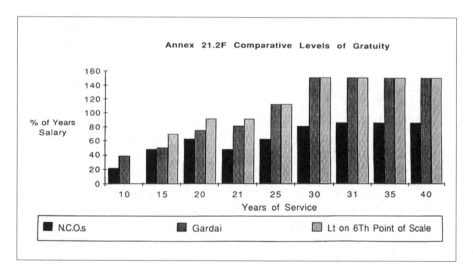

Source: Defence Forces Submission to Gleeson Commission. Dept Defence
Headquarters Newbridge, County Kildare. Copy in possession of author.

Appendix 10

Chronology of Events

February to July 1988	Formation of NASA
October 1988	Eastern Command soldiers discuss representation
December 1988	Inter-Departmental Committee report
January to June 1989	Compilation of PDFORRA constitution in Eastern Command
May 1989	First NASA press conference
4 July 1989	First letters from soldiers seeking establishment of association
28 July 1989	Government announce commission and new consultation structures
28 July 1989	Circulation of letter from Chief of Staff to all military personnel
26 August 1989	Formation of national executive of ad hoc PDFORRA
11 November 1989	Establishment of PDFORRA claiming constitutional legitimacy
8 February 1990	First public interview by PDFORRA PRO from Denmark
13 February 1990	Interim injunction granted in High Court to PDFORRA PRO
14 March 1990	Interlocutory injunction denied in High Court
22 March 1990	Ashling Hotel negotiations and agreement
May 1990	Passing of Defence Amendment Act, 1990
10 July 1990	First formal discussions to create agreed new regulations
31 July 1990	Publication of report of Gleeson Commission
16 May 1991	Enactment of regulation DFR S6 creating statutory body PDFORRA

Notes

PRELIMS

1 T. Bartlett and K. Jeffery (eds), *A Military History of Ireland* (Cambridge, 1996).
2 Sgt Michael Gould (retired), personal interview in County Cork, November 2007.
3 Lt General O'Neill, circular to all Officers, NCOs and Privates of the Defence Forces 27 July 1989. PDFORRA national head office, Dublin.
4 Senior Petty Officer Ger Curley (retired), personal interview in Cobh 18 September 2008.
5 See sections 128–130 Defence Act, 1954.
6 Commander McNamara, navy (retired), personal interview 17 November 2007, Cobh County Cork.
7 Chief of Staff Lt General Dermot Earley, personal interview 26 November 2007, Dublin.
8 *The Soldier and the State: The Theory and Politics of Civil–Military Relations* (Harvard, 1964).
9 See Huntington's chapter on the rise of the military profession in *The Soldier and the State*.
10 Report of the commission on remuneration and conditions of service in the Defence Forces (Dublin, 1990), p.14.
11 Huntington, *The Soldier and the State*, p.1.
12 *Ibid.*, p.1.
13 S.E. Finer, *The Man on Horseback: The Role of the Military in Politics* (London, 1988), p.7.
14 C. Welch and A. Smith, *Military Role and Rule: Perspectives on Military–Civil Relations* (California, 1974), p.13.
15 D. Ralston, *Army of the Republic: The Place of the Military in the Political Evolution of France, 1871–1914* (Cambridge, 1967), p.14.
16 K. Demeter, *The German Officer Corps in Society and State 1650–1945* (Frankfurt, 1962), p.206.
17 Defence Act, 1954, paragraph 131.
18 Lt General G. McMahon, former Chief of Staff, personal interview 2 January 2008, Dublin.
19 McMahon's reference to the 'border' refers to the jurisdictional border between Northern Ireland (officially a part of Great Britain) and the Republic of Ireland where civil conflict had necessitated the deployment of Irish troops.
20 Lt Gen. McMahon interview, January 2008.

21 Col. Brian O'Keefe, General Secretary RACO, personal interview 2 January 2008, Dublin.

22 Jimmy Halligan, former Petty Officer, and chairman of PDFORRA Naval regional committee, personal interview 2 October 2008, Cobh.

23 Finer, *The Man on Horseback*, p6.

24 Welch and Smith, *Military Role and Rule*, p.13.

25 Extract from Defence Force Regulation A7, part VII paragraph 27.

26 Richie Condron, former company sergeant and vice president of PDFORRA, personal interview 16 April 2008, Dublin.

27 D. Gleeson SC, *Report of the Commission on Remuneration and Conditions of Service in the Defence Forces* (Dublin, 1990), p.115–6.

28 Defence Act 1954, paragraph 131.

CHAPTER 1

1 See for examples; S.P. Huntington, *Political Order in Changing Societies* (Yale, 1968), also C. Welch (ed.), *Soldier and State in Africa: A Comparative Analysis of Military Intervention and Political Change* (Evanston, 1970), and S. Webber and J. Mathers, *Military and Society in Post-Soviet Russia* (Manchester, 2006).

2 Welch *Soldier and State in Africa*, pp 6–19.

3 Huntington, *The Soldier and the State*.

4 Finer, *The Man on Horseback*.

5 A variety of perspectives are explored in A. Permulterr and V. Plave Bennet (eds), *The Political Influence of the Military: A Comparative Reader* (Yale, 1980).

6 Finer, *The Man on Horseback*, p.86.

7 Cmdt M. Gannon, *The Advent of Representative Associations in the Irish Defence Forces* (Fort Leavenworth, 1992).

8 Oliver O'Connor, Master of Science, Thesis 'An examination of barrack level representation for enlisted personnel in the Irish Permanent Defence Force', (Dublin, 2002).

9 Report of the commission on remuneration and conditions of service in the Defence Forces, (Dublin, 1990).

10 Commission on remuneration and conditions of service in the defence force, submission by the Defence Forces, 15 November 1989 (Dublin, 1989). Note: Published by DFHQ.

11 Huntington, *The Soldier and the State* (Harvard, 1961).

12 Finer, *The Man on Horseback*.

13 *Ibid.*, p.141.

14 T. Edmunds, A. Cottey, and A. Forster (eds), *Civil–Military Relations in Post-Communist Europe: Reviewing the Transition* (Oxon, 2006).

15 A. Forster, T. Edmunds, and A. Cottey (eds), *Soldiers and Societies in Post-Communist Europe, Legitimacy and Change, One Europe or Several?* (Hampshire, 2003).

16 Philip, P. Everts, *Democracy and Military Force* (New York, 2002).

17 Welch and Smith, *Military Role and Rule*.

18 Larry G. Waterhouse and Mariann G. Wizard, *Turning the Guns Around: Notes on the GI Movement* (New York, 1971).

19 M. Harrell, N. Lim, L.W. Casteneda, and D. Golinelli, *Working Around the Military: Challenges to Military Spouses Employment and Education* (Santa Monica, 2004).

20 Perlmutter and Bennet, *The Political Influence of the Military*.

21 Welch, *Soldier and State in Africa*.

22 Demeter, *The German Officer Corps in Society and State 1650–1945*.

23 Paul Smith (ed), *Government and the Armed Forces in Britain 1856–1990* (London, 1996).

24 Huntington, *The Soldier and the State*, p.viii.

25 Samuel Finer, *Man on Horseback*.

26 Ibid., p.12.

27 Prof. D. Kennedy, in his lecture, *An Invitation to Struggle, the constitution, the military and political accountability*, for the Jefferson Memorial Lecture at University of California, 3 February 2009.

28 Finer, *Man on Horseback*, pp 20–52

29 *Ibid.* p.29.

30 D. Kennedy, *An Invitation to Struggle* (Berkeley, February 2009)

31 *Ibid.*

CHAPTER 2

1 http://acts.oireachtas.ie/print/zza30y1923.1.html#zza30y1923

2 G. Humphreys and C. Graves, *Military Law in Ireland* (Dublin,1997), p.1.

3 J.P. Duggan, *A History of the Irish Army* (Dublin, 1991), p.4.

4 Dáil debates, vol. 1, [152], 20 August 1919.

5 Dáil debates, vol.1 [279], 11 March 1921.

6 Robert Kee, *Ourselves Alone* (London, 1976), p.7.

7 J. Augusteijn, *From Public Defiance to Guerrilla Warfare: The Experience of Ordinary Volunteers in the Irish War of Independence 1916–1921* (Dublin,1996), p.335.

8 Adrian Hardiman, 'Shot in cold blood: military law and Irish perceptions in the suppression of the 1916 rebellion', in G. Doherty and D. Keogh (eds), *1916 the Long Revolution* (Cork, 2007), pp 225–249.

9 Humphreys and Craven, *Military Law in Ireland*, p.2.

10 Dáil debates, vol. 1 [279], 11 March 1921.

11 Kee, *Ourselves Alone*, p.158.

12 Dáil debates, vol. 3 [32-33], 19 December 1921.

13 Dáil debates, vol. 3 [346], 7 January 1922.

14 Comdt Peter Young, 'Michael Collins, a military leader', in G. Doherty and D. Keogh (eds), *Michael Collins and the Making of the State* (Cork, 1998), p.83.

15 Kee, *Ourselves Alone*, pp 158–159.

16 Sheila Lawlor, *Britain and Ireland 1914–23* (Dublin, 1983), p.175.

17 Dáil debates, vol. 4 [181], 16 December 1921.

18 Dáil debates, vol. 4 [182], 16 December 1921.

19 Lawlor, *Britain and Ireland 1914–23*, p.196.

20 Patrick Lynch, 'The Irish free State and the republic of Ireland, 1921–66', in T. W. Moody and F. X. Martin (eds), *The Course of Irish History* (Cork, 1995), pp 324–41.

21 'Against Home Rule', *Weekly Irish Times*, 2 August 1913.

22 A.P. Ryan, *Mutiny at the Curragh* (London, 1956), pp 30–31.

23 D. Fitzpatrick, *The Two Irelands 1912–1939* (Oxford, 1998), p.46.

24 Ryan, *Mutiny at the Curragh*, p.103.

25 Banner 1 -- No Title. 1914. *The Irish Times* (1874–1920), March 21, http://0-www.proquest.com.library.ucc.ie (accessed 28 January 2010).

26 Lead article, *Irish Independent*, 23 March 1914.

27 Finer, *Man on Horseback*, p.29.

28 Lead article, *Irish Independent*, 23 March 1914.

29 M.G. Valiulis, *Almost a Rebellion* (Cork, 1985), p.19.

30 Dáil debates, vol. 6, [1899, 1902] 11 March 1924.

31 B. Kissane, *The Politics of the Irish Civil War* (Oxford, 2005), p.3.

32 See letter to the President from Tobin and Dalton on behalf of the IRA read into Dáil records, vol. 6 [1895] 11 March 1924.

33 Dáil debates, vol. 1 [151–153], 20 August 1919.

34 J.J. Lee, *Ireland 1912 to 1985: Politics and Society* (Cambridge, 1989), p.96.

35 Fitzpatrick, *The Two Irelands*, p.47.

36 Valiulis, *Almost a Rebellion*, p.15.

37 Ibid., p.27.

38 Welch and Smith, *Military Role and Rule*, p.53.

CHAPTER 3

1 See Huntington, *The Soldier and the State*.

2 Valiulis, *Almost a Rebellion*, pp 37–38.

3 Finer, *Man on Horseback*, pp 28–29.

4 Dáil debates, vol. 6 [1895], 11 March 1924.

5 Dáil debates, vol. 6 [1897], 11 March 1924.

6 Gen. Mulcahy, Dáil debates, vol. 6 [1943], 11 March 1924.

7 Dáil debates, vol. 6 [1985], 12 March 1924.

8 Dáil debates, vol. 6 [1988-90], 12 March 1924.

9 Dáil debates, vol. 6 [2000-02], 12 March 1924.

10 Dáil debates, vol. 6 [2009], 12 March 1924.

11 Huntington, *The Soldier and the State*, pp 72–73.

12 Finer, *Man on Horseback*, p.141.

13 Dáil debates vol. 6, [1972], 12 March 1924.

14 Dáil debates vol. 6, [1972], 12 March 1924.

15 Dáil debates vol. 6, [1987], 12 March 1924.

16 Valiulis, *Almost a Rebellion*, p.29.

17 Dáil debates vol. 6, [2216], 19 March 1924.

18 Dáil debates vol. 6, [2218], 19 March 1924.

19 See Dáil debates vol. 6, [2221], 19 March 1924, 'Report on operations Parnell St. Area 18/19 March 1924'.

20 Dáil debates vol. 6, [2226], 19 March 1924

21 Defence Forces (Temporary provisions) Act, 1923, paragraph 36 (a) to (e).

22 Dáil debates vol. 6, [2229-30], 19 March 1924.

23 Dáil debates vol. 7, [2494], 17 June 1924.

24 Kissane, *The Politics of the Irish Civil War*, pp 8–11.

25 See paragraph 36 (b) and (d) of Defence Forces (Temporary provisions) Act, 1923.

26 See Chapter 6 in Kissane, *The Politics of the Irish Civil War*.

27 Fitzpatrick. *The Two Irelands*, p.126.

28 Huntington, *The Soldier and the State*, p.76.

29 Valiulis, *Almost a Rebellion*, p.121.

30 Duggan, *A History of the Irish Army*, pp 84,142.

31 Col M. Walsh, 'The Politics of Irish Defence from the Civil War to the Congo 1923–1964', (MPhil Thesis, UCC), p.118.

32 Duggan, *A History of the Irish Army*, p.147.

33 Defence Force Submission to Gleeson Commission, DFHQ (Dublin, 1989), pp 2–3.

34 D. Gleeson SC, *Report of the Commission on Remuneration and Conditions of Service in the Defence Forces* (Dublin, 1990), pp 241–261.

CHAPTER 4

1 Welch and Smith, *Military Role and Rule*, p. 6–7.
2 Huntington, *Political Order in Changing Societies*, p.239.
3 Finer, *Man on Horseback*, p.14.
4 Article 13, paragraphs 4, 5 and 9, Bunreacht na hÉireann.
5 Former Petty Officer Jim Halligan interview, October 2008, Cobh.
6 Gleeson Commission report, p.21.
7 Finer, *The Man on Horseback*, p.6.
8 Welch and Smith, *Military Role and Rule*, p.10.
9 Brennan, Ornee, Brennan, Keane and Twomey, *A Voyage of Understanding: Effects of Long Term Sea Patrols on Family Life* (Cork, 2006).
10 Gleeson Commission report, p.99.
11 Paragraph 103, Defence Act, 1954.
12 Former Company Sergeant and Vice President PDFORRA, Richie Condron, personal interview, April 2008, Dublin.
13 Col Brian O'Keefe interview, January 2008, Dublin.
14 Welch and Smith, *Military Role and Rule*, p.9.
15 M. Janowitz, *Sociology and the Military Establishment*, revised edition (Chicago, 1965), p.20.
16 M.C. Desch, *Civilian Control of the Military: The Changing Security Environment* (Baltimore and London, 1999), p.5.
17 S. Flynn, *The Irish Times*, 4 February 1988, p.13.
18 S. Flynn, *The Irish Times*, 29 October 1988, p.9.
19 Michael Howard, Secretary General, Department of Defence, personal interview, December 2007, Dublin.
20 Gleeson Commission report, p.2.
21 Gleeson Commission report, p.3.
22 Ralston, *The Army of the Republic*, p.10.
23 Huntington, *The Soldier and the State*, p.27.
24 Defence Force Submission to Gleeson, p.22.16.
25 www.army.mod.uk/training_education/training/20950.aspx
26 Gleeson Commission report, p.40.
27 Gleeson Commission report, pp 40–41.
28 *Ibid.*, p.42.
29 Janowitz, *Sociology and the Military Establishment*, p.29.
30 Ibid., p.27.
31 Finer, *The Man on Horseback*, p.6.
32 Col. B. O'Keefe, General Secretary RACO, personal interview, January 2008, Dublin.
33 Lt Col. A Ryan, Dep. Gen. Secretary RACO, personal interview, January 2008, Dublin.
34 See section entitled 'Career and rank structure', in Defence Forces submission to Gleeson, pp 21.17–21.21.
35 Finer, *Man on Horseback*, pp 24–25.
36 Gleeson Commission report, p.80.
37 Former Squadron Quartermaster Sergeant and founding member of PDFORRA John Wolfe, personal interview, April 2010, Carlow. Expletive deleted.

38 C. Brady *Guardians of the Peace*, second edition (Dublin, 2000), px.

39 Defence Forces Submission to Gleeson, Chapter 12, NCO pay and relativities.

40 See Appendix 9, Comparative levels of gratuity inserted as Annex 21.2F of Defence Forces Submission.

41 Gerry Rooney, General Secretary PDFORRA personal interview, November 2007, Dublin.

42 Richard Dillon, founding chairman of PDFORRA and former Sgt Major 5th Battalion, personal interview, 12 March 2008, Dublin. See also Appendix 13.

43 'Nixering' is a slang word for taking a second job, usually cash-paid and outside of the tax net.

44 Former Squadron Quartermaster Sergeant and founding member of PDFORRA John Wolfe, personal interview, April 2010, Carlow.

45 Richard Dillon interview, March 2008, Dublin.

46 Secretary General Michael Howard, Department of Defence, personal interview, December 2007, Dublin.

47 P. Tansey, *Ireland at Work, Economic Growth and the Labour Market 1987–1997* (Dublin, 1998), p.156.

48 Dáil debates vol. 377, [262–65], 27 January 1988.

49 Source attributed in Tansey's, *Ireland at Work*, p.156, to Labour Market and Social Statistics Division, Central Statistics Office, Cork, September 1997.

50 Dáil debates, vol. 277, [262–280], 27 January 1988.

51 Patrick Gunnigle, Gerard McMahon and Gerard Fitzgerald, *Industrial Relations in Ireland* (Dublin, 2004), pp 13–22.

52 See section 12, paragraph (1), (a) of Employment Equality Act 1977 and section 2, paragraph (1), (d) of Unfair Dismissals Act, 1977.

53 Brian Hillery, Aidan Kelly and A. I. Marsh, *Trade Union Organisation in Ireland*, (Dublin, 1975), pp 1,59.

54 Copy of letter inserted as Annexe 20.1.9 of Submission by Defence Forces to Gleeson Commission (DFHQ Dublin, 1989).

55 Inter-Departmental Committee on Defence Forces pay, allowances and conditions, 1988.

56 Source for civilian rates attributed in Tansey's, *Ireland at Work*, p.161-2, to Department of Finance and Central Statistics Office, Cork. Sources for military rates, see Gleeson Report Appendix 17, p.260.

57 Secretary General Michael Howard interview, December 2007, Dublin.

CHAPTER 5

1 The Garda Representative Association (GRA), the Association of Garda Sergeants and Inspectors (AGSI) and a Superintendents Association (SA).

2 T. Leahy, *Memoirs of a Garda Superintendent* (Clare, 1996), p.161.

3 Defence Force Regulation (DFR) A7 provided under section 26 of Defence Act, 1954 contained in article 27 a provision that made it an offence for any person subject to military law to speak or communicate publicly on any matter concerning the Defence Forces.

4 James Martin, Flight Sergeant (retired) formerly of DFHQ and Air Corps and member of the Gleeson submission team for NCOs, personal interview 2 February 2007, Dublin.

5 Former Squadron Quartermaster Sergeant and founding member of PDFORRA John Wolfe, personal interview, April 2010, Carlow.

6 Defence Forces Submission to Gleeson, p.21.2.

7 D. Keogh, 'Foundation and early years of Irish TUC 1894–1912, pp 19–32, in D. Nevin (ed), *Trade Union Century* (Cork, 1994).

8 www.into.ie/ROI/AboutINTO/AimsandStructure/History/ accessed 3 August 2010.

9 D. Nevin, 'Decades of dissension and division', p.91 in *Trade Union Century*.

10 J. Lynch,'1894–1994 an overview', p.164 in *Trade Union Century*.

11 Paragraph 2, The National Army Spouses Association, constitution and rules, adopted 24 June 1989.

12 Sean Flynn, 'Army spouses are allowed to meet pay committee', *The Irish Times*, 27 October 1988.

13 'Spouses protest at army pay and conditions', *The Irish Times*, 4 November 1988.

14 Carol Tiernan former PRO of NASA, from RTÉ I television interview reshown on video documentary *PDFORRA Ten Years On*, produced by Young communications (Dublin, 2001).

15 Dáil debates, vol. 385 [648], 7 December 1988.

16 Dáil debates, vol. 385 [649], 7 December 1988.

17 Dáil debates, vol. 377 [1755], 10 February 1988.

18 Dáil debates, vol. 376 [456], 2 December 1987.

19 Dáil debates, vol. 377 [1743], 10 February 1988.

20 Dáil debates, vol. 379 [337], 16 March 1988.

21 Dáil debates, vol. 385 [653], 7 December 1988.

22 Colonel E.D. Doyle, 'A pressure group with gun in hand?', *The Irish Times*, 19 August 1988.

23 Cmdr. McNamara interview, November 2007, Cobh.

24 Lt Col Ryan, interview January 2008, Dublin.

25 Ibid.

26 G. McKenna, D. Lavery, 'Defence pay crisis likely to explode in the Dáil', *Irish Independent*, 12 January 1989.

27 Petty Officer (retired) Jimmy Halligan, early activist and former chairman of PDFORRA navy regional committee, personal interview, October 2008, Cobh.

28 Ann O'Loughlin, 'Army promote 30 in bid to up morale', *Irish Independent*, 26 January 1989.

29 D. Lavery, quoting Carol Tiernan, NASA PRO in 'Army wives focus on pay contrast' *Irish Independent*, 14 February 1989.

30 See Appendix 1, copy of letter template used by serving members of the PDF seeking to form PDFORRA. Original copy in PDFORRA archive, Benburb Street, Dublin.

31 Richard Dillon interview, March 2008, Dublin.

32 Senior Petty Officer Sam Fealy, personal interview, November 2009, Cobh.

33 Lorna Reid, 'Election '89', *Irish Independent*, 31 May 1989.

34 Circular in private possession of the author.

35 Para 2f Constitution and rules NASA.

36 *Irish Press*, 31 May 1989.

37 Jim Cusack, 'The voters' choice, the issues of the election', *The Irish Times*, 12 June 1989.

38 Newsletter, NASA Mullingar Branch, 4 May 1989.

39 Ibid.

40 Lorna Reid, 'Election '89', *Irish Independent*, 31 May 1989.

41 www.electionsireland.org [accessed 6 January 2007].

42 Ibid.

43 June Kiernan, founding member of NASA in Mullingar and electoral candidate in

1989 General Election, personal interview 29 July 2008, Mullingar.

44 Jack Kiernan, founding member of PDFORRA and former National Welfare Officer personal interview, 30 July 2008, Mullingar.

45 June Kiernan interview, July 2008, Mullingar.

46 Jack Kiernan interview, July 2008, Mullingar.

47 June Kiernan interview, July 2008, Mullingar.

48 Michael Howard interview, December 2007, Dublin.

49 June Kiernan interview, July 2008, Mullingar.

50 Personal letter to June Kiernan dated 19 April 1989

CHAPTER 6

1 Lt Gen. Gerry McMahon, former Chief of Staff, personal interview, January 2008, Dublin.

2 Henry Abbot 6733, Louis Belton (FG) 6515, Paul McGrath (FG) 4690. Figures from www.electionsireland.org accessed [6 January 2007].

3 Private letter in possession of author dated 3 March 1989.

4 Colm Boland, 'E Europe key priority-Haughey', The Irish Times, 1 January 1990.

5 Jack Kiernan interview, July 2008, Mullingar.

6 Letter from MEP Kirsten Jenson to European Parliament for attention of MEP Barry Desmond, 7 March 1990. See Appendix 5. PDFORRA Archive.

7 Sean Flynn, 'Army Spouses are allowed meet pay committee' The Irish Times, 27 October 1988.

8 Comdt M Gannon, 'The advent of representative associations in the Defence Forces', (Masters of Military Art and Science Thesis, Fort Leavenworth, 1992), p.111.

9 L. O'Neill, Cork Examiner, 27 July 1989.

10 L. O'Neill, Cork Examiner, 28 July 1989.

11 Gleeson Commission report, p.xiii.

12 L. O'Neill, Cork Examiner, 28 July 1989.

13 Letter from Chief of Staff to all members of Defence Forces dated 27 July 1989. See Appendix 2. Author in possession and also in PDFORRA Head office Dublin.

14 M. O'Regan, 'Commission sincere attempt to solve Defence Forces problems', The Irish Times, 28 July 1989.

15 L. O'Neil, 'Commission on Army pay is set up', Cork Examiner, 28 July 1989.

16 J. Martin, member of NCO submission team for Gleeson Commission, personal interview February 2007, Dublin.

17 J. Martin interview, February 2007, Dublin. Note: Author present at meeting.

18 Gleeson Commission report, p.xiii.

19 Former Squadron Quartermaster Sergeant and founding member of PDFORRA John Wolfe, personal interview, April 2010, Carlow.

20 The organisation headquarters subsequently moved and is currently located in Brussels.

21 European parliament resolution 12.4.1984 and parliamentary assembly (fortieth session) of the Council of Europe resolution 903 (1988).

22 H. Rhode, K.V. Christiansen, Euromil 25 Years 1972–1997 (Brussels, 1997), p.11.

23 Defence Force Submission to Gleeson Commission, p.21.4.

24 M. Brennock and J. Cusack, 'Association for Defence Forces to be established', Irish Times 7 February 1990.

25 Former Squadron Quartermaster Sergeant and founding member of PDFORRA John Wolfe, personal interview, April 2010, Carlow.

26 PDFORRA minute book, item 16 in record of minutes dated 11 November 1989. See also J., Cusack, 'Defence Forces association formed', The Irish Times,

12 November 1989; see also lead article in *Daily Star*, 17 November 1989. See extract in Appendix 4.

27 C. Glennon, 'Forces' union is rejected by Government', *Irish Independent*, 17 November 1989.

28 T. Brady, 'Army union talks hope quashed', *Irish Independent*, November 1989.

29 J. Cusack, 'Soldiers call on Taoiseach to allow representation', *The Irish Times*, 28 November 1989.

30 Dáil debates, vol. 393, [1279], 22 November, 1989.

31 Richard Dillon interview, March 2008, Dublin.

32 M. Brennock and J. Cusack, 'Associations for the Defence Forces to be established', *The Irish Times*, 7 February 1990.

33 Richie Condron interview, April 2008, Dublin.

34 Tom McCaughran, personal exchange, 2009 Dublin.

35 Conversation with the author February 1990.

36 Minutes of the meeting of the National Executive Committee PDFORRA 10 February 1990, PDFORRA Archive Dublin.

37 *The Irish Times*, 14 February 1990, p7.

38 Geraldine Martin, Cobh, County Cork, August 2010.

39 *The Irish Times*, 6 March 1990, p.8.

40 *Ibid.*

CHAPTER 7

1 Minutes of the meeting of the National Executive Committee, PDFORRA, 19 March 1990.

2 Dr Brian Hillery, former TD, adviser to the government, personal interview, April 2010, Dublin.

3 Richie Condron interview, April 2008, Dublin.

4 See Appendix 3, Advertisement placed in national newspapers. PDFORRA Archive.

5 Dr Brian Hillery interview, April 2010, Dublin.

6 See Appendix 6. Private collection of Author.

7 Proposed structures within the Permanent Defence Force for consultation and information on pay and conditions of service. Circular from Officer Commanding Naval Base and Dockyard to all military personnel, 10 January 1990. See Appendix 8. Private collection of Author.

8 See Appendix 7. Signatures, Ashling Hotel agreement. PDFORRA Archive.

9 Dr Brian Hillery interview, April 2010, Dublin.

10 Secretary General Michael Howard interview, February 2010, Dublin.

11 Appendix A, minutes of meeting held 10 July 1990 at Department of Defence HQ Dublin. Confidential DOD File P244 part 1, Representative Associations, establishment of non-commissioned officers' and privates' association.

12 Richard Dillon, telephone interview, 17 February 2010.

13 Richard Condron, telephone interview, 17 February 2010.

14 DOD File P244 part 1, minutes 1st meeting between departmental representatives and elected representatives 10 July 1990.

15 DOD File P244 part 1, minutes of 2nd meeting between departmental and representative sides 13 July 1990.

16 DOD File P244 part 1, minutes of 2nd meeting between departmental and representative sides 13 July 1990.

17 DOD P244 part 1, P.230 memo to Secretary Dept.

18 DOD P244 part 1, 'Underlying considerations against the dropping of ranks and the

non-use of uniforms in meetings with commanders in barracks and posts', appended to minutes of meeting between departmental side and representative side 20 July 1990.

19 See Appendix 12, DOD P244 part 1, 'Representation as a military issue', appended to minutes of meeting between departmental side and representative side 20 July 1990.

20 See Appendix 13, DOD P244 part 1, 'Representation as a military issue', appended to minutes of meeting between departmental side and representative side 20 July 1990.

21 Janowitz, *Sociology and the Military Establishment*, pp 37–45.

22 See Appendix 12, DOD P244 part 1, 'Representation as a military issue', appended to minutes of meeting between Departmental side and representative side 20 July 1990.

23 T. Parsons, 'Professionalism and corporatism' in Perlmutter and Bennett *The Political Influence of the Military*, p.27.

24 See Appendix 13, DOD P244 part 1, 'Effect of the uniformed revolving door role', appended to minutes of meeting between departmental side and representative side, 24 July 1990.

25 DOD P244 part 1, minutes of 4th working meeting between departmental and representative sides, 20 July 1990.

26 DOD P244 part 1, minutes of 5th working meeting between departmental and representative sides, 24 July 1990.

27 DOD P244 part 1, minutes of 5th working meeting between departmental and representative sides, 24 July 1990.

28 DOD P244 part 1, minutes of 6th working meeting between departmental and representative sides, 27 July 1990.

29 DOD P244 part 1, minutes of 7th working meeting between departmental and representative sides, 31 July 1990.

CHAPTER 8

1 DOD P244 part 1, 'Representation as a legal issue', LEGAL24 WPMISC July 1990.

2 M. Janowitz, *The Professional Soldier: A Social and Political Portrait* (Illinois, 1960), pp 196–211.

3 DOD P244 part 1, minutes of 8th working meeting between departmental and representative sides, 7 August 1990.

4 DOD P244 part 1, Appendix A to minutes of 9th working meeting between departmental and representative sides, 10 August 1990.

5 DOD P244 part 1, minutes of 10th working meeting between departmental and representative sides, 21 August 1990.

6 DOD P244 part 1, minutes of 12th working meeting between departmental and representative sides, 4 September 1990.

7 DOD P244 part 1, minutes of 13th working meeting between departmental and representative sides, 11 September 1990.

8 Jimmy Halligan interview, October 2008, Cork.

9 Circular dated 19 September 1990 from Deputy Adjutant General, W. X. Phillips to all six military commands.

10 DOD P244 part 1, attached to circular dated 19 September.

11 Letter from PDFORRA head office dated 3 October 1990 to An Tánaiste by Richard Condron. PDFORRA National Archive Dublin.

12 DOD file P244 part 2, Memorandum from G. Gervin, private secretary to the Minister, dated 10 October 1990.

13 DOD P244 part 2, Letter dated 17 October 1990 to An Tánaiste from Chief of Staff.

14 James Martin interview, February 2007, Dublin.

15 Janowitz, *Sociology and the Military Establishment*, pp 55–56.
16 Secretary General Michael Howard interview, December 2007, Dublin.
17 Dr Brian Hillery interview, April 2010, Dublin.
18 DOD P244 part 2, Letter dated 17 October 1990 to An Tánaiste from Chief of Staff.
19 Janowitz, *Sociology and the Military Establishment*, p.59.
20 DOD P244 part 2, Letter dated 17 October 1990 to An Tánaiste from Chief of Staff.

CHAPTER 9

1 DOD File P244 part 2, memorandum 17 January 1991.
2 Letter from Adjutant General N. Bergin to Assistant Secretary Department of Defence Seán Brosnan, dated 19 December 1990 in DOD File P244 part 2, DFHQ Dublin.
3 Memorandum of DJAG attached to letter of 19 December 1990, paragraphs 7–9.
4 Paragraph 12 Memorandum of DJAG attached to letter of 19 December 1990. Note: Memorandum in DOD file P244 part 2, DFHQ Dublin.
5 Note from Assistant Secretary Department of Defence to Adjutant General 18 January 1990.
6 Letter from the Chief of Staff to the Minister for Defence, 6 March 1991.
7 DOD File P244 Part 2, note entitled 'PDFORRA' from Minister for Defence Brian Daly to Secretary DOD dated 12 March 1990.
8 DOD File P244 Part 2, Explanatory paper from the Judge Advocate General to the Deputy Adjutant General dated 23 February 1991.
9 DOD File P244 part 2, minute of the meeting at Dáil Eireann, 24 April 1991.
10 Appendix to agreed arrangements of DFR S6 Paragraphs 16 (1) to (6), PDFORRA Head Office Dublin.
11 DOD File P244 part 2, minutes of 35th working meeting between departmental and representative sides 16 April 1991.
12 DOD File P244, part 2, minutes of 36th working meeting between departmental and representative sides 2 May 1991.
13 Col Brian O'Keefe interview, January 2008, Dublin.
14 Lt Col Ryan, interview, January 2008, Dublin.

Bibliography

PRIMARY SOURCES

Archival

PDFORRA Archives, PDFORRA Head Office, Benburb St. Dublin.
Military Archives, NAI, Cahal Brugha Barracks Dublin.
Department of Defence Archives, Parkgate Dublin.
Private Archival Collection of Author, Cobh.
Defence Forces Submission to the Gleeson Commission.
Department of Defence Files DOD P244, parts I and II, DFHQ Dublin.

Published Primary Sources: Dáil Debates

Dáil Éireann – Volume 1, 20 August 1919.
Dáil Éireann – Volume 1, 11 March 1921.
Dáil Éireann – Volume 3, 19 December 1921.
Dáil Éireann – Volume 6, 11 March 1924, Paragraphs [1895-2229].
Dáil Éireann – Volume 7, 17 June 1924.
Dáil Éireann – Volume 376, 2 December 1987.
Dáil Éireann – Volume 377, 10 December 1987.
Dáil Éireann – Volume 277, 27 January 1988.
Dáil Éireann – Volume 377, 10 February 1988.
Dáil Éireann – Volume 379, 16 March 1988.
Dáil Éireann – Volume 385, 7 December 1988 Ceisteanna – Questions. Oral Answers. –
    Association of Army Spouses.
Dáil Éireann – Volume 385, 7 December 1988 Ceisteanna – Questions. Oral Answers. –
    Early Retirement from Air Corps.
Dáil Éireann – Volume 391, 12 July 1989 Appointment of Taoiseach and Nomination of
    Members of Government.
Dáil Éireann – Volume 391, 19 July 1989, Written Answers. – Pay and Conditions of
    Defence Forces.
Dáil Éireann – Volume 391, 20 July 1989, Vote 37: Defence (Revised Estimate).
Dáil Éireann – Volume 393, 22 November 1989, Ceisteanna – Questions. Oral Answers.
    – Newly Formed Army Representative Body.

Legislation, Official Reports and Letters

Application for 'proposed' formation of Permanent Defence Forces Other Ranks Representative Association. PDFORRA Archive, Benburb St. Dublin.

Chief of Staff letter to all serving members of Defence Forces, 28 July 1989. PDFORRA Archive Benburb St. Dublin.

Temporary Provisions Act (Defence) 1923.

Defence Act 1954.

Defence Amendment Act 1990.

Conroy, John, Justice, Commission on the Garda Síochána, Report on remuneration and conditions of service. (Dublin, 1970).

Gleeson, D., S.C., Report of the commission on remuneration and conditions of service in the defence forces (Dublin, 1990).

Brennan, J., Ornee, R., Brennan, M., Keane, D., Twomey, V., A voyage of understanding, the research results of the effects of long-term sea patrols on family life, (Cork, 2006).

Theses

Gannon, Michael, Commandant., 'The advent of Representative Associations in the Irish Defence Forces', Master in Military Art and Science (Fort Leavenworth, Kansas, 1992).

O'Connor, Oliver, 'An Examination of barrack level representation for enlisted personnel in the Irish Permanent Defence Force,' Master of Science in Education and Training Management (Dublin City University, June 2002).

Walsh, Maurice, Colonel, 'The politics of Irish Defence from the Civil War to the Congo 1923 to 1964,' MPhil thesis (University College Cork, 1997).

Personal Interviews

Dillon, Sgt Maj. R. (retired), founding chairman PDFORRA and Irish Army, personal interview 12 March 2008, Dublin.

Halligan, Petty Officer J. (retired), chairman of Naval Region PDFORRA, personal interview 20 March 2008.

Howard, M., serving Secretary General, Department of Defence personal interviews 14 December 2007 and 17 February 2010, Dublin.

McMahon, Lt Gen. (retired), former Chief of Staff Irish Defence Forces, personal interview 2 January 2008, Dublin.

McNamara, Commd E. (retired), Irish Navy, personal interview 19 November 2007, Cobh.

Rooney, G., serving General Secretary PDFORRA, personal interview 26 November 2007, Dublin.

Secondary Personal Commentary

Condron, Coy Sgt R., former vice president PDFORRA and Irish Army, personal interview 16 April 2008, Dublin.

Early, Lt Gen. D., serving Chief of Staff Irish Defence Forces, personal interview 26 November 2007, Dublin.

Fealy, Petty Officer S., Irish Navy and former activist and representative Naval Region PDFORRA, personal interview 19 November 2007, Cobh.

Hillery, B. Dr, former TD and emissary of government for talks to PDFORRA 1990 personal interview 14 April 2010, Dublin.

Kiernan, Jack, former activist and National Welfare Officer PDFORRA, personal interview 30 July 2008, Mullingar.

Kiernan, June, former NASA activist and candidate for 1989 general election, personal interview 29 July 2008, Mullingar.

Martin, Flight Sgt J. (retired) personal interview 2 February 2007, Dublin.

O'Keefe, Col B., general secretary RACO, personal interview 2 January 2008, Dublin.

Ryan, Lt Col A. serving deputy general secretary RACO, personal interview 2 January 2008, Dublin.

Wolfe, J. founding member PDFORRA and member of NCO Gleeson Team, personal interview 18 February and 10 April 2010, Carlow.

Contextual Background Discussion

Cortejosa, Maria, Perez, founding member of Spanish Spouses group, personal interview 10 December 2007, Seville.

Larson, S.,E., serving treasurer EUROMIL, personal interview 25 April 2008, Madrid.

McCarthy, Chief Petty Officer M., Irish Navy, personal interview 5 March 2007, Cobh.

Ordinez, Maria Angeles, Perez, Spanish Spouses founding member, 9 December 2007, Seville.

Ordellana, Rosario, Fernandez, Spanish Spouses activist, personal interview 9 December 2007, Seville.

Ryan, Commd G., Irish Navy, personal interview 28 June 2010, Cork.

Socota, Rafael Rubio Garcia, retired Spanish Officer, 9 December 2007, Seville.

Sorenson, P., former member of EUROMIL Presidium and political advisor to HKKF Danish representative association, personal interview 25 April 2008, Madrid.

Wiele, Adrian, executive member of the British Armed Forces Federation, (BAFF), personal interview 25 April 2008, Madrid.

Newspaper Articles

'Army group spokesperson faces charges', *Irish Press*, 13 February 1990.

Brady, T., 'Army union talks hope quashed', *Irish Independent*, November 1989.

Brennock M., and Cusack, J., 'Association for defence forces to be established', *The Irish Times*, 7 February 1990.

Cork Examiner, 21 July 1989.

Cusack, J., 'Defence forces association formed', *The Irish Times*, 12 November 1989.

Cusack, J., 'Soldiers call on Taoiseach to allow representation', *The Irish Times*, 28 November 1989.

Daily Star, 17 November 1989.

Glennon, C., 'Forces union is rejected by Government', *Irish Independent*, 17 November 1989.

Lavery M., 'Legal fight looms over army dispute', *Irish Press*, 10 February 1990.

O'Neill, L., Cork Examiner, 27 July 1989.

O'Neil, L., 'Commission on army pay is set up', *Cork Examiner*, 28 July 1989.

O'Regan, M., 'Commission sincere attempt to solve defence forces problems', *The Irish Times*, 28 July 1989.

Sheils, J., 'Soldiers' leader in defiant return, department 'fury' over high profile', *Irish Star*, 10 February 1990.

'Soldiers union man under fire', *Irish Independent*, 9 February 1990.

The Kerryman, 16 February 1990.

SECONDARY SOURCES

Boyd, Andrew, *The Rise of the Irish Trade Unions* (Belfast, 1972).

Brady, Ciaran, (ed.), *Interpreting Irish History: The Debate on Historical Revisionism 1938-1994* (Dublin, 1994).

Cortright, David, *Soldiers in Revolt: The American Army Today* (New York, 1975).

Costello, Con, *A Most Delightful Station: The British Army on the Curragh of Kildare, Ireland*

1855-1922 (Cork, 1996).

Clausewitz von, Carl, (translated by J.J. Graham), *On War* (Hertfordshire, 1997).

Connaughton, Richard, *Military Intervention in the 1990s: A New Logic of War* (London, 1992).

David, Saul, *Mutiny at Salerno 1943: An Injustice Exposed* (London, 1995).

Demeter, Karl, *The German Officer Corps in Society and State 1650-1945* (London, 1965).

Desch, Michael C., *Civilian Control of the Military: The Changing Security Environment* (Baltimore and London, 1999).

Doherty, Gabriel, and Keogh, Dermot, *1916 The Long Revolution* (Cork, 2007).

Edmunds, Timothy, Cottery, Andrew, Forster, Anthony (eds), *Soldiers and Societies in Postcommunist Europe: Legitimacy and Change* (Hampshire, 2003).

Edmunds, Timothy, Cottery, Andrew, Forster, Anthony (eds) *Civil-Military Relations in Postcommunist Europe: Assessing the Transition* (Oxon, 2006).

Edmunds, Timothy and Forster, Anthony, *Out of Step: The Case for Change in the British Armed Forces* (London, 2007).

Elliot, Lorraine and Cheeseman, Graeme, *Forces for Good: Cosmopolitan Militaries in the Twenty-First Century* (Manchester, 2004).

Everts, Philip P., *Democracy and Military Force* (New York, 2002).

Finer, S.E., *The Man on Horseback: The role of the Military in Politics* (Colorado, 1988).

Fisk, Robert, *In Time of War: Ireland, Ulster and the Price of Neutrality 1939-45* (Dublin, 1983).

Harrell, Margaret C., Lim, Nelson, Casteneda, Laura Werber, Golinelli, Daniela, *Working Around the Military: Challenges to Military Spouse Employment and Education* (Santa Monica, 2004).

Hastings, Tim (ed), *The State of the Unions: Challenges Facing Organised Labour in Ireland* (Dublin, 2008).

Hillery, Brian, Kelly, Aidan and Marsh, A.I., *Trade Union Organisation in Ireland* (Dublin, 1975).

Humphreys, Gerard and Craven, Ciaran, *Military Law in Ireland* (Dublin, 1997).

Huntington, Samuel P., *The Soldier and the State: The Theory and Politics of Civil-Military Relations* (Harvard, 1964).

Huntington, Samuel P., *Political Order in Changing Societies* (Yale, 1968).

Janowitz, Morris in collaboration with Little, Roger W., *Sociology and the Military Establishment*, third edition (London, 1959).

Janowitz, Morris, *Sociology and the Military Establishment*, revised edition (New York, 1965)

Janowitz, Morris, *Military Conflict: Essays in the Institutional Analysis of War and Peace* (London, 1975).

Kee, Robert, *Ourselves Alone* (London, 1976).

Keegan, John, *A History of Warfare* (London, 2004).

Kennedy, Kieran, A., (ed), *Ireland in Transition* (Dublin, 1986).

Keogh, Dermot, *Twentieth Century Ireland, Nation and State* (Dublin, 1994).

Keogh, Dermot, *The Rise of the Irish Working Class: The Dublin Trade Union Movement and Labour Leadership* (Belfast, 1982).

Keogh, Dermot and Doherty, Gabriel, *1916 the Long Revolution* (Cork, 2007).

Keogh, Dermot and O'Driscoll, Mervyn, *Ireland in World War Two: Neutrality and Survival* (Cork, 2004).

Kirby, Peader, Gibbons, Luke and Cronin, Michael, *Reinventing Ireland: Culture, Society and the Global Economy* (London, 2002).

Kissane, Bill, *The Politics of the Irish Civil War* (Oxford, 2005).

Lawlor, Sheila, *Britain and Ireland 1914-23* (Dublin, 1988)

Lee, J., J., *Ireland 1912-1985: Politics and Society* (Cambridge, 1989).

Lipset, S.M., Trow, M., Coleman, J., *Union Democracy: What Makes Democracy Work in*

Labor Unions and Other Organisations (New York, 1956).

Logan, John, (ed), *Teachers Union: The TUI and its Forerunners 1899-1994* (Dublin, 1999).

McCarthy, Charles, *The Decade of Upheaval: Irish Trade Unions in the Nineteen Sixties* (Dublin, 1973).

Mitchell, Peter, Schoeffel, John, (ed), *Understanding Power: The Indispensable Chomsky* (London, 2002).

Nevin, Donal, (ed), *Trade Union Century* (Cork, 1994).

Neeson, Eoin, *The Civil War in Ireland 1922-23* (Cork, 1966).

Nichols, Thomas M., *The Sacred Cause: Civil-Military Conflict Over Soviet National Security, 1917-1992* (New York, 1993).

Palokangas, Tapio, *Labour Unions: Public Policy and Economic Growth* (Cambridge, 2000).

Perlmutter, Amos, Bennet, Valerie, Plave (eds), *The Political Influence of the Military: A Comparative Reader* (London, 1980).

Purdon, Edward, *The Civil War 1922-23* (Cork, 2000).

Ryan, A.P., *Mutiny at the Curragh* (London, 1956).

Smith, Paul (ed), *Government and the Armed Forces in Britain 1856-1990* (London, 1996).

Strachan, Hew, *European Armies and the Conduct of War* (London, 1983).

Strachan, Hew, *The Politics of the British Army* (Oxford, 1997).

Tansy, Paul, *Ireland at Work: Economic Growth and the Labour Market, 1987-1997* (Dublin, 1998).

Tzu, Sun, (translated by Thomas Cleary), *The Art of War* (Boston, 2005).

Valiulis, G., Maryann, *Almost a Rebellion* (Cork, 1985).

Video documentary, *PDFORRA Ten Years On*, produced by Young Communications (Dublin, 2001).

Wallace, Joseph, Gunnigle, Patrick and McMahon, Gerard, *Industrial Relations in Ireland* (Dublin, 2004).

Walsh, Maurice, *In Defence of Ireland: Irish Military Intelligence 1918-1945* (Cork, 2010).

Waterhouse, Larry G., Wizard, Mariann G., *Turning the Guns Around* (New York, 1971).

Webber, Stephen, L., Mathers, Jennifer, G., (eds) *Military and Society in Post-Soviet Russia* (Manchester, 2006).

Welch, Claude E. Jnr (ed), *Soldier and State in Africa: A Comparative Analysis of Military Intervention and Political Change* (Evanston, 1970).

Welch, Claude E. Jnr, Smith, Arthur K., *Military Role and Rule* (California, 1974).

Internet Sources

http://acts.ie

http://www.electionsireland.org

http://historical-debates.oireachtas.ie/D/0393/D.0393.198911220014.html

http://www.military.ie

http://www.army.mod.uk/join/terms/3111.aspx

Index

Visit our Website and discover hundreds
of other History Press books.

www.thehistorypress.ie